Fashioning Jews:
Clothing, Culture, and Commerce

Studies in Jewish Civilization
Volume 24

Proceedings of the
Twenty-Fourth Annual Symposium
of the Klutznick Chair in Jewish Civilization
and the Harris Center for Judaic Studies

October 23–24, 2011

Fashioning Jews:
Clothing, Culture, and Commerce

Studies in Jewish Civilization
Volume 24

Editor:
Leonard J. Greenspoon

The Klutznick Chair in Jewish Civilization

Purdue University Press
West Lafayette, Indiana

Dedicated in Memory of

Magda Morsel

Table of Contents

Acknowledgments

The Twenty-Fourth Annual Klutznick-Harris Symposium took place on October 23 and October 24, 2011, in Omaha, Nebraska. The title of the Symposium, from which this volume also takes its title, is "Fashioning Jews: Clothing, Culture, and Commerce."

Most of the chapters in this volume are based on the presentations made at the Symposium. For this collection, Steven Fine and Adam D. Mendelsohn chose to write on topics somewhat different from their Symposium presentations. Two other Symposium presenters were unable to submit articles for this volume. I offer a special thanks to Lisa Silverman, through whose research we found the picture for the cover.

As has been the case for previous Symposia, this Symposium also attracted a large and enthusiastic audience consisting of students, Creighton faculty and staff, members of the Jewish community, and other scholars. Or, to put it another way, the Klutznick-Harris Symposium has not gone out of fashion or out of style.

I cannot recall the exact moment when we decided on "Fashioning Jews" as the topic for the Twenty-Fourth Annual Symposium. Undoubtedly, our decision owes much to the beneficial influence of my wife Ellie, without whose trained eye I would never be able to match shirt with pants, to say nothing of pairs of similarly colored socks.

As in past years, the success of this Symposium owed much to the dedication and wisdom of two of my colleagues, Dr. Ronald Simkins, director of the Kripke Center for the Study of Religion and Society at Creighton University, and Dr. Jean Cahan, director of the Harris Center for Judaic Studies at the University of Nebraska-Lincoln. We were happy to welcome Pam Yenko, who works with both Ron and me. Her unflagging enthusiasm, stamina, and work ethic never failed to energize others. Equally energetic and efficient was Mary Sue Grossman, who is affiliated with the Center for Jewish Life (part of the Jewish Federation of Omaha).

This volume is the fourth in our ongoing collaboration with the Purdue University Press, the staff of which, under Director Charles Watkinson, continues to make us feel welcome in every possible way.

In addition to the Harris Center, the Kripke Center, and the Jewish Federation of Omaha, this Symposium is supported by the generosity of the following:

The Ike and Roz Friedman Foundation
The Riekes Family
Creighton University Lectures, Films and Concerts
The Creighton College of Arts and Sciences
The Center for Jewish Life
The Henry Monsky Lodge of B'nai B'rith
Gary and Karen Javitch
The Dr. Bruce S. Bloom Memorial Endowment
and Others.

This volume is dedicated to Magda Morsel, who persevered in the face of war and persecution.

Leonard J. Greenspoon
Omaha, Nebraska
May 2013
ljgrn@creighton.edu

Editor's Introduction

My mother-in-law, Magda Morsel, was born Magda Guttman in a Czechoslovakian village near the Hungarian border. One of eleven children, she was a teenager when World War II began.

In early 1944, members of her family were taken to Auschwitz. There she was forced to make and mend clothing for the S.S. officers and their families. Together with three of her sisters, Magda survived this concentration camp and other horrors before being liberated by the British at Bergen-Belsen.

From her earliest days as a young girl, Magda showed interest and aptitude in designing and sewing clothes. In the mid-1950s, Magda, her husband Sigi, and their daughter Ellie moved to Richmond, Virginia. During her years there, she worked in the alterations department of an upscale women's clothing store, where she built an appreciative and loyal following as head fitter. We can only imagine what additional opportunities would have been open to her had not war and the Holocaust intervened to cut short her youth and her education.

She also had the time and opportunity to design some of her own clothing as well as clothing for her daughter, including Ellie's wedding dress. Later, Magda took great delight in making dresses for our two daughters, Gallit and Talya. In all of this, Magda never worked from a pattern she purchased; she always made her own.

We dedicate this volume to Magda Morsel. In doing so, we also acknowledge other Jewish women and men who never had the chance to fulfill their talents or their dreams.

The chapters in this volume provide a richly textured picture of many aspects of the relationship between Jews and fashion from biblical times to the contemporary world. Through their choices—what to wear, how to wear it, when to wear it, how to make it, how to sell it, and where to buy it—Jews as individuals and as a group have had wide influence within their own communities and frequently in the larger world they inhabited.

We also recognize that frequently Jews were not given any choice as to what they would wear, how they would wear it, or where they would buy it. In these situations, clothing was one of the means by which Jews were forced into inferior positions. Even when Jews had choices, they were often restricted by those in positions of power.

Thus it is that fashion, which might appear to some as a narrow or even peripheral topic, elicits a series of multidimensional and multidisciplined studies that appreciably enhance our understanding of Jewish history. There are few topics more closely related to daily life and living than the making, procuring, and wearing of clothes.

Today we often speak of a particular person or a particular event as making a fashion statement. But, as should be clear, people use fashion, or more broadly clothes, to make all sorts of statements all the time. As I summarize the contents of this collection, arranged in essentially chronological order, I will to the full extent possible use primary documentation to illuminate the arguments made in each chapter.

Christine Palmer is the author of the first chapter, "Unshod on Holy Ground: Ancient Israel's 'Disinherited' Priesthood." Within the Hebrew Bible, she observes, the detailed descriptions of priestly vestments make no mention of footwear. The classic rabbinic midrash to the book of Exodus, *Exodus Rabbah*, notes the absence and explains it in this way: "Wherever the *Shechinah* [the divine presence] appears one must not go about with shoes on; and so we find in the case of Joshua; Put off thy shoe (Josh. 5:15). Hence the priests ministered in the Temple barefooted." Palmer's explanation, based on a judicious reading of vast numbers of passages from biblical and extra-biblical sources, takes us in another direction, which allows readers to appreciate how bare feet give expression to the subservient role and status of the priest.

The second chapter in this collection that relates to the ancient world is Steven Fine's "How Do You Know a Jew When You See One? Reflections on Jewish Costume in the Roman World." After carefully sifting through the sources, Fine concludes that in antiquity Jews did not dress distinctly. This conclusion, which will likely surprise some readers, is based on a careful reading of well-known sources such as Philo, Josephus, and rabbinic literature. It is also buttressed by a lesser-known funerary inscription in "Greco-Latin" script that reads: "In Memorial of Anastasius and Decusanis and Benjamin, their son." Through these words and the addition of some Jewish symbols, a non-Jewish artifact, complete with images of the deceased, was transformed into a Jewish one.

In the next chapter, Flora Cassen quotes from the sixteenth century Italian poet Battista Guarini: "Why does the Jew wear the letter O / Condemned to eternal torment, the Hebrew bears it as a sign of his grief / Or perhaps this vowel is used as a Zero, indicating his nonentity among men / Or since the Jews get rich through usury, it indicates how they get much out of noting." Throughout her study, "From Iconic O to Yellow Hat: Anti-Jewish Distinctive Signs in Renaissance Italy," Cassen discusses the many nuanced meanings of the O and other markers of their religion that Jews were forced to wear.

In the chapter that follows, Asher Salah also deals with Italy, but in a slightly different period and from a distinctly different perspective. His chapter is titled "How Should a Rabbi Be Dressed? The Question of Rabbinical Attire in Italy from Renaissance to Emancipation (Sixteenth–Nineteenth Centuries)." In appreciably deepening our understanding of these developments, Salah cites, among other contemporary documents, this caption accompanying an engraving of the interior of an early eighteenth-century synagogue: "They [that is, the adult males] put the ritual shawl, with eight strings for each corner, over the shoulders, as a towel, but the rabbis keep it over the head in order to distinguish themselves."

With "The Clerks' Work: Jews, Clerical Work, and the Birth of the American Garment Industry," Adam D. Mendelsohn offers the first chapter in this collection that deals with the United States. Although such positions lacked the adventure and even romance of peddling, work as a clerk served as a rite of passage into America and the American economy for many young Jewish males in the nineteenth century. Spurred on by Mendelsohn's observations, I did a bit of research myself, finding this snippet in *The Encyclopedia of Cleveland History*: "The Jews who settled in Cleveland were primarily shopkeepers and peddlers, although a few were skilled craftsmen. Peddling was a common avenue for entrance into a more stable commercial pursuit. By the 1870s the community had grown and businesses expanded: young or newly arrived Jews no longer peddled goods, but received their business training as clerks or bookkeepers in the firms of relatives or landsmen."

Lisa Silverman takes readers back to Europe with her chapter, "Ella Zirner-Zwieback, Madame d'Ora, and Vienna's New Woman." In the mid-1920s, Zwieback owned what was arguably the most prominent and prestigious department store in Vienna. Madame d'Ora (the pseudonym of Dora Kallmus) was a leading fashion photographer who also made her name through portraits of political and cultural figures of the day. She produced many photographs as ads for Zirner-Zwieback's store, and on occasion she took pictures of the department store owner herself. Silverman evokes one such picture with these words: "[In one portrait] Zirner-Zwieback uses her fur coat to tease the viewer by offering only a partial glimpse of the celebrity they wish to see. But the image of a temptress wrapped in black fur also specifically evokes turn-of-the-century paintings that play upon the notion of the Jewish woman as *femme fatale*. . . . The portrait also playfully utilizes the stereotype of the *belle juive* [beautiful Jewess] that figures woman's 'Otherness' as the basis for her power."

The next two chapters take readers to Germany in the 1920s and the early 30s. The first, by Nils Roemer, is titled "Photographers, Jews, and the

Fashioning of Women in the Weimar Republic." As he points out, Jewish female artists were pioneers in the development of fashion photography during the period. Here is Roemer's description of a characteristic photograph, "Pétrole Hahn," produced by Grete Stern and Ellen Auerbach: "[This] advertisement shows a young blond-haired and dark-eyed female mannequin, wearing an old-fashioned nightgown and holding up the product. A closer looks reveals that the hand belongs to a real woman, thereby fusing the doll-like mannequin with a living woman. The creativeness and artificiality of beauty are being investigated while the advertisement promotes it."

Kerry Wallach's contribution, "Weimar Jewish Chic: Jewish Women and Fashion in 1920s Germany," begins with this observation by a German Jewish satirist in 1927: "Judaism has literally come into fashion: everyone's wearing it again!" Although obviously phrased as an overstatement, this remark broadly conforms to Wallach's assessment that Jewish women played a significant role in creating and popularizing mainstream fashion trends in Weimar Germany. As another Jewish commentator of the time observed: "[The Jewish woman of today] leads fashion trends; serves as a strict judge of taste; and she functions as a critical barometer for the up and coming."

Returning readers to the United States, Ted Merwin joins together two topics of perennial interest—clothing and comedy—in his chapter, "Unbuttoned: Clothing as a Theme in American Jewish Comedy." His joke-rich account spans the twentieth century and, with *Curb Your Enthusiasm*, spills over into the twenty-first. Among the notable quotes, Merwin includes this parody by comedian Allan Sherman, "The Ballad of Harry Lewis" (sung to the tune of "The Battle Hymn of the Republic"): "Glory, glory, Harry Lewis / Glory, glory, Harry Lewis / Glory, glory, Harry Lewis / His cloth goes shining on! / I'll sing to you a story of a great man of the cloth / His name was Harry Lewis and he worked for Irving Roth / He died while cutting velvet on a hot July the fourth / His cloth goes marching on."

Basing herself on a series of one-on-one interviews, Rachel Gordan prepared the next chapter, "'What a Strange Power There Is in Clothing': Women's Tallitot." The women Gordan interviewed, aged fifteen to mid-seventies, were from all over the United States and from many different backgrounds. One woman recalls that, when she was a girl, her rabbi would bring a shofar into the classroom, but exclaim: "I'd rather the girls not touch this." In her own words, such occurrences "chased me away" from Judaism. Another woman associates her wearing a tallit with attendance at an egalitarian minyan at Harvard's Hillel. This turned out to be an ideal environment for her. She says, "I really always wanted it. When I found it, I embraced it fully."

The final chapter in this collection, by Eric K. Silverman, is titled "Aboriginal Yarmulkes, Ambivalent Attire, and Ironies of Contemporary Jewish Identity." A wide-ranging survey from all corners of the world and from all levels of Jewish observance, this chapter highlights the diverse ways in which today's Jews clothe themselves, with references and examples going all the way back to the biblical period. Within the American context, the tension between distinctive dress and the desire to look like everyone else can be seen as early as Mary Anton's *The Promised Land*, from 1912: [We went] to a wonderful country called 'uptown,' where, in a dazzlingly beautiful palace called a 'department store,' we exchanged our hateful homemade European costumes, which pointed us out as 'greenhorns' to the children on the street, for real American machine-made garments."

Within the Hebrew Bible, the first reference to clothing—or the lack thereof—is in Genesis 3:7: "Then the eyes of both of them [Adam and Eve] were opened and they perceived that they were naked; and they sewed together fig leaves and made themselves loincloths." The book of Exodus (here 29:5) speaks of special clothing for Aaron and his sons: "Then take the vestments, and clothe Aaron with the tunic, the robe of the ephod, the ephod, and the breastpiece, and gird him with the decorated band of the ephod."

Elsewhere, a number of the prophets speak of clothing in both positive and negative contexts, for example, in Isaiah 58:7: "When you see the naked, to clothe him, And not to ignore your own kin." In Haggai 1:6: "You have sowed much and brought in little; you eat without being satisfied; you drink without getting your fill; you clothe yourselves, but no one gets warm; and he who earns anything earns it for a leaky purse."

The writers of the Hebrew Bible, we can well imagine, could not have anticipated the varied developments in clothing and fashion that characterized Jewish communities in post-biblical periods. But they would surely have been fascinated, as have we, by the many ways in which Jews have fashioned themselves and been fashioned by others.

Leonard J. Greenspoon

Contributors

Flora Cassen   University of North Carolina
Department of History
Hamilton Hall, CB 3195
Chapel Hill, NC 27599
fcassen@gmail.com

Steven Fine   Yeshiva University
500 West 185th Street
New York, NY 10033
professor.steven.fine@gmail.com

Rachel Gordan   Northwestern University
Department of Religious Studies
Evanston, IL 60208-2164
rachel.gordan@northwestern.edu

Adam D. Mendelsohn   College of Charleston
Jewish Studies
66 George St
Charleston, SC 29424
mendelsohna@cofc.edu

Ted Merwin   Dickinson College
Religion and Judaic Studies
28 N College St
Carlisle, PA 17013
merwin@dickinson.edu

Christine Palmer   Hebrew Union College
3101 Clifton Avenue
Cincinnati, OH 45220
christine@cinci.rr.com

Nils Roemer   University of Texas at Dallas
Arts and Humanities
800 W. Campbell Rd.
Richardson, TX 75080
nroemer@utdallas.edu

Asher Salah

Bezalel Academy of Arts and Design
The History and Theology Department
Mount Scopus, P.O. Box 24046
Jerusalem 91240
oriash@013.net

Eric K. Silverman

Wheelock College
American Studies and Psychology
200 Riverway
Boston, MA 82215
esilverman@wheelock.edu

Lisa Silverman

University of Wisconsin-Milwaukee
History and Jewish Studies
PO Box 413
Milwaukee, WI 53201
silverld@uwm.edu

Kerry Wallach

Gettysburg College
Department of German Studies
300 N Washington St., Box 398
Gettysburg, PA 17325
kwallach@gettysburg.edu

Unshod on Holy Ground:
Ancient Israel's "Disinherited" Priesthood

Christine Palmer

Dress is a prominent motif woven within the writings of the Hebrew Bible. Far from merely covering human nakedness, clothing is a culturally constructed symbolic language that marks ethnicity, signals social status, and even makes a political statement.[1] Nowhere is the symbolic power of dress to communicate ideology more evident than in the ritual attire of Israel's priesthood.[2] Since the earliest interpreters of the biblical text, there has been a fascination with the priesthood's sacral vestments and an attempt to explain their symbolism.[3] One aspect of liturgical dress, however, remains untouched—that of footwear.

The biblical description of priestly dress unfolds in a tapestry of rich detail over forty verses, specifying materials, colors, weave, and ornamentation (Exod. 28). While ordinary priests officiate in linen tunics bound by sashes and linen caps, the high priest ministers in more elaborate apparel reflecting the higher status of his position. He wears a robe of costly blue fashioned of a single piece of cloth and ending in an ornamented hem of alternating golden bells and pomegranates. Over the robe he dons the ephod, fabricated of threads dyed in blue, purple, and scarlet, and interwoven with gold. Its shoulder pieces are embellished with two onyx stones engraved with the names of the tribes of Israel in birth order, six names on each stone. Over the ephod hangs a jewel-encrusted pouch of the same weave containing oracular media used in the priestly ministry. Twelve stones sunk in filigree settings adorn the breastplate, each engraved with the name of a tribe of Israel. Finally, the high priest is crowned in a turban-like linen headdress worn also by kings (Ezek. 21:31). His, however, is distinguished by a rosette frontlet of pure gold inscribed with the dedication "holy to YHWH."

Yet, among the prolific details relating to priestly vestments, there is a striking absence of the mention of footwear. Ancient and modern interpreters alike are in agreement that Israel's priests officiated barefoot within the sanctuary.[4] *Exodus Rabbah* elaborates: "Wherever the *Shechinah* [the divine presence] appears one must not go about with shoes on; and so we find in the case of Joshua; Put off thy shoe (Josh. 5:15). Hence the priests ministered in the Temple barefooted."[5] The practice no doubt is to be traced back to Moses' encounter with YHWH at the burning bush: "Do not come any closer. Remove your sandals from your feet, for the place on which you stand is holy ground" (Exod. 3:5). Moses is the first Levite called to approach the Lord on holy ground, and his brother, Aaron, is the first to serve as high priest. The priestly prerogative to approach God on holy ground reenacts the call of Moses at Sinai.

During the Second Temple period, worshiping with unshod feet appears as regular practice. Maimonides recounts that "the priests were constantly standing barefoot on the pavement of the court."[6] Not only priests, but worshipers as well, are enjoined by Sifre Deuteronomy to remove their shoes upon entering the holy precincts of the Temple Mount.[7] The Mishnah instructs that "a man should not behave himself unseemly while opposite the Eastern Gate since it faces the Holy of Holies. He may not enter into the Temple Mount with his staff or his sandal or with his wallet or with the dust upon his feet" (*Berakoth* 9:5).[8] In addition, the Talmud records that upon visiting the Temple Mount, rabbis removed their sandals and stored them under the doorway (y. *Pesachim* 7:11, 35b).[9] Furthermore, legend has it that when the conqueror Alexander the Great entered Jerusalem, a certain Gabiah urged him to remove his sandals lest he profane the Temple Mount (*Genesis Rabbah* 61:7).[10]

ANCIENT ISRAELITE FOOTWEAR

Our knowledge of footwear in ancient Israel derives mainly from biblical texts and material remains. Sandals were the ordinary footwear of daily life (Exod. 12:11, Josh. 9:5, 13, Song. 7:1[2], Isa. 11:15). They typically were made of leather (Ezek. 16:10) and fastened with a strap or laces (Gen. 14:23).[11] Shod feet display the posture of the Israelites' preparedness on the night of the Passover (Exod. 12:11) or can speak of the invincibility of the Assyrian war machine, of whom "not a sandal thong is broken" (Isa. 5:27). An example of God's merciful care of his people in the wilderness is that their sandals did not wear out (Deut. 29:5[4]).

Roman-era physical remains preserved in the arid climate of the Judean Desert provide the best examples of how sandals were made and worn.[12] Sandals discovered in the Cave of Letters (ca. 145 CE) are made of vegetable-tanned ox hide. Their soles are crafted of several layers of leather, and they are fastened to the foot by leather thongs. Two thick sandal straps attach to the sole near the heel, and through these pass two thongs around the ankle and the length of the foot to join together at the front between the big and second toes. A small, sliding leather band ties around these thongs at the front of the sandal and can be pulled up the foot and adjusted to tighten the sandal or to remove it.[13]

SYMBOLISM OF THE SANDAL IN THE ANCIENT NEAR EAST

The significance of the sandal extends beyond the protection it affords. The foot—specifically, the shod foot— is a symbol of status and dominion in the ancient world.[14] The authority that the foot exercises is observed in both the social and political spheres of the ancient Near East. Although the practice of removing the sandal has been fossilized in religious tradition and become almost exclusively associated with religious practice, the cultural world of the ancient Near East reveals it to have a broader range of social and political implications.

Egyptian royal ideology makes use of the symbol of the sandal to communicate political hegemony. In the Egyptian, the phrase *hr tb(w)t/tbty* [under the sandals], means "to be subject to someone."[15] A pair of sandals from the grave goods of Tutankhamun illustrates this point. The ceremonial sandals, crafted of wood and gilded with gold foil, are embossed on the insoles with images of Asiatic and Nubian captives having their hands bound behind their backs [Fig. 1]. As the pharaoh strides in his sandals, he is symbolically treading his enemies underfoot and asserting he will subdue all foes of his realm. Royal footstools are decorated with similar motifs, the enemies alternately represented as bound human figures or the hieroglyphic equivalent of the nine bows. King Tutankhamun's magnificent golden throne is paired with a wooden footstool overlaid with gold foil. This is adorned with images of the nine traditional enemies of Egypt pictured bound and under his control.[16] The king's reign is unchallenged as his feet are at rest.

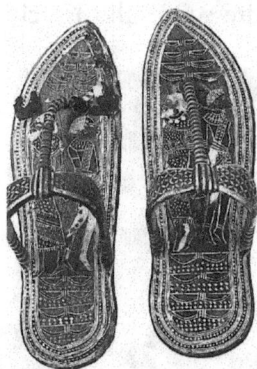

Figure 1. Ceremonial sandals depicting subjugated enemies. Courtesy of Center for Documentation of Cultural and Natural Heritage.

Egypt's monumental architecture puts on display the theme of the victorious pharaoh in countless scenes of trampling his enemies underfoot. Sandals figure prominently in these reliefs. Ramses II is portrayed in an Abu Simbel relief striding upon a fallen foe with his feet shod in upturned sandals.[17] A scene at Medinet Habu depicts Ramses III presenting Libyan captives to Amun-Re, who is recorded as saying in the accompanying inscription: "You have plundered foreign countries and have trampled their towns. You have brought away their captive chiefs according as I decreed for valor and victory, all foreign countries being beneath your sandals forever and ever."[18] All these representations draw upon a culturally understood symbolic language to express political statements of the ruler's dominion and authority.

Mesopotamian renditions on the theme figure prominently in the literature as well as the iconography. Divine sovereignty is articulated in a Sumerian hymn by the goddess Inanna as: "He has given me dominion . . . he has placed the earth like a sandal on my foot."[19] As in Egypt, conquest and control are expressed by bringing enemies into submission under the foot. The Stele of Naram Sin memorializes the victory of the king of Agade over the mountain Lullubi tribe of central western Iran. He stands erect upon a mountain with his sandaled feet planted upon the contorted figures of his enemies. He is armed with an axe, bow, and spear, and he wears a horned headdress typically associated with divinity [Fig. 2].

Drawing from the shared cultural world of the ancient Near East, biblical language is rich with expressions of the military and political power of the foot. David's reign and extension of his kingdom are described as putting his enemies under the soles of his feet (1 Kgs. 5:3[17]). This is not merely poetic speech, but may refer to a literal practice in warfare as seen in Joshua 10:24: "Joshua summoned all the men of Israel and ordered the army officers who had accompanied him, 'Come forward and place your feet on the necks of these kings.' They came forward and placed their feet on their necks."[20] Triumph in the battlefield is vividly portrayed as the staining of a warrior's sandals with the blood of his enemies (1 Kgs. 2:5, Ps. 58:10[11], 68:23[24]),

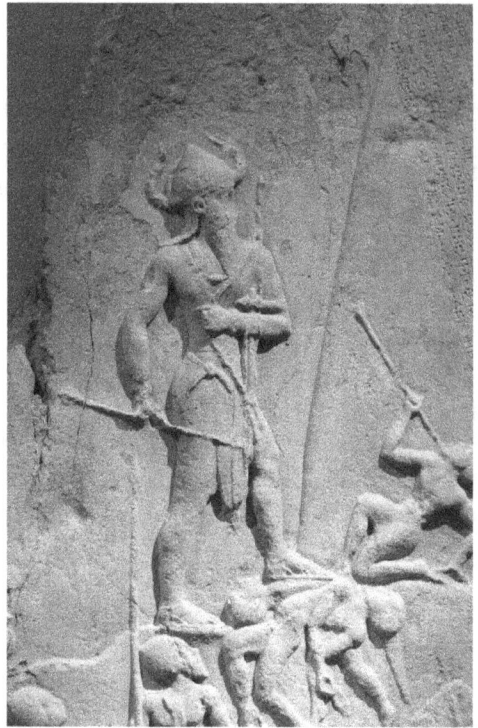

Figure 2. Victory stele of Naram Sin. Public domain.

and victory is heralded when defeated enemies fall at one's feet (Jgs. 5:27, Ps. 18:38–42 [39–43]). Psalm 60 celebrates YHWH as warrior, his sovereignty and territorial conquest marked by the sandal: "Upon Edom I hurl my sandal!" (Ps. 60:8[10]). In the idiom pervasive in the ancient world, the primacy of Judah among the tribes is expressed by making use of the symbol of the feet: "The scepter shall not depart from Judah, nor the ruler's staff from between his feet; so that tribute shall come to him and the homage of peoples shall be his" (Gen. 49:10). Although the staff is easily identified with rule, its placement at the feet is significant in communicating dominion.

As the sandal communicates mastery and authority, its removal is the very image of personal loss, subservience, and defeat. To put one's foot down is to assert dominion, while to go barefoot is to be destitute, vulnerable, and dispossessed. Personal loss is communicated by the removal of the sandal in biblical mourning rites (Ezek. 24:17, 23). David flees from Jerusalem at Absalom's rebellion in a state of mourning and personal distress: "His head was covered and he walked barefoot" (2 Sam. 15:30). The forceful removal of the sandal, furthermore, indicates a loss of status in the community. Deuteronomy stipulates that should a man refuse to perform the duty of a levirate—to take his brother's widow in order to produce an heir—"his brother's widow shall go up to him in the presence of the elders, take off one of his sandals, spit in his face and say, 'This is what is done to the man who will not build up his brother's family line.' That man's line shall be known in Israel as The Family of the Unsandaled" (25:9–10). The man who does not fulfill the moral obligations incumbent upon him by the law of the levirate is shamed. He loses his standing in the community as he loses his sandal. Bare feet signify a loss of social status and perhaps even a loss of self.

The greatest loss of status and self is the loss of freedom and personhood attending captivity. At the time of the Assyrian invasion under Sargon, Isaiah receives a vision: "'Go, untie the sackcloth from your loins and take your sandals off your feet,' which he had done, going naked and barefoot" (Isa. 20:2). Isaiah's prophetic act of shedding his garments and sandals is symbolic of the captivity that is imminent at the hands of the Assyrians. Prisoners of war are depicted in the biblical text as well as in the iconography as stripped and unshod (2 Chr. 28:15a).[21] Some of the most poignant images of Judean captivity come from Sennacherib's palace in Nineveh. Reliefs lining the walls of the Southwest Palace depict the siege and fall of the city of Lachish in 701 BCE. Deportees carrying their belongings slung over their shoulders are pictured exiting the besieged city through a central gate. They go barefoot. To the right of the conquered city are families being led away into captivity. Though they wear distinctive garments and headdresses, both men and women go barefoot. They are driven away from their land and their future; they are disinherited. Another scene focuses on male prisoners singled out for severe punishment; some are paraded before the enthroned king while others are brutally tortured. These captives wear a plain, ankle-length garment and have short, curly hair

Figure 3. Prisoners from Lachish led before Sennacherib. Copyright of Trustees of the British Museum.

and curly beards. They prostrate themselves before Sennacherib with bare feet signaling defeat and abject subjugation [Fig. 3].

THE SHOD FOOT AND LEGAL CLAIMS

Of special interest is the way in which the sandaled foot is utilized in symbolic acts to effect legal claims. The Akkadian *šēpu* [foot] refers to the actual, physical foot, but also, by extension, one's property and those objects in one's possession.[22] To have something beneath one's foot is to lay claim to it and to exercise control over it. Inheritance texts preserve an idiomatic expression referring to one's share in the family estate as *kīma šēpišu* [according to his foot].[23] Traditionally, the eldest son received a double portion, while the remaining sons would receive a share according to their rank. The allotment, which befits one's standing in the family hierarchy, is expressed as "the place he occupies and claims with his foot."[24] Claiming land, whether by right of inheritance or by conquest, is accomplished in the ancient world through symbolic gestures involving the foot.

Some suggest this is the implication of God's command to Abraham: "Up, walk about the land, through its length and its breadth, for I give it to you" (Gen. 13:17).[25] The explicatory clause determines the purpose for which Abraham will walk the land's perimeter: he is to lay legal claim to the parcel of land God will allot to his descendants. This phrase is rehearsed at the conquest. The promise to Moses that "every place on which the sole of your foot treads shall be yours" (Deut. 11:24) is repeated to Joshua (Josh. 1:3). The conquest of Canaan is accomplished by treading the land underfoot, thus legally appropriating and taking possession of the inheritance promised to the forefathers. Tenure in the land is predicated upon faithfulness to the covenant. Should there be a breach of covenant, Israel will be exiled into a foreign land and God will "remove the feet of Israel from the land that I assigned to their fathers" (2 Chr. 33:8).

Legal documents from Nuzi, a Hurrian city of the second millennium BCE, preserve an interesting usage of the foot in a legal symbolic context. Adoption contracts from private family archives record real estate transactions, whereby the adopter's property is transferred to the adoptee.[26] About half of the surviving documents are fictitious adoptions, or "sale adoptions," legally contrived as the inheritance of family property in order to circumvent the Nuzian law of land inalienability. Recorded in every deed is the formula of the current owner raising his foot from the property and placing the foot of the new owner upon it. Some examples are:

> SMN 2390: Ennaya [adopter] lifted up his foot out of his own inherited plot and placed his [adopted son's] therein.
> SMN 2338: My foot from my fields and houses I have lifted up, and the foot of Urhi-Sharri I have placed.[27]

Lifting the foot off the property is a symbolic act of relinquishment, while planting the foot on the parcel of land constitutes the legal act of acquisition. The property is thus regarded as legally conveyed to the adoptee. In this transfer of real estate, the adopter in effect is indicating that he will never again set foot on that property.

It is very likely that this practice informs the customary law behind the biblical narrative of Ruth 4:7. Scripture states there was once such a custom prevalent in ancient Israel: "Now in earlier times in Israel, for the redemption and transfer of property to become final, one party took off his sandal and gave it to the other. This was the method of legalizing transactions in Israel." Taking off the sandal in the presence of witnesses likely corresponds to the lifting of the foot in the Nuzi documents and constitutes a symbolic act with legal consequences. As defined by Meir Malul, "symbolic acts are intentionally performed by the participants in a legal transaction in a solemn prescribed way for the specific purpose of bringing about some legal change."[28]

The biblical narrative relates that Boaz convenes a village court of law by calling together Naomi's kinsman and ten elders to serve as legal witnesses. The issue at stake is a plot of land belonging to Elimelech that Naomi wishes to redeem (Ruth 4:3, 9). The land presumably was sold when the family migrated to Moab under the pressure of famine.[29] Naomi has the legal right to redeem the land, but lacks the means to do so.

The kinsman is initially willing to redeem, since there are no male heirs in Elimelech's line and the property will remain within the kinsman's own estate. When he learns he will also acquire Ruth in the transaction, however, he recognizes the possibility of her bearing children and the land reverting to Elimelech's descendants. The expense of the kinsman will have profited him nothing. He therefore refuses, saying, "'I cannot redeem it lest I damage my own estate'. . . . The redeemer said to Boaz, 'Acquire for yourself,' and he drew off his sandal" (Ruth 4:6, 8). By taking off his sandal, he rescinds his claim on the land.[30] In the presence of witnesses, Boaz may now claim the right of the kinsman-redeemer and have the inheritance legally transferred into his sphere of influence. Boaz intends to "perpetuate the name of the deceased upon his estate, that the name of the deceased may not disappear from among his kinsmen" (Ruth 4:10), that is, raise a future claimant on the land who will be Elimelech's direct descendant and heir to the family's land holdings.[31] The sandal transfers legal authority from one party to another and objectifies the claim.[32]

THE DISINHERITED LEVITES AND SERVICE ON HOLY GROUND

Since the sandaled foot carries such symbolic weight in the culture of the ancient Near East, it becomes important to consider what the unshod feet of Israel's priesthood may have communicated. The nexus of sandals, land claims, and social status is attested in the customs and intellectual world of ancient Israel and must be brought to bear upon the practice of the unshod priest. The question has received relatively little attention in scholarship and the standing suggestions remain unconvincing.

The most frequently proposed *raison d'être* is that the leather of sandals is unclean and therefore incompatible with ministry on holy ground.[33] Sandals are crafted of *tahash* [type of leather] (Ezek. 16:10), typically translated as leather of a dolphin or sea cow based on an Arabic cognate.[34] Not only are these creatures considered unclean (Lev. 11:9–12), but the skin of a dead animal bears ritual impurity that would contaminate the sancta. An objection to this view is that *tahash* leather is prescribed as the outermost covering for the tabernacle structure (Exod. 26:14; 36:19) as well as for the articles of the sanctuary, including the most holy ark of the covenant (Num. 4:6, 8, 10–12, 14, 25). It is unlikely, in the priestly conception and ordering of ritual, that *tahash* could be regarded as unclean if it covers the most holy articles.

Another proposal is that removing the sandals is incidental to not dirtying the sanctuary.[35] William H. C. Propp writes, "The simplest explanation for this restriction is that one should not track dirt into God's house."[36] It is important to note that Moses' encounter with YHWH, where he is instructed to remove his sandals from his feet, occurs out of doors on the bare ground. Prior to the construction of Solomon's Temple, the tabernacle was erected on the ground of the Sinai wilderness and the dust of the land wherever it traveled. The ground is holy because of the numinous presence of God. Yet, holy is not to be equated with free of dirt, as seen in the test for the unfaithful wife, which involves the dust of holy ground (Num. 5:17). What regulates the laws of purity are ceremonial concerns and not concerns for cleanliness.

An avenue of inquiry yet to be explored is to consider the barefoot priests in light of the broader cultural context and symbolism of the sandaled foot in the ancient Near East. If the shoe is a symbol of authority and inheritance, and the bare foot a symbol of dispossession and the relinquishment of inheritance, how does this comport with Israel's ritual practice? Could there be a distant memory of a levitical disinheritance in the priest's unshod feet?[37] If the sandal is the instrument whereby a claim is made and authority over a space is exercised, is there an aspect of biblical religious tradition that rescinds such claims on holy ground?

The biblical text records in the book of Joshua that when tribal allotments were made in Israel, the tribe of Levi did not receive a parcel of land: "But to the tribe of Levi, Moses gave no inheritance" (Josh. 13:33a). The division of land within Israel's kinship-based society is assigned by tribes, clans, and households. As in Nuzi, a family patrimony is inalienable according to Israelite custom (Lev. 25:23). Ideally, the land allotted each tribe at the time of entry into Canaan is to remain within the family's estate (1 Kgs. 21:3). The land is envisioned as the inheritance of Israel, given in fulfillment of divine promise, and is apportioned among the tribes as an estate would be divided among the heirs of a family. The tribes are to live on their share of the land as brothers and coheirs of the patrimony granted to Israel. However, to Levi, no allotment is granted in the patrimony; he is disinherited.[38]

The Testament of Jacob seeks to explain the phenomenon of the landless Levites in terms of their earliest history.[39] According to this tradition, their eponymous ancestor was disinherited when he and his brother Simeon visited vengeance upon Shechem, slaughtering its male inhabitants in retaliation for the rape of Dinah: "Cursed be their anger so fierce, and their wrath so relentless! I will divide them in Jacob, scatter them in Israel" (Gen. 49:7). The dispersal of the tribe is mirrored in the absence of a defined tribal territory in which to settle and their subsequent scattering into levitical cities distributed throughout the land (Num. 35:1–8). The itinerant Levite of the book of Judges (17–18) preserves a picture of a landless class of religious functionaries available to serve at sanctuaries throughout the land. He is a resident alien from Bethlehem who travels north to Micah's shrine in the hill country of Ephraim and then later serves in the tribal territory of Dan. Deuteronomy includes the sojourning Levite within a list of other vulnerable, indigent persons to whom benevolence must be shown. They are grouped together with the resident alien, the fatherless, and the widow as in need of mercy and economic assistance (Deut. 14:29, 16:11, 14, 26:11–13). Their social class is likened to that of the landless resident alien. Since they have no land allotment, they are economically dependent on God in the same way that the widow and the orphan depend on charity.

Another biblical text turns punishment to privilege and interprets the disinheritance of the tribe of Levi as spiritual destiny. The defining moment comes at the foot of Sinai as the Levites rally to Moses and put to death those who worshiped the golden calf. In return, they are granted the role of guardians of the sanctuary (Exod. 32:25–29). The Levites' slaughter of fellow Israelites is in keeping with their ancestral temperament; yet, this act is borne out of zealous loyalty to Israel's God and becomes the underlying reason for their selection (Deut. 33:9). What they do at Sinai is what defines their role as a tribe hereafter: it will be their job to form a cordon around the tabernacle to guard against the desecration of the sanctuary. They are to serve as guards on a plot of land bridging the common and the holy. If anyone encroaches, the Levites are under obligation to put the trespasser to death (Num. 1:53, 3:10, 25:6–9).[40] A clause appended to the statement of their disinheritance transforms their status from a landless class to clients and servitors of YHWH: "But to the tribe of Levi, Moses had given no inheritance; the Lord, the God of Israel is their inheritance, as he promised them" (Josh. 13:33).[41] Though they can lay claim to no tribal inheritance for their livelihood and material sustenance, they are supported by the offerings and tithes of the Israelites (Num. 18:23b–24a, Deut. 18:1–2, Josh. 13:14).

The popular etymology of the tribe's name reflects their role as YHWH's servitors. It is explained in the narrative as deriving from "attachment" when Leah names her third son with this hope in mind: "'This time my husband will become attached to me, for I have borne him three sons.' Therefore, he was named Levi" (Gen. 29:34). Roland de Vaux convincingly argues on the basis of comparative philology that the most plausible etymology of the Hebrew name Levi relates to being a devotee, one given to the service of God. He suggests that the tribal name is most likely a hypocoristic of Levi-El, meaning "attached to God, a client of God."[42] The priesthood's identity and social status is not linked to tribal territory or an ancestral estate, but rather to their attachment and service of YHWH. Hence, the name Levi comes to denote a status and role in addition to a personal, tribal name. The book of Chronicles reflects such an understanding of the Levites, including singers, bakers, and all who serve God under that designation.[43]

The social status of the Levites as devotees and servitors is further communicated by the language and procedures surrounding their consecration to service. Aaron and his sons are ordained to service through rites whereby they receive the same ritual consecration as the tabernacle and its appurtenances—anointing with oil and daubing with blood (Lev. 8:10–12, 23–24). Their ordination transfers them into the realm of the holy and renders them ritually fit for ministry. The high priest is marked as dedicated to God by the gold diadem he wears upon his forehead. It is inscribed "Holy to YHWH," a designation used of goods belonging to God, such as the tithe of produce and flock (Lev. 27:30–32), sacrificial meat offered on the altar (Lev. 6:10[17]), vessels for ritual use (Ezra 8:28, Zech. 14:21), and even spoils of war (2 Sam. 8:11). The priests are integrated into the sphere of the divine as part of YHWH's chattel. What is dedicated to God is no longer available for common use: "But of all that anyone owns, be it man or beast or land of his holding, nothing that he has proscribed for the Lord may be sold or redeemed; every proscribed thing is totally consecrated to the Lord" (Lev. 27:28).[44] Having entered the sphere of the divine, the priests are to comport themselves according to the laws of holiness and maintain ritual purity.

The Levites who assist Aaron's sons are spoken of as dedicated offerings, presented to YHWH as a *tnufah* [elevation offering] (Num. 8:11, 13, 15). The significance of the *tnufah*, Jacob Milgrom explains, "indicates the transfer of the offering from the profane to the sacred, from the offerer's domain to God's."[45] The Levites are thus brought into YHWH's estate as sacrificial offerings. Highlighting their complete conveyance to the realm of God's possessions is the fact that the Levites' dedication is accomplished by the people symbolically placing their hands on them, as is typically associated with sacrifice. This is an act, Baruch A. Levine notes, that "inevitably conveys subservience, even though the context is religious dedication."[46] God claims the Levites from among the tribes of Israel declaring, "The Levites shall belong to me!" (Num. 8:14). The basis for this claim is that they are to satisfy a divine debt. They are taken in substitution of every firstborn Israelite: "For they are formally assigned to Me from among the Israelites: I have taken them for Myself in place of all the first issue of the womb, of all first-born of the Israelites" (Num. 8:16). The Levites live out their lives satisfying YHWH's claim on the firstborn (Exod. 13:2, 11–15). When kings take a census of their fighting men, the Levites must not be included in the muster because they have been transferred from the ranks of the Israelites to be numbered among the possessions of YHWH's household (Num. 1:49, 2 Chr. 21:6).

As with the ordination rites that clearly portray the tribe of Levi as YHWH's possession, the language of their ministry identifies them as servants of his estate. Sanctuary ministry is referred to as *'abodah* [service], deriving from the verb *'bd* [to serve] (Exod. 30:16, Josh. 22:27, 2 Chr. 35:15–16). The descendants of Aaron serve by officiating at the altar while the rest of the clans of Levi are responsible for the physical labor associated with the portable wilderness sanctuary (Num. 1:50–53). The daily ritual priestly ministration includes presenting the morning and evening offerings on the altar, burning incense, tending the lamps, and setting out the bread. In addition, they assist the Israelites in their offerings and perform the annual Yom Kippur purification rite to cleanse the sanctuary. The priests serve as caretakers of God's estate—the daily ordering of his house, the preparations of his table, the kindling of the lamps and cleansing of his house—all reflect a priestly maintenance of the divine estate.

The role of the priest and Levite is expressed in personal terms as God's *mesharet* [servant], an epithet frequently used of priestly service (Isa. 61:6, Jer. 33:21, Joel 1:13). The infinitive of this root is used in like manner in this passage: "At that time the Lord set apart the tribe of Levi to carry the ark of the Lord's covenant, [to stand in attendance] upon the Lord, and to bless in His name, as is still the case. That is why the Levites have received no hereditary portion along with their kinsmen: the Lord is their portion" (Deut. 10:8–9). In secular usage, *mesharet* is a personal attendant of kings, high officials, and prophets (Exod. 24:13, 1 Kgs. 1:4, Est. 2:2), while in political contexts, the verb is used for serving or attending a superior.[47] It is unequivocally clear that the unshod priests of ancient Israel stand as servants of the Lord, satisfying a divine debt claim. Though they have been given no portion in the land, they have been granted a portion at God's table.

CONCLUSION

In the cultural landscape of the ancient Near East, the sandaled foot embodies meanings of sovereignty, authority, and dominion. However this symbol may have been appropriated and accommodated to religious usage in Israel, it maintains its core communicative value. Biblical Israel makes use of the symbols and language that are part of the fabric of their world to communicate their own distinctive beliefs. Rather than attribute the removal of footwear predominantly to a requirement for purification, it is best to understand the unshod foot as a symbol related to acts of relinquishment, servitude, and devotion.

In light of the evidence, it is appropriate to revisit the original occasion for the sandal's removal in Scripture. The context, as now becomes evident, is one of exercising a divine claim—a claim on a chosen people and a promised land (Exod. 19:5–6, Lev. 25:23). Moses' encounter with the divine presence comes at the threshold of YHWH's claiming a people for his very own. They are to no longer *'bd* [serve] Pharaoh (Exod. 1:13), but will be set free to *'bd* [serve] him (Exod. 3:12). This is a divine contest wherein the God of Israel exercises his dominion and asserts his supremacy over the gods of Egypt (Exod. 12:12). Joshua's command to remove his sandal comes outside Jericho at the onset of the conquest where YHWH is making ready to exercise his divine claim on the land. Jericho, the first city of Canaan to be conquered, is wholly dedicated to God and put under the ban (Josh. 6:19). Moses and Joshua remove their sandals in the context of the exercise of a divine claim. In so doing, they acknowledge both YHWH's dominion and their role as his servants. Moses is the servant of YHWH *par excellence* (Exod. 14:31, Num. 12:7, Deut. 34:5), a title likewise given to Joshua (Josh. 24:29). The priestly practice of serving unshod in the sanctuary must be understood as deriving from this dynamic relationship of acknowledging YHWH's sovereignty and their servanthood.

In priestly theology, the symbol of bare feet gives expression to the role and status of the priest. Comparative usage from the ancient Near East suggests that the unshod foot ought to be understood as a posture of submission, humility, and service. Hallowed ground is one that has been in contact with God, the place where the divine presence has alighted and where the gesture of submission and respect is altogether appropriate. Within the social structure of biblical Israel, priestly identity is not to be tied to an ancestral estate, but to YHWH instead. Unshod on holy ground, the priests wear upon their bodies YHWH's claim. The Temple in which they serve is the place from which God exercises his authority over all the earth. It can, therefore, never be the place of any man's feet, but those of YHWH alone: "This is the place of my throne and the place for the soles of my feet, where I will dwell in the midst of the people Israel forever" (Ezek. 43:7).

NOTES

[1] The political significance of the high priest's garments rendered them an issue of contention in Roman-occupied Judaea. Josephus relates how they were kept under lock and key in the Antonia Fortress at Jerusalem and released only through elaborate measures on festivals and holy days (Douglas R. Edwards, "The Social, Religious, and Political Aspects of Costume in Josephus," *The World of Roman Costume* [ed. Judith Lynn Sebesta and Larissa Bonfante; The University of Wisconsin Press, 1994], 156).

[2] Authority to officiate in the sanctuary was conferred upon Aaron at his investiture (Lev. 8:5–9); he may act as priest only when he is dressed as one. The hereditary office is passed down to his son by means of bequeathing the ritual uniform (Lev. 8:13, 30, Num. 20:26). The garments have symbolic power to mediate ritual and invoke remembrance of Israel before the divine presence by virtue of the stones that are inscribed with the names of the tribes of Israel (Exod. 28:9–12, 21, 29).

[3] Early Jewish interpretation has most consistently seen heavenly symbolism in the priestly garments. Philo and Josephus respectively ascribe cosmic significance to each of the layers of priestly dress, perceiving them as an imitation of the cosmos (*Moses, II*, xxiv, 117; and *Ant.*, III, vii, 184–87). Another strand of interpretive tradition views the priestly garments as the primordial glory that clothed Adam in the Garden of Eden. The garments were then passed down through subsequent generations to become the vestments of the priesthood (*Genesis Rabbah* 20.12, *Exodus Rabbah* 38.8, *Numbers Rabbah* 4.8, *The Apocalypse of Baruch* 4:16, *Jubilees* 3:28, and *Ben Sira* 50:6–11).

[4] Menahem Haran, *Temples and Temple Service in Ancient Israel* (Oxford: Clarendon Press, 1978), 166; Cornelis Houtman, *Exodus Vol. I* (Historical Commentary on the Old Testament; trans. Johan Rebel and Sierd Woudstra; Kampen: Kok Publishing House, 1993), 351; Jacob Milgrom, *Leviticus 1–16* (The Anchor Bible 3; New York: Doubleday, 1991), 502.

[5] *Midrash Rabbah: Exodus* (trans. Rabbi Dr. S. M. Lehrman; London: Soncino Press, 1961), 57.

[6] *Mishneh Torah* Vol. 8 (Yale Judaica Series; trans. M. Lewittes; Yale University Press, 1957), 68.

[7] Yaron Z. Eliav, "The Temple Mount, the Rabbis, and the Poetics of Memory," *Hebrew Union College Annual* 74 (2003): 77.

[8] *The Mishnah* (trans. Herbert Danby; Oxford University Press, 1933), 10. The Cambridge manuscript adds the interpretive comment that entering with shod feet "implies lack of respect" (n. 6).

[9] Eliav, *Temple Mount*, 56.

[10] Ibid., 63.

[11] Douglas R. Edwards, "Dress and Ornamentation," *Anchor Bible Dictionary* (ed. David Noel Freedman; New York: Doubleday, 1992), 2:234.

[12] Yigael Yadin, *The Finds from the Bar Kokhba Period in the Cave of Letters* (Jerusalem: The Israel Exploration Society, 1963), 166–68. For photographs, see pl. 57. Also Yigael Yadin, *The Excavation of Masada 1963/4 Preliminary Report* (Jerusalem: Israel Exploration Society, 1965), pl. 22; Yigael Yadin, "The Caves of Nahal Hever," *'Atiqot* 3 (1961), pl. 23.

[13] Yadin, *Finds*, 167.

[14] This also is the case within a broader geographical and chronological landscape. The foot is used in gestures involving dominion, land possession, relinquishment of property, offering homage, and showing respect and submission. See Betty J. Bäuml and Franz H. Bäuml, *Dictionary of Worldwide Gestures* (2nd ed.; Maryland: Scarecrow Press, Inc.), 228–36.

[15] Stendenbach, "רגל," *Theological Dictionary of the Old Testament* (trans. David E. Green; ed. Botterweck, Ringgren, et al.; Grand Rapids: Eerdmans Publishing Company, 1995), 13:309–24.

[16] James B. Pritchard, *The Ancient Near East in Pictures* (New Jersey: Princeton University Press, 1954), 415–17. Abbreviated below as *ANEP*.

[17] Othmar Keel, "Symbolik des Fußes im Alten Testament und seiner Umwelt," *Orthopädische Praxis* 18 (1982), fig. 1.

[18] *Medinet Habu, Vol. VIII: The Eastern High Gate with Translations of Texts* (Oriental Institute Publications 94; The University of Chicago Press, 1970), 6.

[19] A. Falkenstein, "Inannas Erhöhung," *Bibliotheca Orientalis* 9 (1952), 9. The text reads: *Die Herrschaft hat er mir gegeben....die Erde als Sandale an meinen Fuß gelegt.*

[20] *Chicago Assyrian Dictionary (CAD)* s.v. *kabāsu* 5b for Akkadian texts referring to the king as the one "who steps upon the neck of his enemies."

[21] For example, Shasu prisoners on a Megiddo ivory (*ANEP*, 332) and captives on the Balawat gate bands, (*ANEP*, 358–59).

[22] *CAD* s.v. *šēpu* 2b. Texts HSS 14 48:2; HSS 15 271:5; HSS 16 443:3. Expressions of ownership denoted by the foot are also found in the biblical text: "the earth opened its mouth and swallowed them up, with their households, their tents, and every living thing that belonged to them [lit. in *control of* their foot]" (Deut. 11:6).

[23] *CAD* s.v. *šēpu* 5. Texts HSS 9 24:16; HSS 5 21:10, 67:1, 72:9.

[24] Meir Malul, *Studies in Mesopotamian Legal Symbolism* (Alter Orient und Altes Testament 221; Neukirchener Verlag, 1988), 388 n. 23.

[25] Keel, *Symbolik des Fußes*, 534. Early Jewish exegesis is consonant with ancient Near Eastern practices, understanding this as a symbolic act of legal acquisition termed *hazakah* in rabbinic Hebrew (Nahum M. Sarna, *Genesis* [The JPS Torah Commentary; Philadelphia: The Jewish Publication Society, 1989], 100).

[26] Texts HSS 5, 58; 13, 143; JEN 59; 206; SMN 2338; SMN 2336; SMN 2390.

[27] Quoted in E. R. Lacheman, "Note on Ruth 4:7–8," *Journal of Biblical Literature* 56 (1937), 54.

[28] Malul, *Legal Symbolism*, 27.

[29] Herbert Chanan Brichto, "Kin, Cult, Land and Afterlife: A Biblical Complex," *Hebrew Union College Annual* 44 (1973): 1–54; Robert Gordis, "Love, Marriage, and Business in the Book of Ruth: A Chapter in Hebrew Customary Law," in *A Light Unto My Path: Old Testament Studies in Honor of Jacob M. Meyers* (ed. Bream, et al.; Philadelphia: Temple University Press, 1974), 256. Raymond Westbrook, *Property and the Family in Biblical Law*, (JSOTSup 131; Continuum International Publishing Group, 1991), 79.

[30] Brichto clarifies that this is not yet a land purchase, but a transfer of the *right* of redemption: "A right, a presumptive privilege, is yielded or surrendered to the claimant next in line" (*Kin*, 19).

[31] See also Numbers 27:4. Westbrook understands the raising of a name for the deceased as the title to the inheritance. He notes that since the son takes the name of the biological father in genealogical lists (Ruth 4:21), "name" must refer to the title of the land parcel (*Property and the Family*, 74–76).

[32] Gordis, *Book of Ruth*, 247.

[33] Houtman, *Exodus*, 351; Milgrom, *Leviticus 1–16*, 654.

[34] JPS, as well as most Bible translations. Tur-Sinai proposes male goat (Haran, *Temples*, 162 n. 28). Jacob Milgrom suggests "yellow-orange" as the color of the *dušu* stone (*Numbers* [The JPS Torah Commentary; Philadelphia: The Jewish Publication Society, 1989], 26).

[35] Ringgren, " נעל," *Theological Dictionary of the Old Testament* (trans. David E. Green; ed. Botterweck, Ringgren, et al.; Grand Rapids: Eerdmans Publishing Company, 1995), 9:466; Umberto Cassuto, *A Commentary on the Book of Exodus* (trans. Israel Abrahams; Jerusalem: The Magnes Press, 1997), 33.

[36] William H. C. Propp, *Exodus 1-18* (The Anchor Bible 2; New York: Doubleday, 2006), 200.

[37] It is not the purpose of this paper to present a reconstruction of the history of Israel's priesthood, but rather to observe traditions alluding to their social status and role that aid in the interpretation of the unshod priest.

[38] The Levites receive no tribal inheritance and no land in a strict sense. They are, however, given forty-eight cities and their surrounding pasturelands in which to dwell (Num. 35:2–5).

[39] The tribe of Simeon, cursed alongside of Levi, is not listed among the tribes in the Blessing of Moses (Deut. 33) or in the Song of Deborah (Jgs. 5), but appears to have become assimilated into Judah (Josh. 19:1, 1 Chr. 4:24–43).

[40] Jacob Milgrom, *Studies in Levitical Terminology I* (University of California Press, 1970), 48.

[41] The patron-client relationship may be defined as a personal relationship between a dominant and servient party in which the patron offers support and protection in exchange for the client's loyalty (Raymond Westbrook, "Patronage in the Ancient Near East," *Journal of the Economic and Social History of the Orient* 48 [2005]: 210–33).

[42] Roland de Vaux, *Ancient Israel* (New York: McGraw-Hill Book Company, 1965), 359. Kellerman, " לוי," *Theological Dictionary of the Old Testament* (trans. David E. Green; ed.

Botterweck, Ringgren, et al.; Grand Rapids: Eerdmans Publishing Company, 1995), 7:490.

[43] Kellerman, "לוי," 499. This is also seen with the Gibeonites, who become servants of the house of God though they have no specific ethnic or hereditary right (Josh. 9:22–23).

[44] Dedicated items belong to YHWH alone and may not be used in the sphere of the common. This is true of offerings (Exod. 28:38), furniture (1 Kgs. 8:4), anointing oil (Exod. 30:31–33), incense (Exod. 30:37–38), Korah's censers (Num. 16:37–38), and priestly garments (Ezek. 44:19).

[45] Jacob Milgrom, *Studies in Cultic Theology and Terminology* (Studies in Judaism in Late Antiquity Vol. 36; ed. Jacob Neusner, Leiden: E. J. Brill, 1983), 158.

[46] Baruch A. Levine, *Numbers 1-20* (The Anchor Bible 4; New York: Doubleday, 1993), 278.

[47] Terence E. Fretheim, "שרת" *Dictionary of Old Testament Theology and Exegesis* (ed. Willem A. VanGemeren; Grand Rapids: Zondervan Publishing House), 4:256–57.

How Do You Know a Jew When You See One?
Reflections on Jewish Costume
in the Roman World

Steven Fine

Recently I opened the American *Wikipedia* page for Josephus, to find a sculpture at the Ny Carlsberg Glyptotek in Copenhagen at the top of the page, identified as "Josephus" [Fig. 1].[1] Soon I found that this bust appears in a broad range of *Wikipedia* articles on the first-century author, from French to Spanish, Arabic to German. Oddly, a different image, an early modern print, illustrates the Esperanto and Russian pages, and the Danish language article is unillustrated.[2] This sculpture is well known and appears in a number of scholarly and popular publications as "Josephus."[3] Most recently, a guide to the excavations at the Western Wall in Jerusalem, written by noted archaeologist Eilat Mazar, contains a drawing of this "Josephus" portrait bust.[4]

The bust was listed as "some unidentified Jew" in a 1925 Ny Carlsberg collection catalog.[5] In 1930, Austrian Jewish art historian, biblical scholar, and follower of the psychology of Carl Gustav Jung, Robert Eisler identified this "Jew" as Josephus.[6] Eisler embraced this identification, and it has mostly stuck, especially—but in no way exclusively—in antisemitic discourse.[7] What is it that prompted the identification of this sculpture with the Jewish historian Josephus? It was certainly not his haircut or the styling of his facial hair, which are standard Roman fare. Rather, Eisler suggested a physiognomic reason, focusing on the unusually large nose of this statue.[8] Since the Nazi era, this kind of racial interpretation is, of course, (mostly) out of vogue. We tend to

Figure 1. Roman Portrait erroneously identified as Josephus. Courtesy of the Ny Carlsberg Glyptotek.

downplay physiognomic distinctiveness of European populations—and particularly of Jews.

What is perhaps most interesting about the Copenhagen "Josephus" is the way that a stereotype about large Jewish noses—not altogether out of place when Ashkenazi Jews are compared as a group with more Nordic populations—was retrojected into antiquity as a kind of racial type and ascribed to a bust that in fact does have a prodigious nose.[9] The Ny Carlsberg Glyptotek long ago dropped the "Jewish" identification.[10] It is likely not coincidental that Danish scholar Per Bilde already unpacked the underlying racism inherent in this identification in 1988, which today is mainly purveyed over the Internet (though not the Danish *Wikipedia*), and is no longer taken seriously by scholars.[11]

In a similar way, assumptions about Jewish costume are often projected backward from the modern situation.[12] This logic assumes that if Chasidim today, for example, dress distinctively, then Jews in antiquity certainly must have done the same. This is not just an "outsiders'" instinct. Contemporary pedagogic materials used in fervently Orthodox schools portray the biblical characters and the rabbis dressed as contemporary *haredim.* They follow on illustrations of Jews in medieval Hebrew manuscripts, an approach tacitly assumed in medieval Jewish literature.

Medieval scholars transformed a late antique text in *Leviticus Rabbah* (fifth–sixth centuries), which has it that the "redemption" of the Jews from Egypt was assured by four acts—that they maintained circumcision, Jewish names, Hebrew language, and did not engage in sexual improprieties.[13] In medieval rabbinic sources, however, the foursome was transformed, "sexual improprieties" replaced with "their [distinctive Jewish] dress." Medieval European Jews did, in fact, dress distinctively (often not by choice).[14] In antiquity, by contrast, Jews did not dress distinctly. Nowhere in Philo, Josephus, rabbinic literature, or in visual culture is there evidence that Jews dressed in ways profoundly different from others. In fact, the overwhelming evidence is that they did not.

An excellent point of departure is a large stone funerary monument, *dated to* the first half of the fourth century. With a height of 1.81 meters, this tombstone was purchased in Pest in the 1830s or 40s and hails from this region—some have suggested *ancient Aquincum, now a section of Budapest* [Fig. 2].[15] The monument resides in the Hungarian National Museum in Budapest (where I examined it in 2007). The focal point of this architectonic, gabled monument is the image of a family, with the father to the right, the mother to the left, and a boy holding a bird before the mother. All are dressed in typi-

Figure 2. Jewish Tombstone from Pannonia, detail. After B. Kaniel, *Die Kunst der antiken Synagogue, Munich/Frankfurt a/m,* 1961, fig. 57.

cal Roman garments, and the folds of the garments are clearly portrayed. The artifact has not been scanned for color, and no painted surface decoration is evident.[16] Below, a smaller register presents a well-known scene in tombstones of this sort, a table at the center flanked by men raising their cups. A large panel below contains a Latin inscription that identifies the dead:[17]

> To the good memory of Claudia Maximilla, who lived 25 years, and
> of Domitio Domnionus who died in Retia, her husband, who lived
> 37 years. Aurelia Urbana and Ingenua [have erected this memorial]
> to their well-deserving sister.

There is no reason to think that Claudia Maximilla and Domitio Domnionus were Jews, nor that the mourners were either. The inscription mentions only this couple, and the boy of the portrait relief is unmentioned, not an uncommon situation in Pannonian funerary monuments. Sometime later the stone was acquired by another family, who added new inscriptions in a "Graeco-Latin" script. The longest of these translates: "In Memorial of Anastasius and Decusanis (?) and Benjamin, their son." Between the heads of the parents is a large menorah with a triangular base, and there are two more menorahs, on the chests of the son and the father. Near each of the family members appears the inscription *Eis Theos,* a Greek term used rarely by Diaspora Jews, more often by Christians. Through the addition of these three menorahs and three inscribed expressions of fealty to Judaism, a Jewish family in late antiquity was able to see itself in the images of a non-Jewish family that had died years before.

The only markers of Jewishness are to be found through these additions, which transform a non-Jewish artifact into this Jewish one, a non-Jewish family into Anastasis and Decusanis and Benjamin. David Noy, Alexander Panayotov, and Hanswulf Bloedhorn are quite correct that the literal translation of our text suggests a family of four. They translate: "Anastasius and Decusanis (?) and (*et baneiami*) Benjamin and our son (*et feileio nostro*)," a family of four, which would suggest that the Jewish mourners reused a monument with three images for a family of four.[18] I would be more comfortable with this interpretation if it did not depend on the literacy of a carver writing Latin in Greek script, who could just as well have added *et,* "and," before each noun. Either way, the costume and coif of the newly Jewish family portrayed on the tombstone are not altered. The Jewish family buried with this monument bore enough physical resemblance to the original polytheistic family commemorated that Jewishness could be superimposed—as kind of palimpsest—without any changes to the actual portraits.

Thus, Baruch Kanael is completely correct when he claims: "This is the only known Jewish group portrait on a grave stone of the Roman period."[19] Indeed, no other portraits of named Jews are extant from late antiquity, not even a palimpsest. Reflecting on the uniqueness of this tombstone, Leah Di Segni hazards that our monument, with its portraits, represents "an un-kosher mixture if ever there was one." The presence of a Latin inscription written in Greek script (which might have been taken to be a traditional Jewish epigraphic language in the West, as it was) suggests a family deeply embedded in its own place and time, while still expressing Jewishness. While our stone does reflect a decision to decorate a Jewish tombstone with images of the dead, is this necessarily "un-kosher"?

Similarly with the expression of *Eis Theos,* "One God." Rarely used in Jewish contexts, it is common among Samaritans and Christians. The trifold insertion of the menorah—undoubtedly painted, as the incision in the stone is very shallow—is the sure sign of Jewishness (or perhaps Samaritan-ness?). It is the one God of Israel to whom this family—the parents with Greek names, the child with a biblical one—display allegiance. I am reminded, though, of the thousands of Jewish tombstones in twentieth-century Eastern European cemeteries adorned with photographs of the deceased—my own grandparents, buried in Rochester, New York, among them. "Un-kosher," perhaps not. The *Mekhilta of Rabbi Ishmael,* a mid-third-century Palestinian midrash, describes people—perhaps Jews—keeping images of their deceased parents with no adverse judgment:[20]

> "Who does wonders" (Exod. 15:12).
> The attributes of flesh and blood are not like the attributes of God.
> Flesh and blood goes to a maker of images and says to him: Make me a likeness of my father.
> He (the craftsman) says to him: Bring me your father and place him before me, or bring me his picture and I will make one like it.
> But He who spoke and the world was created is not so.
> He gives this man a son resembling his father from a drop of water (semen).

Such images were, of course, quite common in Roman times, the best preserved being a group of mummy portraits discovered in Egypt and along the Mediterranean coast.[21] For Samaritans, however, our memorial stone might certainly have been "un-kosher"—at least in terms of what we know of rigorous Samaritan aniconism from synagogue discoveries in this period. Then again, if Samaritans did live in Pannonia (there is evidence of their presence in not-so-distant Dalmatia, modern Albania[22]), they would have been a very, very small minority—otherwise unattested in this region. In such a situation, anything is possible. I point out that Samaritans today decorate their homes with images of their ancestors, while their synagogues are without human, animal, or mythological imagery. While mosaic portrayals of individuals do not appear in Jewish contexts in the land of Israel, images of biblical figures and the signs of the zodiac found in Palestinian synagogues do appear—as they do in Christian contexts—dressed as good late Romans.

The same may be said of the Dura Europos synagogue, completed ca. 244/5 CE. Images of biblical characters appear there dressed as either Romans or Persians in ways that are appropriate to the story being told.[23] Thus, in the panels depicting Esther and Mordecai and the Valley of the Dry Bones, the biblical characters appear dressed as Persians, and in scenes not specifically related to Persia, Greco-Roman garments are used. This cognizance of the "difference" between Persian dress and "normal" Roman clothing likely reflects the reality of Dura itself—a Roman city on the Persian border. It particularly reflects the makeup of the synagogue community, where Aramaic and Greek inscriptions predominate, but Persian language graffiti appears throughout. There is nothing "Jewish" about the garments of the biblical characters. In fact, a *chiton* similar to those worn by Moses, Elijah, David, and other characters, decorated with two vertical stripes, was uncovered in the Dura Europos excavations. It is my sense that these images of biblical characters project the garments worn by Jews at this time in the eastern Empire, including at Dura, into the biblical past.

One element of the paintings, however, does reflect a specifically Jewish costume. In the panel of Moses crossing the Red Sea and again in the image of Moses holding a Torah scroll, small strings hang from the corners of Moses' toga [Fig. 3]. It has been suggested that these strings represent the ritual fringes, *tsisiot* (singular, *tsisit*), known from rabbinic sources to have been attached by at least some Jews of this time to the corners of their four-cornered garments in observance of Numbers 15:37–41.[24] That the artists at Dura imagined Moses with fringes parallels rabbinic assumptions about the biblical heroes. Babylonian Talmud *Baba Batra* 73b–74a, for example, describes the Babylonian rabbi Rabbah bar bar Hannah on a trip in the Sinai desert, where he finds the remains of "those who died in the desert." He unsuccessfully tried, we are told, to take a bit of the blue string from their ritual fringes.[25]

A particularly humorous tradition preserved in a roughly contemporary Hebrew language text, *Sifre Numbers,* a mid-third-century Palestinian midrash, describes a student of the sages going down to the "cities of the sea" from some rabbinic enclave inland to visit the "most beautiful prostitute in the world." Just before he could perform the act, his *tsisiot* flew up as "four witnesses [or, men] against him" and hit him in the face—souring the moment and shocking him to his senses.[26] On a formal level, the strings of the fringes on Moses' garment at Dura are related to an image in the Temple of the Palmyrenes. The specifically Jewish strings

Figure 3. "Moses," wall painting, Dura Europos Synagogue. Photograph by Fred Anderegg. From E. R. Goodenough, *Jewish Symbols in the Greco-Roman Period* [New York: Pantheon, 1964], 11, pl. v.

Figure 4. "Julius Terentius Performing a Sacrifice," wall painting, Temple of the Palmyrene Gods, Dura Europos. Photographs by Steven Fine.

of Moses there are thus not out of place when viewed in terms of the belts of figures that appear in a wall painting called today the "Wall Painting from The Temple of the Palmyrene Gods of Julius Terentius Performing a Sacrifice" [Fig. 4].[27] What is most fascinating, though, is the way that a typical Roman garment is judaized and that Jews at Dura wished to see Moses depicted with this Jewish detail visible—one that no Roman author finds sufficiently distinctive to mention as a Jewish peculiarity.[28]

How did you know a Jew when you saw one in the Greco-Roman world? Jews did not have any particular physiognomic qualities, unless perhaps when males were nude in a mixed group—and only then if other Semites and Egyptian priests, groups that also circumcised, were not present.[29] Archaeological and literary remains are hard-pressed to provide the kind of nuanced distinctions for which this question calls. After all, insider knowledge of distinction may be incomprehensible to outsiders of any group. So, too, Jews. While their garments were just like those of everyone else, it is likely that only an insider would notice fringes like those of Moses at Dura; or the particular tip of a fedora that today informs any Jewish insider that the Orthodox Jew to whom they speak is a Chabadnik; or the knitted *kippah* balanced at the front of the denim, knee-length skirt that identify a Bnei Akiva-oriented modern Orthodox teen today; or the way that the color and size of a turban and beard have meaning for contemporary Sikhs; or the code that dictates the color (grey, black, or blue), styling, and fabric quality of a suit worn by Manhattan lawyers. This kind of nuance is invisible in the sources available to us for antiquity, but this kind of distinction was certainly very real—as it continues to be today.

NOTES

[1] http://en.wikipedia.org/wiki/Josephus

[2] http://da.wikipedia.org/wiki/Josefus

[3] For example, Robert Eisenman, *James the Brother of Jesus: The Key to Unlocking the Secrets of Early Christianity and the Dead Sea Scrolls* (New York: Viking Penguin, 1997), fig. 18.

[4] Eilat Mazar, *Complete Guide to the Temple Mount Excavations* (Jerusalem: Shoham, 2000), 19 [Hebrew].

[5] Frederik Poulsen, *Katalog over antike skulpturer,* (Copenhagen: Nielsen & Lydiche, 1940), VIII 225 28/86, "Josephus Flavius" Ny Carlsberg Glyptotek, 646. The 1925 catalog was unavailable to me, and is cited from the 1945 catalog.

[6] Robert Eisler, "Deux sculptures de l'antiquité classique representant des juif," *Arettwse* 26 (1930): 34. On Eisler, see: http://en.wikipedia.org/wiki/Robert_Eisler (accessed March 2013).

[7] Sander Gilman, *The Jew's Body* (New York and London: Routledge, 1991), 169–93.

[8] A number of recent scholars have pointed out this antisemitic trope. See: Per Bilde, *Flavius Josephus Between Jerusalem and Rome: His Life, His Works and Their Importance* (Sheffield: Sheffield Academic Press, 1988), 60; Magen Broshi, *Bread, Wine, Walls and Scrolls* (New York: Continuum, 2002), 46–47; Jonathan P. Roth, "Distinguishing Jewishness in Antiquity," in *A Tall Order: Writing the Social History of the Ancient World: Essays in Honor of William V. Harris* (ed. Jean-Jacques Aubert, Zsuzsanna Várhelyi; Berlin: DeGruyters, 2005), 54.

[9] See Shaye J. D. Cohen, *The Beginnings of Jewishness: Boundaries, Varieties, Uncertainties* (Berkeley: University of California Press, 1999), 28–30, who discusses the lack of an explicitly Jewish physiognomy in antiquity.

[10] Frederik Poulsen, *Katalog over antike skulpturer,* op. cit.

[11] Bilde, *Flavius Josephus,* 60. See now: Roth, "Distinguishing Jewishness in Antiquity," 54.

[12] Cohen, *The Beginnings of Jewishness,* 30–35.

[13] This tradition appears across rabbinic literature. The first to notice this point was Solomon Buber, *Pesiqte de-Rav Kahana* (Leipzig, O. Schulze, 1885), 83b, n. 66. See also S. Lieberman, "Ḥazanut Yannai," *Sinai* 4 (1939): 227 [Hebrew]; Samuel Safrai and Ze'ev Safrai, *Haggadat Ḥazal* (Jerusalem: Koren, 1998), 133 [Hebrew].

[14] See, for example, the articles by Flora Cassen and Asher Salah in this volume.

[15] David Noy, Alexander Panayotov, and Hanswulf Bloedhorn, *Inscriptiones Judaicae Orientis 1: Eastern Europe* (Tubingen: Mohr Siebeck, 2004), 6–7, provide a thorough and up-to-date literature survey on this artifact. See also Dorottya Gáspár, *Christianity in Roman Pannonia: An Evaluation of Early Christian Finds and Sites from Hungary* (Oxford: Archaeopress, 2002), 21–22; Nagy Mihály, *Lapidarium: a Magyar Nemzeti Múzeum régészeti kiállításának vezetője; Római kőtár* (Budapest: Hungarian National Museum, 2007), 170–71.

[16] On polychromy in ancient Jewish art, see: Steven Fine, "Menorahs in Color: On the Study of Polychromy in Jewish Visual Culture of Roman Antiquity," *Images: A Journal of Jewish Art and Visual Culture* 6 (2012), forthcoming.

[17] Erwin R. Goodenough, *Jewish Symbols in the Greco-Roman Period* (New York: Pantheon, 1953), 1: 60.

[18] Noy, Panayotov, and Bloedhorn, *Inscriptiones Judaicae Orientis 1.*

[19] My translation, "Es ist dies die einzige jüdische Bildnisgruppe auf einem Grabstein der römischen Verträge Period, die bisher bekannt ist." Baruch Kaniel, *Die Kunst der Antiken Synagoge* (Munich and Frankfurt am Main: Ner Tamid Verlag, 1961), 70.

[20] Mekhilta of Rabbi Simeon Bar Yohai, *be-Shalaḥ* 15:11 (ed. J. N. Epstein and E. Z. Melammed; Jerusalem: Sumptibus Hillel Press, 1955), 93–94; Steven Fine, et al., eds., *Art and Judaism in the Greco-Roman World* (Cambridge: Cambridge University Press, 2010 [second revised edition]), 99.

[21] See Susan Walker, ed., Ancient Faces: Mummy Portraits in Roman Egypt (London and New York: Routledge, 2000).

[22] Noy, Panayotov, and Bloedhorn, *Inscriptiones Judaicae Orientis 1.*

[23] The principal publication of the Dura synagogue is C. H. Kraeling, *The Synagogue,* with contributions by C. C. Torrey, C. B. Welles, and B. Geiger (New Haven: Yale University Press, 1956). See Fine, *Art and Judaism,* 174–85; Steven Fine, "Jewish Identity at the *Limus*: The Jews of Dura Europos between Rome and Persia" is updated from an earlier version that appeared in E. Gruen, ed., *Cultural Identity and the Peoples of the Ancient Mediterranean* (Malibu: J. Paul Getty Museum Press, 2011), 289–306.

[24] Fine, *Art and Judaism,* 181. See R. Pfister and L. Bellinger, *The Textiles: The Excavations at Dura-Europos, Final Report IV, Part 2* (New Haven: Yale University Press, 1945), 10–12, especially tunic no. 1, pl. 5. Even as they provide concrete parallels to the garments illustrated in the wall paintings, our authors caution that the paintings "may be copied from earlier models" (p. 10). See B. Goldman, "The Dura Synagogue Costumes and Parthian Art," in *The Dura-Europos Synagogue: A Re-evaluation* (ed. J. Gutmann; Atlanta: Scholars Press, 1992), 52–77; B. Goldman, "Greco-Roman Dress in Syro-Mesopotamia," in *The World of Roman Costume* (ed. J. L. Sebesta and L. Bonfante; Madison: University of Wisconsin Press, 1994), 163–81; L. A. Roussin, "Costume in Roman Palestine: Archaeological Remains and the Evidence of the Mishnah" in *The World of Roman Costume,* 182–90.

[25] Dina Stein, "Believing is Seeing: Baba Batra 73a–75b," *Jerusalem Studies in Hebrew Literature* 17 (1999): 9–32 [Hebrew]; Fine, *Art and Judaism,* 181.

[26] Sifre Numbers *Shelaḥ* 115 and parallels (ed. M. Friedmann; Vienna: Holwarth, 1864), 35b.

[27] Maura K. Heyn, "The Terentius Frieze in Context," in *Dura Europos: Crossroads of Antiquity* (ed. L. R. Brody and G. L. Hoffman; Boston: McMullen Museum of Art at Boston College, 2011), 221–33, and the bibliography cited there.

[28] See Cohen, *The Beginnings of Jewishness,* 30–34, and my review of this volume in *Archaeological Odyssey* (November/December 2000): 56, 58.

[29] Seth Schwartz, "Political, Social, and Economic Life in the Land of Israel, 66–c. 235," in *The Cambridge History of Judaism: The Late Roman-Rabbinic Period* (ed. S. Katz; New York: Cambridge University Press, 2006), 34–35.

From Iconic O to Yellow Hat:
Anti-Jewish Distinctive Signs in Renaissance Italy

Flora Cassen

INTRODUCTION

In 1516 Cardinal della Rovere forced the famous Hebrew printer Gershom Soncino to print a verse by the Italian poet Battista Guarini. The title and the first line of the poem repeated the same question: "Why the Jews wear the letter O," and "Why does the Hebrew wear the fourth vowel on his breast."[1] Guarini's question was not rhetorical. Starting in the fifteenth century, the governments of northern Italy forced the Jews to wear a yellow circular badge on their clothing. In the documents and edicts that imposed it, the yellow badge of the Jews was not verbally described. Instead, as this article will show, it was invariably represented by an "O" in the text. The representation of the Jewish badge by the O was a phenomenon unique to Italy, where it became a well-known and widely used symbol. Yet as the sixteenth century wore on, authorities replaced it with a yellow hat, thereby moving the mark of the Jews from their chests to a more conspicuous location on their heads.

The discriminatory marks represented a difficult challenge for an Italian Jewry who had previously been allowed to dress as they pleased. Studies of sumptuary law have revealed that Renaissance Italy was in the midst of a fashion revolution.[2] New styles of dress and clothing were on the rise, and as the popularity of costume books suggests, they fascinated men and women at all levels of society.[3] But although diversity of clothing may have been the norm, it also served as a source of anxiety.[4] Secular and religious authorities justified their attempts to control the Jews' appearance as a means to protect the purity of Christian society.[5] Not only was this often mere rhetoric, but precisely why such authorities chose to enact such protection with a yellow O or a yellow hat, rather than another sign, is not obvious. Nor, as Guarini's question reveals, was it clear to contemporaries.

Scholars have offered different interpretational strategies for the phenomenon of anti-Jewish sartorial discrimination. Some attempt to elucidate the meaning and implications of anti-Jewish symbols in artistic representation, while others, such as Diane Owen Hughes, combine the art historical approach with an examination of the social and cultural situation of the Jews in society, showing, for example, that their treatment bore similarities to that of prostitutes or lepers.[6] Other scholars have explored the political implication of the Jewish badge and analyze how it affected power relations between the Jews and the authorities.[7] And some, like Michel Pastoureau, even take a biological perspective, using examples from the animal world to explain why stripes or patches are so often used as discriminating signs.[8]

Building on these studies, this article adds a new methodological approach: a visual analysis of the written documents dealing with those badges or hats. It analyzes not only the contents of these documents, but the graphic and typographic choices made by their compositors, revealing the rhetorical implications of such easily overlooked elements as the placement of the text on the page and how individual letters represented the Jewish badge—aspects of composition that often carried significant meaning in medieval and early modern contexts. Thus my analysis clarifies the meaning of Jewish distinguishing marks in both their textual and physical contexts, and it shows that there was an intriguing, inversely proportional relation between the two. The textual representations were clearer and symbolically more powerful when the physical manifestations of the badge were small and hardly visible. When the physical mark of the Jews was conspicuous, its description in the documents became imprecise and confusing. Following the shifts between the two captures the tensions between the law and its application and reveals that while the textual representations inform us of the ambiguities of the legislative authorities, the physical symbol reflects how Italian society perceived the Jews. But to fully appreciate the intricacies of anti-Jewish sartorial legislation in Italy, it is useful to first examine prior efforts to mark the Jews by the Papacy or other European countries.

THE FOURTH LATERAN COUNCIL AND ITS CONSEQUENCES

The Fourth Lateran Council of 1215, convened by Pope Innocent III, was the first to order that Jews and Muslims living in western Christendom wear distinctive clothing. Its reasoning was that although in some areas of western Christendom Jews and Saracens were easily distinguishable from Christians, there were some regions where they all dressed alike, which could result in sexual intercourse between Christians and Jews or Muslims.[9] In practice, though, the regulation applied primarily to Jews who, unlike Muslims, could be found across the European Continent. The wording of the Lateran decree also specifically referred to the Law of Moses and to Jewish sartorial regulations.[10]

Surprisingly, however, the Council did not specify how the distinction should be carried out. By being vague, it gave wide latitude to local rulers to decide how to implement the distinction. This led to a diversity of Jewish signs and marks: blue stripes in Sicily, a red cape in Rome, the tablets of the Law in England, a yellow wheel in France, a pointed hat in Germany, a red badge in Hungary.[11] To ensure their uniformity and reproducibility, the edicts and decrees that imposed these signs needed to precisely specify color, shape, size, and material. Long and detailed description of the Jewish mark appeared in legal documentation throughout Europe. For instance, in 1269 Louis IX ordered the Jews of France to wear:

> A wheel made of yellow cloth or rag, sown on their outer garment on chest and back to ensure their visibility. This wheel, which has to be four fingers wide, has to be large enough to contain a palm [of a hand].[12]

Edward I of England's Statute of Jewry, issued in 1275, demanded:

> That each Jew after he shall be seven years old, shall wear a badge on his outer garment; that is to say, in the form of two tablets joined, of yellow felt, of the length of six inches, and of the breadth of three inches.[13]

Given Italy's political fragmentation, one might have expected a similar situation to prevail. This was the case in the south of the peninsula and Rome. In Sicily, Jewish men had to wear a blue linen garment and grow their beards; women wore blue bands on their upper garment and on their heads.[14] In Naples, the badge was a yellow circle, while in Rome, starting in 1360, the Jews were required to wear a red tabard or cape.[15] However, in the north and center of the peninsula, the situation was different. From Florence and the cities of Umbria to Milan and Venice, the Jews all had to wear one and the same badge: a yellow circle.

JEWS, FRIARS, AND SUMPTUARY LAWS

In northern Italy, the Jewish badge was introduced only at the end of the fourteenth century, almost three hundred years after the decree of the Fourth Lateran Council. The immigration and settlement of the Jews was one of the main factors leading up to it. Until the end of the thirteenth century, most Jews lived in Sicily, Naples, and Rome, but during the fourteenth and fifteenth centuries, the centers of Italian Jewish life gradually shifted northward. By the middle of the sixteenth century, the majority of the Jews lived in the center and north of the peninsula.[16] This was the result of episodes of anti-Jewish violence in and outside of Italy, combined with new economic opportunities.[17] Northern Italy was in the process of developing a flourishing economy that offered prospects and a livelihood to Jews, though mostly as moneylenders or physicians. The first settlers to move to a city or town, sometimes after being invited, were often moneylenders. Once they were established, others followed and small Jewish settlements slowly formed. Although there were larger communities in Venice and Florence, most were small, sometimes just a family or two, and Jewish life was spread out across the region.[18]

Another factor was the fanatical activity of Franciscan and Dominican preachers. Following their sermons on the alleged immorality of Renaissance life, which included prostitution, sodomy, witchcraft, gambling, and the presence of indistinguishable Jews, a terrified population often demanded action. According to Hughes, this pressure directly led the friars to introduce the Jewish badge in the peninsula. Robert Bonfil echoes this charge, arguing that these preachers had "a decisive say in determining the fate of the Jews of the period."[19] Recent research has called into question the extent of the friars' ability to influence Jewish policy.[20] Nonetheless, their pronouncements on the Jews were vitriolic in tone and intent on establishing clear boundaries between Christians and Jews.

These were also the peak years for sumptuary legislation in the peninsula. In an effort to regulate the dress of each and every member of society, Italian cities were producing treatises on sumptuary laws in rapidly increasing numbers.[21] This, too, was a response to the anxieties that Renaissance life, with its growing wealth and diversity, generated. Authorities worried about excessive consumption and tried to prohibit luxury items, control the appearance of women, and maintain tight boundaries between social groups.[22] But no sooner had a sumptuary law been issued than Italians circumvented it by introducing new or modified types of clothing not included in the prohibition. Paradoxically, therefore, rather than curbing consumption, sumptuary laws often increased it.[23] Like the Jewish distinctive sign laws from France, Spain, or England, Italian sumptuary legislation contained elaborate and detailed descriptions that were constantly amended and expanded upon to respond to the appearance of new styles.

ANTI-JEWISH SARTORIAL DISCRIMINATION
IN RENAISSANCE ITALY

Once the cities and towns of northern and central Italy decided to implement the Jewish badge, they had a wide variety of distinctive signs from which to choose: the French wheel, the English tablets, the Sicilian blue stripes, or the Papal States' red tabards. They had also access to the ever-widening vocabulary of fashion developed for sumptuary legislation. But neither source seems to have inspired them. Instead, from the moment the Senate of Venice issued the first edict in 1394, the Jewish badge imposed all over northern Italy for the next one hundred years would invariably be a thin circle made of yellow cloth, called the O in the documents. Not only was the badge the same, so too were its textual descriptions. The Venetians described it as "unum O zallum"—a yellow O.[24] In Florence in 1446, it was to be an O-sign, made of yellow cloth and at least as large as one sixth of an arm.[25]

Sabatto and his family were exempted from wearing the O-sign in Verona in 1464: "non ferendi signum .O."[26] Not so the Jews of Assisi who had to wear: "uno .O. de colore giallo."[27] Similarly, in the towns of the Duchy of Milan, the Jews were instructed to wear the "literam O pro insigne" in Piacenza and a "signi .O." in Cremona.[28] From Milan in the north to the cities of Tuscany and Umbria, authorities thus designated the letter O as the sign to be worn by the Jews. It was, as can be seen in the corresponding figures, graphically represented by a circle inscribed in the text.[29]

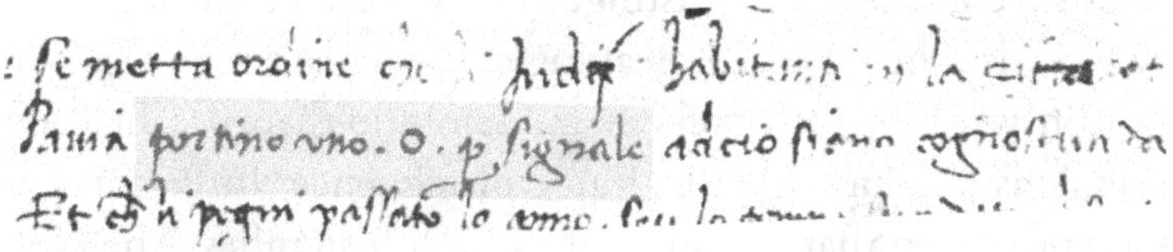

Figure 1. Highlighted text reads "portino uno .O. p signale."

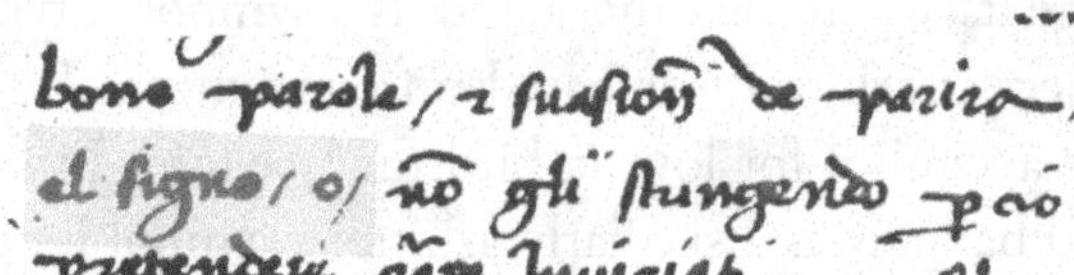

Figure 2. Highlighted text reads "el signo /O/."

The Italian Renaissance states were powerful, independent, and, during the first half of the fifteenth century, in a state of constant internal and external warfare.[30] The apparent ease with which they all adopted the yellow O suggests that it had become a well-established symbol for the Jews. Illustrating just how common the O badge had become is the case of Leone Musirilli, a Jew caught stealing two shirts from another Jew in Florence in 1485. Musirilli was sentenced to be banned from Florence for five years, but before his banishment took effect, he was to undergo a humiliating public punishment. On the next Saturday morning, he would be paraded through the city on a donkey wearing a miter. On the miter, there would be the yellow O, with a black L inside.[31] The L referred to *ladrone*, a thief, but to all the spectators of his sentence, the O showed that Leone was not simply a thief; he was a Jewish thief.

Musirilli's case shows that the O had quickly taken on the kind of iconic status that made it a meaningful part of public punishment; however, how familiarity with the O spread so broadly and rapidly remains a question. One possibility is that the Franciscan friars, who were traveling and preaching around the region, facilitated its dissemination. Although it is unclear whether they consistently used the O to talk about the badge, it is likely that their vigorous preaching across the region helped its rapid propagation. For example, Bernardino da Siena, one of the most influential preachers, regularly demanded that the Jews dress distinctively. He did not usually specify the appearance of the badge, but in one sermon at Padua, he harshly criticized the Jews' failure to wear the O: "Oh! Is there any Jew here? I do not know since I do not recognize them; if they had an O on their chest, I would recognize them."[32]

The representation of the yellow badge by an O in the documents is an intriguing and unique phenomenon. It sets these Italian states apart from other European countries and distinguishes Jewish badge legislations from sumptuary laws, but because the meaning of symbols can be elusive, we need a framework in which to comprehend it. Semiotic theory, a field devoted to the study of signs, can provide this frame of reference. In Peircean semiotics, an icon is a type of sign that resembles the object it signifies. The O in the text resembles the badge outside of the text; therefore, it is an icon of that badge. The physical badge itself, on the other hand, is a symbol, a type of sign whose relation to its object is arbitrary or based on convention. In our culture, for example, a rose is a symbol for love, a bird for freedom. In fifteenth-century Italy, the yellow O badge was a similarly arbitrary symbol for the Jews.[33] This is not to say that fifteenth-century Italians had a working knowledge of semiotics, but simply that the concepts and categories devised by modern semioticians can be used to understand the signs of the past. In this case, the semiotic categories of icon and symbol establish that there were two signs, the icon O in the text and the symbol O in the physical world, each raising its own sets of questions.

Moreover, the relation between the two highlights the tensions between theory and practice, between issuing a decree and actually implementing it. The laws typically mandated that the O badge be the size of a palm with a yellow rim the width of a finger. Given that only the rim was visible, the Jews could easily conceal the badge or let it disappear amidst the folds of their clothes. Time after time, the ruling authorities insisted that the badge be visible, evident, and uncovered. In Florence in 1439, the sign had to be "evidens, discopertum et manifestum."[34] In Città di Castello, in 1480, the O had to be worn, "publice et manifeste, omnibus videntibus eos."[35] But that does not seem to have solved the problem. While the icon O provided clarity and simplicity in the texts, in real life the yellow O badge was hardly visible. To remedy this situation, authorities eventually replaced the yellow O with a yellow hat, but the relation between the written and material forms of the Jewish marks remained ambiguous.

SHIFTING SIGNS:
THE YELLOW HAT IN THE SIXTEENTH CENTURY

Beginning at the very end of the fifteenth and through the sixteenth century, the authorities of the northern Italian city-states ruled that the Jews had to wear a yellow hat. Venice again led the way. In 1496, its Senate ruled that because the Jews were hiding the O badge, they would henceforth have to wear a yellow beret: "in luogo del dicto O portar debino . . . le berete over alter foce de teste ache siano zale."[36] Other cities soon followed. In 1518 in Cremona, Jewish men were compelled to wear "the yellow beret on their head and women, the O on their sleeves."[37] A few years later in Genoa, the Jews had to wear "their yellow beret on the head."[38] Still in Genoa, in a strange twist, Jewish men were made to wear a yellow badge, called *fresetto*, on their berets and caps—*biretis et pileis*. Women had to wear the *fresetto* on their ornamented head coverings.[39] By mid-century in Milan, Jewish men had to wear a yellow beret or wide-brimmed hat, and women a yellow collar: "che li hebrei portino una baretta o cappello gialdo et le donne uno coletto."[40] Similarly, in Piedmont in 1584, men had to wear a yellow beret or wide-brimmed hat, while women were required to put on a yellow veil, described as "vello o cendallo."[41]

Although both were means to distinguish Jewish men and women from the rest of the population, there were differences between the O and the hat. First, the hat was not iconically represented in the documents. Second, whereas the rationale for choosing the O had never been clarified, the ruling authorities explained that the hat was a response to the fact that Jews were hiding the O badge. One has to wonder why the authorities devised a small badge in the first place, why they did not try to remedy this situation by enlarging the size of the O, and why it took a century for effective action to be taken. Regardless, a yellow hat was difficult to hide and dramatically increased the visibility of the Jewish distinctive mark. It was a means to bring clarity to the physical world.

Meanwhile, in the textual world, some confusion arose. There were a variety of hats and styles of veils that the Jews used to wear. These could be neither easily drawn nor iconically represented in the text. In the documents, as a result, elaborate descriptions and increased vocabulary replaced the icon

O. Where there was just one sign before, there were now at least seven words, referring to six different types of head coverings and a collar: *beretto, capello, pileus, cappuccio, colletto, cendallo,* and *vello*. The documents had to be precise and accurately describe or name the different types of yellow hats that the Jews could wear, and it became necessary to assign distinct signs to men and women, since they were wearing different headgear. But despite the authorities' best efforts to be clear, there remained significant uncertainty. The story of a Piemontese Jew, Leone Segele, traveling in the Duchy of Milan, illustrates the perplexing nature of the situation. In November 1560, Segele went on a journey to visit his sister and conduct business. Upon arriving in the Duchy of Milan, a young Jewish man informed him that the Jews had to wear a yellow hat. Segele, who was wearing a black hat, responded he did not know of this law, but the next day he went to a hatmaker and said to him: "Maestro, I want to travel to Lodi and then on to other places, so make me a hat according to the law . . . regarding the hats of the Jews."[42]

Segele then traveled in the Duchy of Milan for several days, presumably wearing his new hat, until one morning the *podestà* of Lodi arrested him. The precise color of his hat was the question his trial hinged on, but the witnesses' testimonies reveal great confusion. The *podestà* claimed, of course, that Segele was not wearing a yellow hat. Sara of Verona, a fellow traveler, testified that he was wearing an "orange-golden" hat. Moses Sacerdote, another witness, declared that he was wearing a "silver and golden" hat. Segele himself argued that although he was not familiar with Milanese laws, and that the hatmaker had assured him his hat was the right color. At a loss, the *podestà* sent Segele's hat to the Duke of Milan, so that he himself could to evaluate it and decide whether Segele should be punished.[43]

Reduced clarity in the written documents was the price to pay for a sign more visible and easier to enforce. While the hat solved the problem of the conspicuousness of the distinctive sign, confusing descriptions replaced the iconic and unique qualities of the O in the text. Given the tenacity with which the various Italian governments had held on to the O for a century, it is ironic that it was precisely its iconic qualities that they replaced, but this irony probably follows from the dynamic and inverted relation between the textual representations of the Jewish signs and their physical manifestations. As it became easier to distinguish the Jews in the real world, insistence on their iconic representations in the laws diminished. When the symbol or physical mark grew larger, its iconic status in the text faded away, and vice versa. Because the symbol is part of the physical world, it reflects upon society's perception of the Jews. The icon, on the other hand, echoes the ambiguities of the ruling authorities who authored the laws. Nevertheless, the meanings of the icon and the symbol, which will be elaborated upon below, were intimately related. As Umberto Eco has written: "At a certain point the iconic representation, however stylized it may be, appears to be more true than the real experience, and people begin to look at things through the glass of iconic convention."[44]

THE SYMBOL O

Establishing the precise meaning of symbols is difficult, for they can change over time, have multiple connotations, and depend heavily on context. Even Battista Guarini, the Italian poet who wrote about the O badge in the early sixteenth century, did not find its sense self-evident. In answer to his question "Why does the Jew wear the letter O," he offered three possible answers, though none was presented as conclusive:

Condemned to eternal torment,
the Hebrew bears it as a sign of his grief;
Or perhaps this vowel is used as a Zero,
indicating his nonentity among men;
Or since the Jews get rich through usury,
it indicates how they get much out of nothing.[45]

The first is a theological explanation referring to the Jews' rejection of Jesus and their subsequent exile and servitude. Just like Cain, who was exiled and marked on his forehead for murdering his brother, the Jews must be exiled and branded for their guilt in Jesus' death.[46] However, this traditional interpretation of the Jews' condition does not relate specifically to the appearance of their badge.

Guarini's second and third explanations directly link the icon O to the round shape of the badge and provide an intriguing insight into how early modern Italians dealt with numbers and letters. Even though Guarini calls the badge the "letter O" and "the fourth vowel," he tells us that it should in fact be read as a zero, standing for both the low status of Jews and their practice of usury. Here, too, Guarini refers to traditional Church teachings. The Jews' inferior condition, or "nonentity" as he calls it, followed from their continued disbelief, and charging interest, the Church argued, was tantamount to selling time or sinfully creating wealth "out of nothing."[47]

More significantly, though, Guarini relates both explanations to people's fears about the number zero. Medieval Europe understood zero as nothingness and had developed a deep terror of it. Void was equated with evil, with the absence of God. Nothing was the state of oblivion where unbelievers and heretics ought to be dispatched.[48] In the sixteenth century, when scholars started using the zero in scientific work, these fears abated. But the Church soon reacted by declaring the zero heresy.[49] The problem with following Guarini in reading the O as zero is that in some edicts the O is specifically referred to as a letter, for example "literam O pro insigne."[50] However, in many other manuscripts, the O is referred to as "lo .O." or "uno .O.," the masculine pronoun suggesting that it was a number rather than a letter. If the icon O was in fact a zero, it would explain why legislators, scribes, and copyists preferred it to the verbal descriptions; it created an immediate association between void, evil, and Jews.

The circular shape of the O could also be related to heraldry. Coats of arms appeared in Europe in the middle of the twelfth century and soon became one of the main attributes of the nobility. By the fourteenth century, they had spread to other classes of the population and taken a place in literature and imagination. Usually their shape was triangular, and they contained the family insignia, but in paintings and fictional narratives, wicked characters—Saracens, bastards, and pagan kings—always bore round coats of arms.[51] Inasmuch as circular coats of arms served to emphasize a character's inferiority and malevolence, the O badge, which was round too, probably tapped into the same reservoir of symbolic associations, linking them to the Jews.

Another way of understanding the O badge is to focus on its color, which, whether in Italy or abroad, was most often yellow. Although much has been written about the association of Jews and yellow, so far no scholarly consensus has emerged. In the Muslim world, the Jews had to wear a yellow sign too, and some have argued that that was the origin of the color.[52] But within Christendom, yellow was utilized to marginalize other groups as well, and by the fifteenth century, it had become the color of treason, felony, avarice, envy, and laziness.[53]

In several Italian cities, namely Venice, Bologna, Brescia, and Pisa, prostitutes had to be distinguished by a yellow badge.[54] Hughes studied the connection between the marking of Jewish women and prostitution. In her pioneering study of laws issued in Umbria in 1432 and 1436 that forced Jewish women to wear golden circular earrings, she shows that these earrings branded Jewish women as sexually promiscuous and likened them to prostitutes.[55] Given that the same edicts also required men to wear the O badge, the earrings are related to the O and may even have to be looked at within its context. Surely, the earrings were in gold (and not in cloth) and were worn in the ears (instead of on the chest), but inasmuch as they were circular in shape and yellow in color, they were another version of the yellow O. Building on Hughes' contribution, it appears that through the yellow O, the association between Jewish women and deviant sexual behavior extended to Jewish men as well.

In sum, when worn by the Jews, the yellow O badge distinguished them from Christians, but also had the potential to evoke the depreciatory associations related to its color, shape, or both. The icon O, on the other hand, was not yellow, nor did the Jews wear it. Rather, it was a black ink representation of the badge, a textual phenomenon that instructs us about those who wrote and authored the laws, the ruling class of Renaissance Italy.

THE ICON O: FROM PAPAL POLICY TO RENAISSANCE ITALY

To understand the meaning of the icon O and what the relation between iconic and verbal representation of the Jewish badge implies about the authors of those edicts, it is helpful to briefly examine papal legislation. Ever since Gregory the Great in the sixth century, the official papal policy toward the Jews had been that the Jews had the right to live in Christian society but had to be subservient to Christians.[56] In this context, the distinctive signs could be seen as an effective means to implement this policy. Not only would they prevent sexual intercourse, but they also visibly maintained the Jews in an inferior position, separated from the rest of the society.

Even though the Papacy first introduced the Jewish badge in the thirteenth century, the popes themselves did not consistently enforce it. But there was a pattern in their inconsistencies. According to a wide-ranging collection of papal bulls and briefs compiled by Shlomo Simonsohn, from 1215 to the end of the fifteenth century, thirty-eight popes wrote over seventy-five letters on the matter of distinguishing clothing.[57] All but fifteen letters were exhortations to bishops and civil rulers across Europe and Italy to compel the Jews to dress distinctively. Papal policy, expressed in two letters from 1419 and 1439, was to insist that the Jews wear a sign but to let local rulers chose its appearance. "Jews," they declared, "cannot be made to wear a sign different than the one customary in their city."[58]

The fifteen letters that did not demand that the Jews wear the sign were addressed to localities comprised within the Papal States.[59] There the popes did describe the sign—a red tabard or cape—and instead of being adamant that the Jews wear it, they alternated between enforcing and relaxing the rules for one or more privileged individuals or for the whole community.[60] This reveals a difference between the popes' local policies concerning Rome and their universal policies regarding Christendom. In the Papal States where the popes acted as direct rulers, they adapted to the complex realities of Renaissance life and agreed to compromises about the Jewish badge. However, in their universal role, they adopted a more consistent and dogmatic stance. There was a tension between doctrine and practice that manifested itself around the subject of the Jewish badge and was played out through the dual role of the popes.

Secular authorities of fifteenth-century Italy were often subject to the same dilemma, having to comply with the popes' standards and the friars' demands on the one hand, while pragmatically running complex societies on the other. Unlike the popes, they did not have a dual universal and local role through which this quandary manifested itself. Yet it appears that some of their ambiguities were embedded within the texts of the distinctive sign legislation that they issued. The widespread adoption of the O in the Italian peninsula suggests a desire for obvious boundaries between Jews and Christians.

In practice, however, society was complex, and interreligious mixing even had some advantages: the Jews could perform a useful economic role, be good neighbors, and, sometimes even, be good citizens. To effectively implement the badge, a strong and sustained political determination was necessary, but absent that, enforcement tended to be unequal and inconsistent. Perhaps one way, then, of understanding the popularity of the textual icon O is to see it as a means to satisfy a need for strict religious boundaries that was difficult to achieve in real life.

Renaissance society could be complex and confusing. So too were the long-winded descriptions of the yellow hat. But the icon O did not require any further explanation; it was simple and unmistakable. In 1436, the priors of Todi decided that Jewish men had to wear a yellow O and women golden earrings. In the texts, they juxtaposed a drawing of the earrings and the O to their written description, which contained three different words—"anelum vel circulum sive circulium."[61] In spite of this detailed description, the O sign was drawn in the margin because it offered a clarity that only icons could provide. Just as the Jews ought to look different from Christians, the icon O was easily distinguishable from the rest of the written document. It stood for a social order in which religious groups were plainly separated, but that situation really existed only on paper, only in the text. The iconic textual O created in texts the clear and graphic sense of separation that law could not fully establish in real life.

CONCLUSION

By paying close attention to the descriptions of the Jewish badge in Italian documents and comparing those to Jewish distinctive sign legislation from across Europe and the intricacies of papal policy, I have attempted to offer a broader perspective on anti-Jewish sartorial discrimination in Italy. My investigation indicated that to understand the significance of this legislation, it is instructive to pay attention to both the iconic and symbolic representations of the signs that the Jews were required to wear. As a symbol the O badge expressed strong anti-Jewish sentiments, but its textual representations contained some of the dilemmas of the ruling authorities.

The yellow, round badge imposed on the Jews of north and central Italy during the fifteenth century appears to have had an intrinsically negative meaning that its material characteristics—color and shape—reinforced. Contemporaries, as Guarini's verse shows, were not entirely certain what it meant, but that it had negative connotations was not in question. The different cities and towns of the region adopted it without hesitation or discussion and kept it in place for a century even though it was ineffective—the badge was rather small and Jews could easily hide it. It is surprising that authorities did not introduce the hat earlier, but the popularity of the O badge was probably associated with its icon in the text. The circle on the written page stood for an ideal achievable only at the legislative level, but one of which the authorities were not ready to let go.

When the Italian cities replaced the yellow O with a yellow hat during the sixteenth century, they made a concrete effort to finally effectively implement the discrimination by imposing a sign that the Jews could not conceal. From that perspective, it was an improvement. At the documentary level, however, it involved a concession: the icon O was replaced by elaborate verbal descriptions and a multiplicity of different words that could lead to confusion. Such were the paradoxes of distinctive sign legislation: an obvious icon all over the texts but a badge that was barely visible in the real world; a yellow head covering that everybody could see but a loss of clarity in the written document. Indeed, making the Jews more readily distinguishable in the physical world appears to have necessitated the undoing of their iconic and idealized separateness in the world of text and legislation.

ACKNOWLEDGMENTS

I would like to thank Brigitte Bedos-Rezak, Robert Chazan, Sean Field, Benjamin Ravid, as well as Leonard Greenspoon and the participants at the 24th Klutznick-Harris Symposium for their helpful comments.

PERMISSIONS

Images reproduced with the permission of the *Ministerio per i Beni e le Attivita Culturali* and the *Archivio di Stato di Milano* in Italy where they are preserved (protocollo 3404/28.13.11, recorded in the Institute's Register nr. 26/2013).

NOTES

[1] David Werner Amram, *The Makers of Hebrew Books in Italy*, 2nd ed. (London: Holland Press, 1963), 121.

[2] Diane Owen Hughes, "Sumptuary Law and Social Relations in Renaissance Italy," in *Disputes and Settlements: Law and Human Relations in the West* (ed. John Bossy; Cambridge: Cambridge University Press, 1983), 69–99; Carole Collier Frick, *Dressing Renaissance Florence: Families, Fortunes, and Fine Clothing* (Baltimore: The Johns Hopkins University Press, 2002), 179–200.

[3] See, for example, Cesare Vecellio, *Habiti Antichi, Et Moderni Di Tutto Il Mondo* (Venetia: Appresso i Sessa, 1598); François Deserps, *A Collection of the Various Styles of Clothing which are Presently Worn* (Minneapolis: James Ford Bell Library, 2001).

[4] See, for example, the anxiety that accompanied the introduction of the passport, due to the difficulty of recognizing people and establishing one's identity. Valentin Groebner, "Describing the Person, Reading the Signs in Late Medieval and Renaissance Europe: Identity Papers, Vested Figures, and the Limits of Identification, 1400–1600," in *Documenting Individual Identity: The Development of State Practices in the Modern World* (ed. Jane Caplan and John Torpey; Princeton University Press, 2001), 15–27; Valentin Groebner, *Who Are You?: Identification, Deception, and Surveillance in Early Modern Europe* (Boston: Zone Books, 2007).

[5] Two edicts issued in Florence in 1439 and 1446 argue that the Jews must wear the yellow badge to prevent them from having sexual intercourse with Christians and committing evil deeds that might harm or disrespect Christianity. Umberto Cassuto, *Gli Ebrei a Firenze Nell'età Del Rinascimento* (Firenze: L.S. Olschki, 1965), 366–68. The letter written in 1468 by the Bishop of Cremona to the Duke of Milan explains that three Christians were injured by Jews who did not wear their badge: "che li fano portare lo .O. como vole a ragione et per che tre cristiane sonno state vituperate da tri judei parte per che non li cognoscano del che e grandissima pena et scandalo in questa citate." Archivio di Stato di Milano, Carteggio Sforzesco, Potenze Sovrane, 1633. See also the declaration by the Venetian Senate that Jews who do not wear or hide their badge commit many evil atrocities: "quelli zudei non possendo eser cognoscuti da christiani stano ad beneplacitum suum in questa nostra citta commetendo varie enormita . . ." Archivio di Stato di Venezia, Senato, Terra, reg. 12, c. 135, 1496 march 26.

[6] On artistic representation of the Jewish badge: Ruth Mellinkoff, *Outcasts: Signs of Otherness in Northern European Art of the Late Middle Ages* (California Studies in the History of Art; Berkeley: University of California Press, 1993); Sara Lipton, *Images of Intolerance: The Representation of Jews and Judaism in the Bible* (The S. Mark Taper Foundation Imprint in Jewish Studies; Berkeley: University of California Press, 1999); Marc Michael Epstein, "Review Essay: Re-Presentation of the Jewish Image: Three

New Contributions," *AJS Review* 26, no. 2 (2002): 327–40; Diane Owen Hughes, "Distinguishing Signs: Ear-Rings, Jews and Franciscan Rhetoric in the Italian Renaissance City," *Past and Present*, no. 112 (August 1986): 3–59; Danièle Sansy, "Marquer la différence: L'imposition de la rouelle aux XIIIe et XIVe siècles," *La rouelle et la croix*, no. 41, Medievales (2001): 15–36; Danièle Sansy, "Signe distinctif et judéité dans l'image," *Micrologus* 15 (2007): 87–105.

[7] Benjamin Ravid, "From Yellow to Red: On the Distinguishing Head-Covering of the Jews of Venice," *Jewish History* 6, no. 1–2 (1992): 179–210; Stefanie B. Siegmund, *The Medici State and the Ghetto of Florence: The Construction of an Early Modern Jewish Community* (Stanford: Stanford University Press, 2006). On pp. 68–69, Siegmund writes "the law-abiding Jews confirming the authority of the Duke and his power over them with their own bodies."

[8] Michel Pastoureau, *The Devil's Cloth* (trans. Jody Gladding; Simon and Schuster, 2003); Steven Connor, "Maculate Conceptions," *Textile: The Journal of Cloth and Culture* 1, no. 1 (2003): 48–63.

[9] Norman P. Tanner, *Decrees of the Ecumenical Councils* (London: Sheed & Ward, 1990), 266; and the translation by Solomon Grayzel, *The Church and the Jews in the XIIIth Century: 1198–1254*, 2nd ed. (New York: Hermon Press, 1966), 308–9: "Whereas in certain provinces of the Church the difference in their clothes sets the Jews and Saracens apart from the Christians, in certain lands there has arisen such confusion that no differences are noticeable. Thus it sometimes happens that by mistake Christians have intercourse with Jewish or Saracen women, and Jews and Saracens with Christian women. Therefore, lest these people, under the cover of an error, find and excuse for the grave sin of such intercourse, we decree that these people (Jews and Saracens) of either sex and in all Christian lands and at all times, shall easily be distinguishable from the rest of the populations by the nature of their clothes."

[10] Tanner, *Decrees of the Ecumenical Councils*, and the translation by Grayzel, *The Church and the Jews in the XIIIth Century: 1198–1254*, 308–9. Although the mention of the Mosaic Law has led Guido Kisch to argue, correctly I think, that the distinctive sign was aimed at Jews, Cutler contends that it has to be understood in the context of Innocent's millennial beliefs and that, as such, the primary targets were the Muslims of the Middle East. Guido Kisch, "The Yellow Badge in History," *Historia Judaica*, no. 4 (1942): 109–10; Allan Cutler, "Innocent III and the Distinctive Clothing of Jews and Muslims," *Studies in Medieval Culture* 3 (1970): 92–115.

[11] Shlomo Simonsohn, *The Jews in Sicily* (Studia Post-Biblica; Leiden; New York: Brill, 1997), 448–49; Elizabeth Pearl, ed., *Anglia Judaica, or, A History of the Jews in England/ Tovey, D'Blossiers* (London: Weidenfeld and Nicolson, 1990), 208; Solomon Grayzel, *The Church and the Jews in the XIIIth Century: 1254–1314* (Detroit: Wayne State University Press, 1989), 205–1; Kisch, "The Yellow Badge in History," 107–8.

[12] Jourdan, Decrusy, and Isambert, eds., *Recueil Général Des Anciennes Lois Françaises, Depuis L'an 420 Jusqu'à La Révolution De 1789* (Paris: Belin-Le-Prieur, 1822), 345; and for more on the introduction of distinctive sign legislation in France, Robert Chazan, *Medieval Jewry in Northern France: A Political and Social History* (Baltimore: Johns Hopkins University Press, 1973), 149–51; Joseph Shatzmiller, *La deuxième controverse de Paris*.

Un chapitre dans la polémique entre chrétiens et juifs au Moyen-Age (Collection de la Revue des Études Juives 14; Louvain: Peeters, 1994).

[13] Mundill, *England's Jewish Solution: Experiment and Expulsion, 1262–1290*, 291–93. These are only a few examples. Among others, in 1363, the French king required the Jews to wear a badge the size of the great royal seal, colored half in red and the other half in white. Jourdan, Decrusy and Isambert, *Recueil general*, v. 5, 134: "Que tous juifs . . . porteront une grant rouelle bien notable, de la grandeur de nostre grant seel, partie de rouge et de blanc." In a Castilian law of 1313, the Jews had to wear a yellow, round badge on chest and back: "sinal de panno amariello en los pechos en las aspaldas." Baer, *Die Juden im Christlichen Spanien*, vol. 2, 131. In Germany and Austria, badges were not mentioned until the fifteenth century, but as early as 1265, Jews were required to wear pointed hats. Kisch, "The Yellow Badge in History," 107–8.

[14] Shlomo Simonsohn, *The Jews in Sicily* (Leiden; New York: Brill, 1997), 448–49: "edictum Iudeis . . . super vestimenta que induet gestet lineum vestimentum clausum undique et tinctum colore celesti, et secundum sue tempus etatis barbam nutriat et barbatum inceda . . . sancimus ut mulieres hebree, super rudello vel pallio quo se tegunt bendam deferant tinctam colore celesti, quo deposito, bendam eiudem coloris portent super capitis ligamenta." Frederick II issued this decree in 1221.

[15] Toaff, "The Jewish Badge in Italy during the Fifteenth Century," 275.

[16] Roberto Bonfil, *Jewish Life in Renaissance Italy* (Berkeley: University of California Press, 1994), 1–19; Shlomo Simonsohn, *The Jews in the Duchy of Milan* (A Documentary History of the Jews of Italy; Jerusalem: Israel Academy of Sciences and Humanities, 1982), xiii–xxvii; Ariel Toaff, "Gli insediamenti ashkenaziti nell'Italia settentrionale," in *Gli ebrei in Italia* (ed. Corrado Vivanti; Storia d'Italia 11; Turin: Einaudi, 1996), 155–71.

[17] For example, Jews fled German lands after the plague of 1348 and were expelled from France in 1394 and from Spain in 1492. Bonfil, *Jewish Life in Renaissance Italy*, 1–19; Shlomo Simonsohn, "la condizione giuridica degli ebrei nell'Italia centrale e settentrionale (secoli XII–XVI)," in *Gli ebrei in Italia*, 97–120.

[18] On Jewish economic activities and money lending, see Bonfil, *Jewish Life in Renaissance Italy*, 20–79; Ariel Toaff, "Il commercio del denaro e le comunita ebraiche 'di confine' (Pittigliano, Sorano, Monte San Savino, Lipiano) tra cinquecento e seicento," in *Italia Judaica: Gli ebrei in Italia tra Rinascimento ed Età barocca* (Rome, 1986), 99–117; Salvatore Foa, "Banche e banchieri ebrei nel Piemonte dei secoli scorsi," *Rassegna Mensile di Israel* 21 (1955): 93–50; Léon Poliakov, *Jewish Bankers and the Holy See: From the Thirteenth to the Seventeenth Century* (London: Routledge & K. Paul, 1977); Moses A. Shulvass, *The Jews in the World of the Renaissance* (Leiden: Brill, 1973), 114–33.

[19] Hughes, "Distinguishing Signs," 19–20; Bonfil, *Jewish Life in Renaissance Italy*, 20.

[20] Franco Mormando argues that current historiography on the friars lacks in thoroughness. He shows that Bernadino, for instance, had not written or preached about the Jews as much as was previously thought, and that his overall impact on Jewish policy needs to be reassessed. Franco Mormando, *The Preacher's Demons: Bernardino of Siena and the Social Underworld of Early Renaissance Italy* (Chicago: University of Chicago Press, 1999); Franco Mormando, *The Friar's Solution: Bernardino of Siena and the Jews* (American Society of Church History Papers; Portland: Theological Research Exchange Network

[TREN], 1995); Nirit Ben-Aryeh Debby, "Jews and Judaism in the Rhetoric of Popular Preachers: The Florentine Sermons of Giovanni Dominici (1356–1419) and Bernardino da Siena (1380–1444)," *Jewish History*, no. 14 (2000): 180; Nirit Ben-Aryeh Debby, *Renaissance Florence in the Rhetoric of Two Popular Preachers* (Turnhout: Brepols, 2001)

[21] Hughes, "Sumptuary Law and Social Relations in Renaissance Italy," 71: "it has been calculated that the Italian cities produced eighty-three substantial sumptuary laws in the fifteenth century and more than double that number in each of the following centuries."

[22] Alan Hunt, *Governance of the Consuming Passions: A History of Sumptuary Law* (New York: St. Martin's Press, 1996), 77–101; Maria Giuseppina Muzzarelli and Antonella Campanini, eds., *Disciplinare Il Lusso: La Legislazione Suntuaria in Italia e in Europa tra Medioevo ed Età Moderna* (Studi storici Carocci 40; Roma: Carocci, 2003); Ronald E. Rainey, "Sumptuary Legislation in Renaissance Florence" (Ph.D. diss., Columbia University,1985), 617–23; Gabriel Guarino, "Regulation of Appearances During the Catholic Reformation: Dress and Morality in Spain and Italy," in *Les Deux Réformes Chrétiennes: Propagation Et Diffusion* (ed. Ilana Zinguer and MyriamYardeni; Studies in the History of Christian Thought 114; Leiden: Brill, 2004), 492–510.

[23] Hughes, "Sumptuary Law and Social Relations in Renaissance Italy," 69–72.

[24] I thank Benjamin Ravid for his transcriptions of the archival documents. Archivio di Stato di Venezia, Senato, Misti, reg. 43, c. 24r, 1394 agosto 27. In 1408, the law required the Jews to wear a yellow O made of a thin rope of spun fiber a finger in width: "*judei stantes in Venetiis debeant portare O in pectore . . . quod O sit de una cordella zalla lata de uno digito.*" Senato, Misti, reg. 46, c. 55v, 1402 novembre 7. See also Ravid, "From Yellow to Red: On the Distinguishing Head-Covering of the Jews of Venice," 182. For reasons of clarity, I capitalized the O. This was sometimes done in the original documents, but, more consistently, the O was separated from the rest of the text by a dot or slash on each side.

[25] Umberto Cassuto, *Gli Ebrei a Firenze Nell'età Del Rinascimento* (Firenze: L. S. Olschki, 1965), 367–68, 72: "unum O cuius latitudo rotunditatis sit per directum unius sexti brachhi ad minus ad mensuram florentinam, panni vel nastri gialli." A few years later in, 1463, the law was repeated and the size of the badge was doubled to a third of an arm: the Jews had to wear "el segno del O," which was "uno grande O giallo . . . la circumferenza uno terzo di braccio, et la larghezza sia uno ditto communale." The *braccio* is a unit of length of about 60 cm. One-sixth is a badge of 10 cm circumference; one-third is 20 cm.

[26] Alberto Castaldini, *Mondi Paralleli: Ebrei E Cristiani Nell'italia Padana Dal Tardo Medioevo All'età Moderna* (Firenze: L. S. Olschki, 2004), 80–81.

[27] There are many other examples in Umbria. In Amelia in 1468: "signo coloris croci per modium unius .O." or "lu signo de lu .O." Norcia specifically referred in 1478 to the sign as the letter O, and, interestingly, Jews could wear it in yellow or green: "signum in formam littere .O. coloris viridis gialli granulini." In Citta di Castello in 1485, the Jews had to wear the "segno del .O." and a year later in Perugia, they were compelled to wear "lo .O. giallo." See Ariel Toaff, *The Jews in Umbria* (Leiden; New York: E. J. Brill, 1993), 154–57, 788–89, 982–83, 1006–7.

[28] Archivio Storico Communale di Piacenza, Provisioni, cart. 2, reg. 11, fol. 24r. Archivio di Stato di Milano, Carteggio Sforzesco, Potenze Sovrane 1633. Other examples include: Milan 1473: "debiano portare un O nel pecto," and Pavia 1478: "uno O pro signale."

Carteggio Sforzesco 914; and Missive 131, Mf bob 76. Also listed in Simonsohn, *The Jews in the Duchy of Milan*, v.1, 54, 429, 615.

[29] Archivio di Stato di Milano, Missive 4, fol 131b, Mf bob2. Archivio di Stato di Cremona, Fragmentorum B.9/1, 000714.

[30] For more information on the conflicted interactions of Renaissance States, see Nicolai Rubinstein, *The Government of Florence Under the Medici (1434–1494)* (Oxford-Warburg Studies; Oxford, Clarendon Press, 1966); Robert Finlay, *Politics in Renaissance Venice* (New Brunswick: Rutgers University Press, 1980); Gregory Lubkin, *A Renaissance Court: Milan Under Galeazzo Maria Sforza* (Berkeley: University of California Press, 1994); Trevor Dean, *Land and Power in Late Medieval Ferrara: The Rule of the Este, 1350–1450* (Cambridge: Cambridge University Press, 1988).

[31] I thank Michele Luzzati for bringing this story to my attention. Archivio di Stato di Firenze, Otto di Guardia e Balia della Repubblica n. 69, cc. 72v–73r, 2 gennaio 1485: "cum mitria in capite picta et plena karakteribus .O. croceis et in quolibet dictorum karakteribus .O. croceis cum karakteribus .L. nigris."

[32] Debby, "Jews and Judaism in the Rhetoric of Popular Preachers," 185.

[33] Charles S. Peirce, *Charles S. Peirce: The Essential Writings* (New York: Harper & Row, 1972); Bronwen Martin and Felizitas Ringham, *Dictionary of Semiotics* (London, New York: Cassell, 2000), 73, 128. Thomas Albert Sebeok, *Signs: An Introduction to Semiotics*, 2nd ed. (Toronto Studies in Semiotics and Communication; Toronto, Buffalo: University of Toronto Press, 2001), 81–88.

[34] Cassuto, *Gli Ebrei a Firenze Nell'età Del Rinascimento*, 367.

[35] Toaff, "The Jewish Badge in Italy during the Fifteenth Century," 277. On the problem of concealment and how Venice dealt with it, see Ravid, "From Yellow to Red: On the Distinguishing Head-Covering of the Jews of Venice," 183.

[36] Archivio di Stato di Venezia, Senato, Terra, reg. 12, c. 135, 1496 march 26. Ravid, "From Yellow to Red: On the Distinguishing Head-Covering of the Jews of Venice," 183.

[37] Archivio di Stato di Cremona, Fragmentorum B.9/1, 000714: "la beretta gialda in capo li maschii et le femine lo O sopra la spalla."

[38] Archivio di Stato di Genova, Archivio Segreto n. 755, c. LXVIIIIr-v, M. D. S.: "birretum suum in capite coloris gialdi."

[39] Archivio di Stato di Genova, Archivio Segreto n. 755, c. LXVIIIIr-v, M. D. S., 1587. Archivio di Stato di Genoa, Archivio Segreto n. 833, c. 156, M. D. S., 1587. And Urbani et al., *The Jews in Genoa*, 194–95: "omnes hebrei . . . debeant portare super biretis et pileis a modo in antea portare nastrum seu, ut vulgo dicitur, fresetto crovis coloris, et eedem mulieres hebree idem frexetum portare teneantur super ornamentum capitis."

[40] Archivio di Stato di Milano, Fondo Culto 2159. Listed in Simonsohn, *The Jews in the Duchy of Milan*, 1449–50.

[41] Archivio di Stato di Torino, Art. 693, par. 1, reg. 1580–1589, nr. 6, fol. 78: "gl'homeni berette o cappello gialli et le donne vello o cendallo giallo in cappo." Listed in Segre, *The Jews in Piedmont*.

[42] Archivio di Stato di Milano, Fondo Culto 2159: "Maestro, io voglio andare sin a Lodi et più oltri anchora pero fattime un capello secondo l'ordine . . . circa il portar de berette et capelli per li hebrei."

[43] Archivio di Stato di Milano, Fondo Culto 2159. Unfortunately, the duke's response was not preserved.

[44] Umberto Eco, *A Theory of Semiotics* (Bloomington: Indiana University Press, 1976), 205.

[45] Amram, *The Makers of Hebrew Books in Italy*, 121.

[46] In 1208, just seven years before the Fourth Lateran Council, Innocent III wrote a letter to the count of Nevers, in which he associated Cain and his sign with the Jews and their guilt: "Ut esset cain vagus et profugus super terram, nec interficeretur a quoquam, tremorem capitis signum Dominis imposuit super eum; quare Iudei, contra quos clamat vox sanguinis Ihesu Christi, et si occidi non debeant, ne divine legis obliviscatur populus Christianus, dispergi tamen debent super terram ut vagi, quatinus facies ipsorum ignominia repleatur, et quadrant nomen Domini Ihesu Christi." Shlomo Simonsohn, *The Apostolic See and the Jews* (Toronto: Pontifical Institute of Mediaeval Studies, 1988), 92–93; Jeremy Cohen, *Living Letters of the Law: Ideas of the Jew in Medieval Christianity*, 1st ed. (University of California Press, 1999), 28–29, 55, 249 n.90, 361 n. 118; Ruth Mellinkoff, *The Mark of Cain* (Berkeley: University of California Press, 1981); Gilbert Dahan, "L'exegese de Cain et Abel du XIIe au XIVe siecle en Occident," *Recherches en Theologie ancienne et medievales* 49–50 (1982): 21–89, 5–68

[47] The socioeconomic conditions and consequences of the Jews' involvement in money lending have been studied extensively. Here I am primarily interested in the idea that the O badge can symbolize it. For more on Jews and money lending, Luciano Allegra, *La Città Verticale: Usurai, Mercanti e Tessitori Nella Chieri Del Cinquecento* (Dipartimento di storia dell'Universita di Torino 2; Milano: F. Angeli, 1987); Benjamin Ravid, "'Contra Judaeos' in Seventeenth-Century Italy: Two Responses to the 'Discorso' of Simone Luzzatto by Melchiore Palontrotti and Giulio Morosini," *AJS Review* 7 (1982): 301–51; F. R. Salter, "The Jews in Fifteenth-Century Florence and Savonarola's Establishment of a Montis Pietatis," *Cambridge Historical Journal* 5, no. 2 (1936): 193–211; Kenneth R Stow, "Papal and Royal Attitudes toward Jewish Lending in the Thirteenth Century," *AJS Review* 6 (1981): 161–84; Ariel Toaff, "Il commercio del denaro e le comunita ebraiche 'di confine' (Pittigliano, Sorano, Monte San Savino, Lipiano) tra cinquecento e seicento"; Joseph Shatzmiller, *Shylock Reconsidered: Jews, Moneylending, and Medieval Society* (Berkeley: University of California Press, 1990).

[48] Charles Seife, *Zero: The Biography of a Dangerous Idea* (New York: Viking, 2000), 60–61; John D Barrow, *The Book of Nothing* (London: Jonathan Cape, 2000), 72–73. Medieval fears of zero were based on those of Greek thinkers such as Aristotle, but there was an inherent contradiction because the Judeo-Christian creation story started with a void.

[49] Seife, *Zero*, 82–83; Barrow, *The Book of Nothing*, 91–93.

[50] Archivio Storico Communale di Piacenza, Provisioni, cart. 2, reg. 11, fol. 24r.

[51] Michel Pastoureau, "Figures et Couleurs Péjoratives en Héraldique Médiévale," in *Figures et Couleurs: Études sur la symbolique et la sensibilité Médiévales* (Paris: Léopard d'or, 1986), 115–37; Michel Pastoureau, "L'image héraldique," in *Figures et Couleurs*, 193–209.

[52] Kisch, "The Yellow Badge in History," 104. But see also Rubens, *A History of Jewish Costume*, 110. Mark R. Cohen, *Under Crescent and Cross: The Jews in the Middle Ages* (Princeton: Princeton University Press, 1994), 61–64.

[53] Mellinkoff, *Outcasts: Signs of Otherness in Northern European Art of the Late Middle Ages*, 35–47; Pastoureau, "Formes et couleurs du désordre. Le jaune et le vert," 23–43, and "Les couleurs médiévales: systèmes de valeurs et modes de sensibilité," 35–49.

[54] Ravid, "From Yellow to Red: On the Distinguishing Head-Covering of the Jews of Venice," 182, 203. Owen Hughes, "Distinguishing Signs: Ear-Rings, Jews and Franciscan Rhetoric in the Italian Renaissance," 25, 29–38.

[55] Hughes, "Distinguishing Signs," 50–59.

[56] Cohen, *Living Letters of the Law*, 19–94, 271–313.

[57] Simonsohn, *The Apostolic See and the Jews*, v.1, vii–viii. This work assembles 3,250 bulls and briefs containing references to the Jews. Due to the immensity of the Vatican archives, Simonsohn and his collaborators limited the scope of their research to a thorough investigation of the major Vatican archival collections and of those lesser ones that they expected to contain information on the Jews. For references to the relevant documents, see the index at "Badge."

[58] Ibid., 68, 79–80, 858–59.

[59] On the Popes' dual role: Paolo Prodi, *The Papal Prince: One Body and Two Souls: The Papal Monarchy in Early Modern Europe* (Cambridge: Cambridge University Press, 1987), 17–67.

[60] For example in 1360, the Jews were required to wear a red tabard or cape. After the Pope's return from Avignon, the rule of the red tabard was kept in place, as can be deduced from a papal letter of August 1391, in which a Jewish member of the papal household, Benedictus Melis, was granted an exemption from wearing it: "Nec te invitum ad portandum cappam vel tabardum rubea." In 1401, three more Jewish members of the papal household were granted the same privilege, and in 1402, all the Roman Jews were freed from the obligation of wearing the tabard: "Iudei . . . possint ire, stare et redire libere et sine tabbardo rubeo." A few years later, the red tabard was reinstated but soon new exemptions were being granted. See Simonsohn, *The Apostolic See and the Jews*, v.2, 510, 530, 541

[61] Archivio Communale Todi, Statuti 4, Addictiones, rub. 224, foll. 324a–324b. See also Ariel Toaff, *The Jews in Umbria: 1435–1484* (Leiden: Brill Academic Publishers, 1993); Ariel Toaff, "La vita materiale," in *Gli ebrei in Italia*, 239–67; Hughes, "Distinguishing Signs," 23–24.

How Should a Rabbi Be Dressed? The Question of Rabbinical Attire in Italy from Renaissance to Emancipation (Sixteenth–Nineteenth Centuries)

Asher Salah

The promulgation of sumptuary laws, regulating specific items of dress that might be worn by various individuals on certain occasions, is a well-known chapter of European social history from the late Middle Ages to the eighteenth century.[1] Within the Jewish communities these decrees were often issued by the rabbis or by the communal authorities and have been used by scholars in order to study different aspects of the material culture of the Jews in early modern Europe.

From these sources two general conclusions have been drawn, as far as Italy is concerned. First, that the Jews in Italy imitated in their clothes the fashion of the upper classes of the Christian society.[2] Second, that "Jewish clothing is uniform and reflects a social homogeneity that is a prime characteristic of Jewish life."[3]

Should we hence infer that rabbis dressed like all the other Jews in their communities? Whatever answer we could be tempted to give to this question, one thing is sure: no sumptuary law known to us says anything about how a rabbi was supposed to be dressed.

In what follows I would like to tackle the question of rabbinical dress in Italy from the vantage point of the visual evidence provided by portraits of Jews and Italian rabbis from the Renaissance to the beginning of the twentieth century. This material has been somehow overlooked by previous scholarship, unaware of the relatively large number of extant depictions of Italian rabbis.

In the past decade, while dealing with the intellectual history of Italian Judaism in the early modern period, not once did I run into portraits of rabbis and physicians, which constitute an invaluable source of information about clothes and fashion.

I have been able to collect some forty portraits, spanning over a period of three hundred years, from the early seventeenth to the late nineteenth century. Forty portraits are not many compared to the 1,100 names of rabbis and physicians catalogued in my bibliographical dictionary of eighteenth-century Jews,[4] but still they can provide a sufficiently broad basis from which to make some general considerations about Jewish portraiture of the time and rabbinical garments in particular.

Material of this kind lends itself to different sorts of inquiries related to the question of fashion and Jews, from the custom of covering one's head,[5] to the use, or should we rather say disuse, of the beard among Italian Jews in early modern period,[6] from the social functions of clothes, to issues pertaining to the aesthetic values of the Jews in the past. However important, these are not topics I will address here.

Rather, I am interested in another, more relevant question. I will try to pinpoint the problem as follows: did the rabbis in Italy in the exercise of their functions make use of specific garments that distinguished them both from the rest of their congregation and from other religious clergy? And in the affirmative, from which moment is it possible to ascertain the use of a distinctive cassock, under which circumstances and what forms and shapes did it take?

But before getting to the heart of the matter, some preliminary methodological comments concerning the use of iconographic sources are necessary.

First, we should be suspicious of the apparent immediacy of the visual image and of its documentary value. It is well known that art is always about representation and imagination. As such, it can be an extremely fruitful field for the historian of mentalities, of prejudices, and of stereotypes, but it can also be misleading and fallacious for the scrutiny of material culture.

Figure 1. Moshe Gentili Hefetz in second "corrected" edition of his Melekhet Mahashevet, Konigsberg, 1819

Early modern portraits belong to a pictorial genre subject to rigid conventions, from the pose of the figure depicted to the objects surrounding it. The simple fact of being portrayed with a certain dress does not tell us by itself whether it was worn daily or on special occasions only.[7] Moreover, we must be very careful and remember that many rabbinical portraits in our collection were painted without the knowledge or the consent of the person portrayed, and therefore, they correspond more to the artist's image of how a rabbi should be dressed than how he actually dressed.

An interesting instance of the fallacious nature of the image can be found in the portrait of Rabbi Mosheh Gentili (1663–1711) that appears in the frontispiece of the second edition of his book *Melekhet Mahashevet* [Intentful Work], printed in Königsberg in 1819 [Fig. 1]. There a

Figure 2. Mosheh Gentili Hefetz in the original first edition of Melekhet Mahashevet, Venice, 1710.

black *kippah* [hemispherical cap] has been placed on his head in order to make him look more like an Eastern European Chasid than an Italian scholar of the late seventeenth century. Luckily enough, we can still refer to the first edition, where the rabbi appears bareheaded [Fig. 2], but this is not always the case.[8]

Figure 3. Avraham Cohen da Zante, rabbi, poet, and physician (Zante, 1670–Venice, 1729).

Second, our information is derived from a wide range of different iconographic sources, belonging to disparate stylistic registers, realized with different techniques, of which the degree of precision and realism can vary considerably from one portrait to the other. Some of them are lavish paintings on canvasses commissioned by the portrayed persons; others are extremely stylized engravings appearing on title pages of books, such as the portrait of the poet and physician from Padua named Avraham Cohen da Zante (1679–1729) [Fig. 3]. Others are depicted on *ketubot* [wedding contracts]—sometimes the same portrait of the groom and the bride in richly decorated prenuptial agreements was reused for different couples [Fig. 4]—or on medallions or in lithographs distributed postmortem for celebratory purposes, such as the one depicting Rabbi Ishmael HaKohen from Modena (1723–1811) [Fig. 5].

Figure 4. Detail of the Ketubbah with the portraits of the groom, Dr. Shemuel HaCohen Cantarini, and the bride, Colomba Aziz, Padua, 1732.

In one case we have also a caricature by Pier Leone Ghezzi (1674–1755) of famous Roman Rabbi Tranquillo Corcos (1660–1730) [Fig. 6].[9] The Corcos portrait can be read as one of the earliest instances of the formation in Europe of a new kind of antisemitism, where a racial stereotype (the hooked nose) replaces the religious one.[10]

Therefore, not every testimony has the same degree of reliability, especially when stereotypes related to the artist's background, most of whom were non–Jews,[11] can interfere with the representation of clothes used by Jews. This should induce us to be prudent, since in the representation of Jewish scenes, there could be at work two con-

Figure 5. Ishmael Ha-Cohen (Laudadio Sacerdote), chief rabbi of Modena (1723–1811).

Figure 6. Tranquillo Corcos, chief rabbi of Rome (1660–1730).

trasting but equally deforming principles.

On the one hand, there could be at work the attempt to transform foreignness into something more familiar and, subsequently, less threatening,[12] as happens paintings of synagogues and in the paintings by Alessandro Magnasco (1667–1749) [Fig. 7], where the only detail indicating the fact that we are observing a Jewish prayer is the tallit [ritual shawl] over the head of the preacher, while none of the other congregants wears any distinctively Jewish dress.

Figure 7. Prayer in a Synagogue (1710) by Alessandro Magnasco, (Genoa 1667–1749), at Galleria degli Uffizi, Florence (photograph by Asher Salah).

Such distinctive dress could have been the red hat that Jews were obliged to wear, as can be seen in the apparently more realistic depiction of a Jewish wedding in Venice by Marco Marcuola (1740–1793) [Fig. 8].

Figure 8. Jewish wedding in Venice, Marco Marcuola, (Verona, 1740–Venice, 1793) (photograph by Asher Salah).

Figure 9. Funeral wake in Reggio Emilia, 1740.

On the other hand, we have the drive to exaggerate the depiction of the exotic, of the uncanny, and of the curious detail, as can be seen in Figure 9, where the anonymous artist has introduced several Jews with Oriental dress, a quite unexpected sight in a small Italian Jewish community such as Reggio Emilia, where no local Jew went around with this kind of accoutrement.

Lastly, portraits become fashionable among Italian Jews only in the late seventeenth century.[13] It is true that we have earlier evidence of pictures hanging on the walls of Jewish homes, such as Leone da Modena's (1571–1648) when, in his *Historia de' Riti Hebraici*, he writes that "in Italia molti [ebrei] si fanno lecito tener ritratti e pitture in casa, massime non essendo di rilievo ne di corpo compito [in Italy many Jews allow themselves to keep in their homes portraits and pictures, especially if they are not in relief or represent the full body]."[14] We know of at least one case of a Jewish woman sending her portrait to a Christian writer,[15] and it is highly probable that some rabbinic figures had in their studies images of their masters as early as the sixteenth century, though none of these portraits have survived.[16]

In any case in the Jewish world, even in the much acculturated Italian communities, these are still isolated occurrences attested with a considerable delay compared to other social categories in the Christian environment, where the birth of portraiture is considered a definitive feature of the early fifteenth century.[17] After the first few attested instances in the seventeenth century— such as the portrait of the cabalist Menahem Azariah da Fano (1548–1620)[18] [Fig. 10] and Leon da Modena, which appears in the frontispiece of his book

רבינו מנחם עזריה מפאנו זצ״ל
נולד הוא שח-תנאמף אל עמיו ד׳ אב ש״ף-במנטובה.

Figure 10. Menahem Azari-
ah da Fano, rabbi and kaba-
list (Fano, 1548–Mantua,
1620).

Figure 11. Detail of frontispiece of Historia de Riti
Hebraici, Venice, 1638, with the portrait of its
author, Rabbi Leone da Modena (1574–1648).

devoted to Jewish ritual, *Historia de' Riti Hebraici* (Venice, 1638)[19] [Fig. 11]—
it is only during the eighteenth century that it is possible to speak about widespread Jewish patronage of arts and of prominent Italian Jews asking renowned
artists to paint their portraits. This was the case in the northern European
Sephardic communities, with paintings commissioned from renowned artists
such as Rembrandt, Reynolds, or Gainsborough.[20]

From what precedes, it should be clear that in order to benefit as much
as possible from the analysis of this kind of iconographical source, much
prudence is needed. When we use this material, we must compare it to other
forms of documentary evidence, such as the communities' *taqanot* [decrees],
the rabbinical responsa, and the *prammatiche,* that is, dispositions regulating
the life of the community and its institutions, always being attentive to what
happens in other cultural and religious contexts in a perspective both dia-
chronic and synchronic.

Yet it is not possible to do without the visual evidence for at least two
reasons. The first one is linked to the high degree of precision and realism usually found in the depictions of Jewish life by Christian artists from the early
sixteenth century,[21] notwithstanding the aforementioned antisemitic biases.
Second, because the written testimonies through which we can get an idea
of how rabbis dressed in the crucial period of Jewish history when traditional
society was being overrun by modern tendencies are surprisingly scant.

Unfortunately, the question of the rabbinical dress, an important aspect of material culture of the Jews in Italy, has not been the object of deep scrutiny by scholars and historians of early modern and modern Italian Judaism.[22] As far as Italy is concerned, we must rely almost exclusively on Alfred Rubens' classical contribution, though much outdated, that refers to Italian Jews clothing habits only sporadically.[23] Rubens summarizes the issue as follows:

> There is no traditional rabbinical robe and the robes worn at the present time are derived from the black Geneva gown and white bands of the Calvinist or Reformed Church, while the round black hat, which was adopted during the nineteenth century in Austria and Germany, must be derived ultimately from the similar headgear of the Greek Orthodox clergy.[24]

Rubens does not say anything about the reasons for the appropriation of the Protestant cassock by rabbis, an even more surprising appropriation considering that it concerns not only the Jews living in areas inhabited mainly by Protestants, but also, as in the case of the Italian peninsula, in states where the official religion was Catholicism. Moreover, he seems to have been led astray by the still widespread but inexact assumption that the adoption of a specific dress by rabbis was a nineteenth-century innovation done under the auspices of the Jewish reform movement in Central Europe.

In fact, there is substantial evidence that the thrust to create a distinctive dress for rabbis emerges already in the late Renaissance and mainly in the communities of Italy and the Netherlands. Before that time, rabbis apparently dressed as the rest of the Jews in their congregations. This is at least the conclusion reached by the Israeli historian Roberto Bonfil in his essential work on rabbis and Jewish communities in Renaissance Italy: "For the sixteenth century I have not found that the ordained Rabbis in Italy wore special garments unique to their status."[25]

Nevertheless it seems, from a disposition of Verona's community in 1557, that cantors and all those who led the prayer, except the rabbi, had to wear a special mantle.[26] On the nature of this mantle little is known, but to judge from sixteenth-century Ashkenazi legal sources, it seems to have been either a particularly sumptuous *tallith* of silk or a garment similar to the *cappa*, the mantle worn by university doctors.

The main halakhic authorities of the time were critical of this use, considered to be a sign of haughtiness and presumption to be avoided,[27] but the thrust to establish a vestimental difference between officiants and the rest of the congregation is evidently already in action in the different way of wearing the tallit by rabbis.[28] Concerning the tallit, Paolo Medici (1671–1738), a Florentine apostate, writes that "the rabbis keep

Figure 12. Jewish burial by Marco Marcuola (Verona, 1740–Venezia, 1793), made around 1780, oil 41,9 x 81 cm (Israel Museum).

Figure 13. David Nieto, chief rabbi of London (Venice, 1654–London, 1728).

it over their heads in order to distinguish themselves from the rest of their congregation and act in this way more for lavishness than for religious zeal"[29] [Fig. 12]. Apparently, in the second half of the seventeenth century, this desire for distinctiveness had become a reality, since most of the rabbinical portraits in Italy of the time show the rabbis wearing a characteristic dress, with the clerical bands and the black gown.

Figure 14. Salomon Aylion, Rabbi in Amsterdam (1660–1728).

Figure 15. Shabtai Marini, Rabbi and physician in Padua (1662–1748).

Among the most remarkable and earliest examples of this dress we have the portraits of Moshe Gentili and David Nieto (1654–1728) [Fig. 13]. Since we are dealing with rabbis from Venice

Figure 16. Shimshon Morpurgo, rabbi in Ancona (1681–1740).

and Leghorn, cities with strong ties with the Jewish communities of England and the Netherlands, it is quite likely that the adoption of such a garment was made under northern European Sephardic influence, where we have several examples of rabbis dressed likewise [Fig. 14] at least a decade before Italy and where Protestantism was the majority's religion.

Should we consider this a dress specifically conceived for rabbis? Although this dress is not widespread to other categories of Jews, it bears a strong resemblance to academic and medical costumes of the time. These are professions that in Italy used to wear a collar similar to the one of the reformed clergy in Protestant countries, though a little bit longer and not necessarily white (as can be seen in the Shabtai Marini [1685–1762] and Shimshon Morpurgo's [1681–1740] portraits [Figs. 15 and 16]). The influence of the medical garb on the rabbinical cassock is even more plausible, since rabbis are similar to physicians insofar as their social status is concerned in the edicts of many northern Italian Jewish communities.[30]

Nevertheless, later on in the eighteenth century, this kind of garb became exclusively rabbinical, since physicians and other classes of people discontinued its wearing. When in 1775 Pope Pius VI (1775–1799), in his *Editto sopra gli Ebrei* [Edict about the Jews], forbids the rabbis to use a distinctive cassock and obliges them to wear the same clothes as the rest of the community members,[31] this can be read as an evidence that rabbis were indeed wearing a special dress, not dissimilar from the one that appears in many portraits of the time. For instance, at about the same time of the edict, in 1777, Rabbi Zecharia Padova from Modena:

> after a quarrel with the leaders of his community, caricatured them
> in an etching, in which he depicted himself seated in his study and
> his elegantly-dressed opponents advancing on him, one of them—
> his bitterest enemy—having a dog's body.[32]

The dress by itself suffices to identify the rabbi from the lay community leaders [Fig. 17].

From the second half of nineteenth century, the dress of the rabbis and of the ministers in Italian synagogues (see the example of Yitzhaq Shemuel Reggio [1784–1855] [Fig. 18]), with the adoption of the square hat with the addition of a small pompon and the belt, has remained almost unchanged until today.[33] At this point we can legitimately speak of a uniform, and as such, it was conceived in the circles of Reformed Judaism in Germany around 1840.

Attilio Milano, in the last paragraphs of his *History of the Jews in Italy*, dedicated to rabbinical dress, records the aforementioned transformation and writes:

Though most of those Italian Jews—who today refer to the synagogue as the "temple," to the prayer book as the "hymnary," to the rabbinical assemblies as "synods," and call the rabbis "reverends"—may have forgotten the origin of such a lexicon, there is little doubt about the fact that these are terms belonging to the religious sphere of the reformed churches and not of Catholicism.

Figure 19. Round hat of Jacques Kahn, chief rabbi of the Moselle in 1930 (1868–1944).

Figure 20. David Sintzheim, chief rabbi of Strasbourg and chairman of the Grand Sanhedrin in Paris (1745–1812).

Third and lastly, rabbinical garments show us a European Judaism that follows the same fashion all over the continent, notwithstanding some local, national, and religious differences. Italian, German, French, and British rabbis dress in similar ways, with slight and insignificant

Figure 21. Abraham de Cologna, vice-chairman of the Grand Sanhedrin in Paris (Mantua, 1755–Triest, 1832).

Figure 22. Visit of Pope John Paul II at the synagogue of Rome, 1986.

particularities, such as the round clerical hat in France (*chapeau clerical*) [Fig. 19] as opposed to the hexagonal one in Italy (*toque*).

Therefore, we should not be surprised that the question of how rabbis should be dressed was not a central issue in the debates that otherwise raged among European Jews concerning reform of Judaism, at least in the first half of the nineteenth century. The clerical garb had long been an established custom among rabbis in most western European synagogues.[39] Champions of the Orthodox camp, from David Sintzheim (1745–1812) [Fig. 20] to Samson Raphael Hirsch (1808–1888), are dressed in the same way as their opponents

among the reformers, from Abraham Cologna (1755–1832) [Fig. 21] to Abraham Geiger (1810–1874).

In fact, in a Württemberg document of 1847, the white collar bands of the rabbinic garb are called "Moses Tablets," including them in a specifically Jewish semantic field of reference rather that stressing their dependence on a foreign religious model.[40] An attack condemning the by then traditional canonical robes of rabbinical dress will come only later, in the second half of the nineteenth century, from elements inside Jewish society that rejected modernity *in toto*. These elements reinvented a supposedly original tradition through a vehement opposition toward anything that was considered an effect of emancipation even when, such as was the case of the cassock, it did not constitute a divide between a liberal and conservative milieu.[41]

Perhaps we should introduce a distinction between a programmatic reform (that actively fights for a change in liturgy, its musical accompaniment, the structure of the synagogue—whether the *bimah* [raised platform] should be in the center or not—and the compulsory character of traditional Jewish law) and an underground and unconscious reform, linked to a deep and therefore imperceptible change in mentalities and religious behavior.

The rabbinical cassock was not debated, since nobody deemed it debatable and no one considered, at least in Italy, its use an instance of a dangerous imitation of the mores of the Gentiles. Quite the opposite, since no Catholic priest ever dressed like an Italian rabbi.

During the Pope's visit to the Rome synagogue in 1986, even the choir members were dressed with the rabbinical cassock, something quite unusual on normal occasions, but this was done precisely with the purpose of affirming the distinctiveness of the Jewish attire from the Catholic one [Fig. 22]. This is a most striking example of how the Protestant clerical dress has been definitively Judaized by Jews living in a Catholic environment. Ironically enough, sometimes common patterns of civilizations and of cultures emerge when we scrutinize what each one of them claims to be its distinctive characteristics.

NOTES

[1] On Jewish sumptuary legislation in general, see Salo Wittmayer Baron, *The Jewish Community: Its History and Structure to the American Revolution*, 3 vols. (Philadelphia: Jewish Publication Society, 1942); Louis Finkelstein, *Jewish Self-Government in the Middle Ages* (New York: Jewish Theological Seminary, 1924). For Eastern Europe, see Elliott Horowitz, "Sumptuary Legislation," in *YIVO Encyclopedia of Jews in Eastern Europe* http://www.yivo-encyclopedia.org/article.aspx/Sumptuary_Legislation; for Italy, Roberto Bonfil, *Jewish Life in Renaissance Italy* (Berkeley: University of California Press, 1994), 104ff; Ariel Toaff, "La

vita materiale," in *Storia d'Italia. Annali 11/1* (ed. Corrado Vivanti; Torino: Einaudi, 1996), 239–67; Maria Giuseppina Muzzarelli, "Il vestito degli ebrei," *Zakhor* 4 (2000): 161–68. On Italy but without much information on Jews, Catherine Kovesi Killerby, *Sumptuary Law in Italy. 1200–1500* (Oxford: Clarendon Press, 2002). Yehudah Da Modena, *Ziqnei Yehudah.*

[2] Thérèse Metzger, *Jewish Life in the Middle Ages: Illuminated Hebrew Manuscripts of the Thirteenth to the Sixteenth Centuries* (Secaucus: Chartwell Books, 1982), 138, and Toaff, "La vita materiale," 257. This is what already appears in Leon da Modena, *Historia de riti hebraici* (Paris, 1637), 19, when he writes that the Jews are dressed like the Christians "secondo il paese ove si trovano [following the uses of the country where they live]." Further, since the Christians consider it an expression of respect to take out their headgear, Jewish men do likewise: "gli uomini ancora non hanno ben fatto l'andar con il capo scoperto . . . essendo tra Christiani, dove si costuma per riverir i maggiori [togliersi il cappello], lo fanno anch'essi." See also da Modena's famous responsum on the permission of walking bareheaded, in Yehudah Da Modena, *Ziqnei Yehudah* (ed. S. Simonsohn; Jerusalem, 1956), 33–38, siman 21.

[3] Kenneth Stow, *Theater of Acculturation: Roman Ghetto in the Sixteenth Century* (Seattle: University of Washington Press, 2001), 184.

[4] Asher Salah, *La République des Lettres: Rabbins, médecins et écrivains juifs en Italie au XVIIIe siècle* (Leiden/Boston: Brill, 2007).

[5] Raphael Straus, "The Jewish Hat as an Aspect of Social History," *Jewish Social Studies* 4 (1942): 59–72.

[6] Elliott Horowitz, "The Early Eighteenth Century Confronts the Beard: Kabbalah and Jewish Self-Fashioning," *Jewish History* 8 (1994): 95–112; Idem, "Visages du judaisme: De la barbe en monde juif et de l'élaboration de ses significations," *Annales. Histoire, Sciences Sociales* 49 (1994): 1065–90.

[7] A striking example of the discrepancy between visual documents and reality is the beard. In Christian iconography in the Middle Ages, Jews were depicted almost invariably wearing a beard, for the symbolic purpose of underscoring the obsolescence of their faith, while it is known from other sources that the vast majority of the Jews in Christian lands were barefaced and clean-shaven. See Bernard Blumenkranz, *Le juif medieval au miroir de l'art chretien* (Paris, 1966), 18–20.

[8] This case has been studied by Aviad Hacohen, "Melekhet Mahashevet Le-Rabbi Mosheh Hefetz," *Mahanaim* 4 (1993): 265–75.

[9] Reproduced in Attilio Milano, *Il ghetto di Roma* (Roma: Carucci, 1988). Other satirical portraits of Jews from Italy are found in A. Rubens, *A Jewish Iconography* (London: The Jewish Museum, 1954), 59. It is worthwhile to remember that the first representations of Jews in the history of art are grotesque antisemitic drawings, such as the one of Isaac of Norwich, dated 1233 and mentioned in Cecil Roth, "Portraits of Jews," *Encyclopedia Judaica*, vol. 13, fol. 915.

[10] Isaiah Shachar, "The Emergence of the Modern Pictorial Stereotype of 'The Jews' in England," in *Studies in the Cultural Life of the Jews in England presented to Avraham Harman* (Jerusalem: Magnes, 1975), 331–66, situates in the mid-eighteenth century the emergence of a new stereotype of the Jew, which is economic (the Jew as a peddler), cultural (the bearded Jew with a turban-like hat in a strange garb and speaking a broken

English), and racial (hooked nose, dark complexion, with a peculiar cast of eyes) more than religious. From this moment on the dichotomy will be between the "fashionable" local Jew and the stranger Jew in ragged clothes, between the Jew as emblem of wealth and the beggar.

[11] Although from the late eighteenth century on we begin having examples of Jewish portraitists, such as the engraver and draftsman Samuele Jesi (1788–1853) from the little northern Italy village of Correggio. Andrea Balletti, *Gli ebrei e gli estensi* (Reggio Emilia, 1930), 250; Laura Giannoccolo, *Samuele Jesi (1788–1853) incisore* (Correggio: Areastampa, 2007).

[12] According to what Anthony Pagden has defined as "the principle of attachment," a strategy at work also among other eighteenth-century depictions of alterity, such as those studied by Samantha Baskind, "Bernard Picart's Etchings of Amsterdam's Jews," *Jewish Social Studies* 13 (2007): 40–64.

[13] On the background of this phenomenon, see Richard Yerachmiel Cohen, *Jewish Icons* (Berkeley: University of California Press, 1998), especially chapters 1 and 3 that are based on two articles originally published in Hebrew in *Zion* 57 (1992): 275–340; and 58 (1993) 407–52. Some of Cohen's assumptions have been criticized by Aviad Hacohen, "Diuqanaot Hakhamim—Bein Halakhah UMaaseh [Images of Scholars—Between Halakhah and Reality]," *Mahanayim* 2 (1995): 100–21.

[14] Leon da Modena, *Historia de Riti Hebraici*, 10.

[15] The Venetian Sarra Coppia Sulam to the Genoese Ansaldo Ceba. See Don Harran, *Sarra Coppia Sulam: Jewish Poet and Intellectual in seventeenth Century Venice* (Chicago: University of Chicago Press, 2010), 23–24.

[16] Moses A. Shulvass, *The Jews in the World of the Renaissance* (Leiden: Brill, 1973), 235, mentions portraits of Meir ben Isaac Katzenellenbogen, the Maharam of Padua, and his son, a lost médaillon of Leon da Modena, and even a statue of Judah Minz. Yet Elliott Horowitz's remarks suggest more prudence about the possibility of the Maharam of Padua having being portrayed. See Elliott Horowitz, "Speaking of the Dead: The Emergence of the Eulogy among Italian Jewry of the Sixteenth Century," in *Preachers of the Italian Ghetto* (ed. D. Ruderman; Berkeley: University of California Press, 1992), 157. In any case, these are rare and exceptional instances in the seventeenth century, as rightly stressed by Aviad Hacohen, "Melekhet Mahashevet Le-Rabbi Mosheh Hefetz," *Mahanaim* 4 (1993).

[17] Andrew Martindale, *Heroes, Ancestors, Relatives and the Birth of the Portrait* (Maarssen & The Hague: SDU, 1988); Joanna Woodall, *Portraiture: Facing the Subject* (Manchester: Manchester University Press, 1997).

[18] David Kaufmann, "Menahem Azarya da Fano et sa familie," *Revue d'Etudes Juives* 35 (1897): 84–90.

[19] Though he graduated in Padua, the physician Joseph Delmedigo, whose portrait can be seen in Mozes Heiman Ganz, *Memorbook: History of Dutch Jewry from the Renaissance to 1940* (Baarn, 1977), 44, was originally from Crete and lived most of his life in the Netherlands. Another portrait of an Italian Jew, though not a rabbi, Maggino di Gabriello, appears in the frontispiece of his book. See Dora Liscia Bemporad, *Maggino di Gabriello hebreo venetiano: i Dialoghi sopra l'utili sue inventioni circa la seta* (Firenze: Edifir, 2010). The first portrait of an Italian Jew who can be identified with a historical personality is most likely the one portraying the banker Daniel da Norsa and his family

at the foot of the Madonna executed for the Basilica of Sant'Andrea in Mantua in 1495. See Dana Katz, *The Jew in the Art of the Italian Renaissance* (Philadelphia: University of Pennsylvania Press, 2008).

[20] For England, see Alfred Rubens, *Anglo-Jewish Portraits* (London: The Jewish Museum, 1935). For Altona-Hamburg, see Peter Freimark, "Portraets von Rabbinern der Dreigemeinde Altona-Hamburg-Wandsbek aus dem 18. Jahrhundert," in *Juden in Deutschland. Emanzipation, Integration, Verfolgung und Vernichtung* (ed. P. Freimark, et al.; Hamburg: H. Christians Verlag, 1991), 36–57. One of the most remarkable examples in Italy is the Jacob de Joseph Barukh Carvalho portrait, the first Italian Jew to have been portrayed with his whole body. See Vivian B. Mann, ed., *Gardens and Ghettos: The Art of Jewish Life in Italy* (New York: The Jewish Museum, 1989), 313.

[21] As has been noted by Richard Cohen, *Jewish Icons. Art and Society in Modern Europe* (Berkeley: University of California Press, 1998), 67. Cohen has characterized this phenomenon as the result of the "movement in art from symbolism toward realism," interpreting it as a sign of an "increasing openness and tolerance to Jews" enhanced by "the primacy of the eye's image."

[22] Among the first, and to date the very few who devoted themselves to this subject, we should mention Leopold Löw, "Die Amstracht der Rabbinen," in *Gesammelte Schriften*, IV (Szegedin, 1889), 217–34.

[23] Rubens, *A History of Jewish Costume*. The same critique can be addressed to the more recent work by Cohen, *Jewish Icons,* focused on the history of northern and central European Judaism.

[24] Rubens, *History of Jewish Costume*, 190.

[25] Roberto Bonfil, *Rabbis and Jewish Communities in Renaissance Italy* (Oxford: Oxford University Press, 1990), 76.

[26] Ibid., 118.

[27] Mordechai Breuer, "Ha-Semikhah Ha-Ashkenazit," *Zion* 33 (1968): 42. The Italian rabbi from the Renaissance, Messer David Leon, also opposes the use of this dress (he calls it "sudar shel begged"), worn by some Sephardi rabbis and their disciples in Constantinople. He does so in a responsum published by Salomon Schechter, "Notes sur Messer David Leon," *Revue d'Etudes Juives*, 24 (1892): 137. An ambivalent, though lenient, attitude toward the *cappa* characterizes the responsa of Rabbi Joseph Colon, a contemporary of Messer Leon, due apparently to his ignorance of the exact shape of this dress. See Moses Avigdor Shulvass, "Mahlokotav Shel Messer Leon Im Rabbanei Doro Ve-Nisiono Lehatil Maruto Al Yehudei Italia," *Zion* 12 (1946): 17. This mantle cannot be compared in any case to the later development and specialization of the rabbinic cassock, though it is another early testimony to a probable assimilation of the semantic value of intellectual distinction between the doctor's exterior attire and the rabbi's.

[28] In the Middle Ages, only the beard could have been a distinctive sign of piety worn by certain cantors and rabbis, and even this quite seldom. See Elliott Horowitz, "Visages du judaisme: De la barbe en monde juif et de l'élaboration de ses significations," *Annales. Histoire, Sciences Sociales* 49 (1994): 1082. In the eighteenth century, the beard ceased almost completely to function as a sign of the rabbinical class. See Horowitz, "The Early

Eighteenth Century Confronts the Beard: Kabbalah and Jewish Self-Fashioning,'" *Jewish History* 8 (1994): 103.

[29] Paolo Medici, *Riti e costumi degli ebrei* (Venezia, 1801), 58. A similar statement, though limited solely to cantors, can be read in Leon da Modena, *Historia de riti ebraici* (Venezia, 1638), 29: "fuori che il cantarino [i.e., the hazan] che si mette il taled [besides the cantor who wears the ritual shawl]" also during the afternoon prayers, while the rest of the congregation does not wear it. Also Giulio Morosini, *Via della fede mostrata agli ebrei* (Roma, 1683), 249, and the caption accompaning the engraving of an interior of synagogue at Reggio in 1730: "sulle spalle mentre orano tengono il Talet, ch'e' come un scigatojo, con un fiocchetto d'otto fili per angolo, ma i Rabbini a distinzione degli altri lo tengono sopra il capo [they put the ritual shawl, with eight strings for each corner, over the shoulders, as a towel, but the rabbis keep it over the head in order to distinguish themselves]." See Rubens, *A Jewish Iconography*, plate number 1325.

[30] Bonfil, *Rabbis and Jewish communities in Renaissance Italy*, 76, quotes a Mantua document from the year 1599 that reads: "the excellent ordained rabbis, by the agreement of the Committee, are allowed to dress as they please, as are the honorable physicians."

[31] Attilio Milano, "L'editto sopra gli ebrei," *Rassegna Mensile di Israel* 19 (1955): 118–25.

[32] Cecil Roth, *Jewish Art: An Illustrated History* (New York: McGraw-Hill, 1961), 521. The picture was in Cecil Roth's personal collection and today is located at the Brotherton Library in Leeds.

[33] The rabbinical dress was therefore codified in the community's statutes. An example from late nineteenth-century Rome is found in Gianfranco Di Segni, "Innovazioni nel culto religioso a Roma nella seconda metà dell'Ottocento," *Zakhor* 8 (2005): 72, where it is written: "Art. 5: Tutti gli ufficanti e i sagrestani dovranno presenziare la celebrazione di tutte le funzioni religiose, indossando sempre l'abito talare [all ministers should be present at all religious services wearing always the cassock]. Art 20: I sefarim saranno sempre portati dai Celebranti vestiti dell'abito talare [The sefarim should be always held by the ministers dressed with the cassock]." Di Segni remarks that "è interessante notare che la sollecitazione affinché i chazannim indossino l'abito talare viene dal presidente della comunità non dal rabbino (a cui probabilmente la questione non interessava molto) [it's interesting to note that the request to dress the cantors with the cassock comes from the president of the community and not from the rabbi, who probably was not particularly interested in the question]."

[34] Attilio Milano, *Storia degli ebrei in Italia* (Torino: Einaudi, 1963), 442.

[35] Auguste Zeiss-Horbach, "Kleider machen Leute. Der Streit um den Rabbinertalar in Bayern im 19. Jahrhundert," *Aschkenas* 20:1 (2010): 71–118, studies the opposition in Bavaria of Protestant church representatives to what they considered to be an offensive imitation of their cassock by liberal rabbis.

[36] Daniel Roche, *The Culture of Clothing: Dress and Fashion in the Ancien Régime* (Cambridge, 1999), 454, writes: "The progress from lay clothes to the clothes of the modern clergy can be seen as part of the history of the widening gap that increasingly separated ecclesiastics from everybody else. The role of the councils, especially Trent, has to be emphasized in order to express the trend toward differentiation, accentuated in the seventeenth century."

[37] Michael A. Mayer, *Response to Modernity: A History of the Reform Movement in Judaism* (Oxford: Oxford University Press, 1988); and Auguste Zeiss-Horbach, "Kleider machen Leute," 71–118.

[38] See, for instance, the appreciation of Unitarism by one of the most important Italian rabbis of the nineteenth century, Marco Mortara (1815–1894). See Asher Salah, *L'epistolario di Marco Mortara: un rabbino italiano tra riforma e ortodossia* (Firenze: Giuntina, 2012), 35–36.

[39] The differences between the dress of the cantors, the rabbis, and in some places also other community officials should be further investigated as well as the codes of dress in particular circumstances of the liturgical calendar.

[40] Mayer, *Response to Modernity*, 103.

[41] In the *psak* [rabbinical decree] of Michalovce in 1865, the canonical robes for the cantor were included among the innovations that were severely forbidden. See Michael Silber, "The Emergence of Ultra-Orthodoxy: The Invention of a Tradition," in *The Uses of Tradition* (ed. Jack Wertheimer; New York: Jewish Theological Seminary, 1992), 40.

The Clerks' Work: Jews, Clerical Work, and the Birth of the American Garment Industry

Adam D. Mendelsohn

By the end of the nineteenth century, Jews dominated significant portions of the ready-made men's clothing trade in the United States. Manufacturers in New York, Chicago, Cincinnati, and Philadelphia drew on a reservoir of recent eastern European Jewish immigrants in a low-wage, high-volume industry focused on the seasonal production of cheap garments. Gimbels, Filene's, Macy's, Rich's, and numerous other Jewish-owned stores great and small carried these fashions to the middle class and those who aspired to join it. While Jews were not new to the garment trade—the collection and sale of secondhand clothing had long allowed impecunious Jews in Europe to maintain a tenuous grip on the lower rungs of the economic ladder—in America the garment industry offered extraordinary new opportunities for Jews.[1]

Before the arrival of ever-increasing numbers of central European Jews in the United States from the 1820s—roughly 100,000 in number by 1880—few Jews were involved in the clothing business. Many of those who arrived as young men seeking to improve their economic fortunes trod a familiar path from peddling to storekeeping, and, in some case, on to manufacturing. Beginning in the middle decades of the century, a series of technological, commercial, and social changes opened the way for their sustained economic ascent. Demand for garments accelerated on plantations in the American South, in boomtowns on the western frontier, and among urban workers with disposable income in soot-stained industrial cities. Merchants and manufacturers began to jettison familiar patterns of doing business for new ways of making and marketing clothing. The trade shifted decisively from skilled tailoring by artisans and the extensive reuse of castoff garments to its modern incarnation of mass production, mass consumption, and consumerism. For most, these changes enabled only a modest climb up the economic ladder, but a few attained giddy heights of prosperity. Others found their livelihoods undercut by disruptive new methods and technologies.

John Higham, an influential historian of ethnicity and immigration, identified the central European Jews who settled in America in the middle decades of the nineteenth century as the most successful immigrant group in American history.[2] He and others have offered several different theories to explain the striking trajectory of this cohort of newcomers. Several—most

recently Hasia Diner—have emphasized the role of peddling as a transformative and enabling occupation for central European Jewish immigrants. Diner
has argued persuasively that peddling of clothing, fabric, and notions offered
several attractions to young men seeking to sink roots into American soil:
independence and self-employment, the prospect of advancement through
hard work, and the promise of eventually owning a store. [3] It was a niche that
expanded because of the market and transport revolutions—peddlers sold
mass-produced, cheap merchandise to farmers who fell within the interstices
of an expanding railroad, canal, and road network—and positioned Jews well
for changes in the ways that Americans bought, sold, and consumed goods
after the Civil War.

While peddling by Jews has attracted scholarly attention, no scholarship has adequately recognized the significance of clerking as a priceless
apprenticeship in the modern ways of business. This article argues that
clerking was the neglected coequal of peddling in terms of its impact on the
upward march of Jews within the ready-made clothing business. As two new
studies have demonstrated, in the nineteenth century clerking was highly
sought after as preparation for a career in business and became a modern
occupation that transformed American capitalism. [4] Clerking was common
within the central European Jewish immigrant cohort. By examining clerking closely, this article argues that it provided training in a variety of fungible
skills and created personal and business connections that proved crucial as
Jewish immigrants moved from peddling into the sale and manufacture of
ready-made clothing.

Although itinerant trading was a formative experience for Jewish immigrants in the antebellum period—the typical newcomer was far more likely to
lift a peddlers' pack than a ledger book during their first years in America—the
early careers of successful immigrant entrepreneurs were often punctuated by
periods spent clerking. Stints of clerical work appear in countless life stories of
those who went on to become clothiers and wholesalers. Jewish immigrants to
the United States often identified peddling as a rite of passage in their mem-
oirs; time spent behind the counter usually received little more than passing
mention. [5] Dreary and routinized bookkeeping understandably did not capture
the imagination in the same way as pack peddling.

Once the aches of peddling were dulled by the curative effects of
memory, they could be transformed into marks of pride. Stories of a distant
footsore youth could make economic prosperity later in life seem all the more
extraordinary. Toting a pack accorded more closely with an American mythol-

ogy of adventure, self-making, rugged individualism, and pioneering than did totaling a ledger. There was little romance associated with clerical work; time did not add the same lacquer to bookkeeping that it did to carrying a pack. Later in life, a peddler might imagine himself as part of a fraternity whose stooped labor contributed to the more epic story of the building of America; at most, a clerk could claim to have served as a cog in the wheels of emerging organizational capitalism or express pride in the success of a firm that offered him employment.

While the basic methods of those who peddled in the nineteenth century were little different from the Yankee peddlers of the colonial period, clerical work underwent dramatic change. The centipedal march of railroads, telegraph lines, turnpikes, and canals across the country facilitated a new kind of commerce carried out at a faster pace, in greater volume, and over longer distances. Remote markets were inexorably drawn into the national economy. Technological change and infrastructural improvement provided a boon to Jews involved in the clothing trade in seemingly contradictory ways. Instead of being marginalized by more efficient methods of transportation, peddlers—the foot-soldiers of the distribution system—came to depend on this infrastructure to access inexpensive merchandise. An inexpensive train or river boat ticket could extend the reach of a peddler, allowing him to use a larger town as staging area and depositing him close to customers otherwise inaccessible by shanks' pony. Itinerant traders thrived by bridging the last mile between manufacturers in distant cities and remote customers, carrying packs laden with cheap merchandise from railheads and market towns to frontier and backcountry farmers along poorly maintained rural roads.

Although these customers lived in the outer orbit of the national consumer economy, they were sufficiently attuned to fashion that they chose to buy goods from a passing peddler rather than sew their own. Jewish peddlers relied on many of the features of modern markets—factories to mass produce cheap fabric, clothing and notions, wholesalers to supply credit, a legal system to protect their transactions, and customers hungry for consumer goods—but at the same time thrived in the narrow interstices of an incompletely integrated and imperfect economic system. Peddling had a Goldilocks-like relationship with the transportation system. If customers were at too far a remove or roads impassable, it was difficult for an itinerant trader to earn a reliable income. If rural customers had easy access to the marketplace, they had little need to purchase from a peddler. But if customers were remote *and* accessible, the conditions were just right for a peddler's progress.

Even as peddlers depended on the limitations of America's railroad and road network to earn a living, the train and telegraph transformed how manufacturers and wholesalers did business. Railroads and telegraph lines advantaged those able to efficiently access, organize, and respond to information about supply and demand. Historians Michael Zakim and Brian Luskey have pointed to clerks as the handmaidens of an increasingly sophisticated and specialized economy born in the decades immediately prior to the Civil War. As the scale and speed of commerce increased, those who made and marketed goods came to rely on an ever-growing class of clerks to manage their inventories, balance their books, record their sales, and correspond with suppliers, creditors, and customers.

By 1855, clerical work had become the third most common male occupation in Manhattan, behind only petty laborers and servants.[6] Ironically, the proliferation of clerical positions in major cities generated considerable new demand for the kinds of inexpensive clothing offered by manufacturers and retailers of ready-made garments. A clerk wishing to keep up appearances and emulate the fashions of urban men of means would be straightjacketed by a meager salary if not for the cut-price imitations of the latest styles offered at the show-shops of ready-made clothiers.

Just as the concentration of peddlers varied depending on locale, so too did the proportion of the Jewish population employed as clerks. While in several towns and cities "clerk" was the third-most commonly reported occupation for Jewish men on census returns (behind merchant and peddler), their numbers varied considerably by place and time. In Charleston, a port city that had long prospered by trading cargos of cotton, rice, and people, just under a third of adult Jewish men identified themselves as merchants in 1850. This capacious category might encompass anything from humble grocer to shipping tycoon, but in this case appears to have most often meant proprietor of a clothing store. Collectively, these businesses employed a large number of bookkeepers and salesmen; roughly one in four Jewish men employed in the city identified themselves as clerks. By contrast very few Jews supported themselves by peddling, a consequence of onerous licensing laws and brighter prospects for itinerant tradesmen elsewhere.

This correlation between mercantile occupations and clerking held true in the Carolinas after the Civil War; eighty percent of Jewish men whose occupations were recorded on the census during Reconstruction were either merchants or store clerks.[7] The picture was reversed in Boston in 1850 and 1860, a city where Jews as latecomers struggled to break into the vibrant merchant community. There a handful of lonely Jewish merchants and clerks were outnumbered many times over by peddlers.

Unsurprisingly, Jewish wholesalers and clothiers in Cincinnati—whose extensive sale of garments to storekeepers and peddlers across the West and South necessitated careful record keeping and voluminous correspondence— employed ink-stained armies of clerical workers. Between 1850 and 1860, Cincinnati's Jewish population grew more than threefold to around 10,000 as the city boomed. Demand for cheap clothing soared in the South along with the cotton prices. As the frontier galloped westward, thousands of potential new customers settled in towns and farms accessible to those who distributed clothing sewed in Cincinnati. The brightening horizons of Queen City cloth- iers were reflected in their need for ever more underlings able to fill orders and tabulate accounts. By 1860, clerks outnumbered peddlers more than two to one; a little under one in five Jewish men who worked in the city were employed as clerks and salesmen.[8]

In this age of the account book, there was considerable demand for those adept at figuring, filling, and filing orders. Even businesses modest in scale employed clerks. But more than offering a stable salary and hope of prefer- ment, clerical work was seen to supply young men—plenty of women worked behind the counter, but they rarely enjoyed the status, remuneration, and opportunities for advancement available to their male counterparts—with the kind of practical apprenticeship that would firmly plant both of their feet on the ladder of success. Even though there was often a substantial gulf between the expectations of clerks and the realities of their dreary work, for many young men who flocked to America's burgeoning cities in the middle decades of the century, clerical work held far more appeal than working on a family farm, laboring in a factory, or carrying a peddler's pack.

As with peddling, bookkeepers and salesmen often viewed their occupa- tion as a temporary way station on the path to proprietorship. For those buf- feted by financial misfortune, clerical work provided a port of refuge. Ernst Feuchtwanger, described in 1867 by an anonymous agent for a credit reporting agency in Georgia as the "leading merchant of this part of Macon," resorted to clerking after a failed attempt to recover from bankruptcy just four years later.[9]

While a period spent in peddling undoubtedly supplied immigrants with a rough-and-ready introduction to American capitalism, clerical work offered tutelage in operating a larger and more complex business. If repetitive clerical routines trained clerks in fungible skills essential for success in modern commerce—record keeping, planning, inventory, personnel and credit management—it was doubly important for recent Jewish immigrants. Not only did clerical work provide socialization in the American way of efficiently and effectively conducting business, but it also introduced newcomers to potential future suppliers, distributors, creditors, and partners. Since clerical positions were in great demand, young Jewish immigrants with imperfect English (but ample ambition) most often seem to have found employment in firms operated by their Jewish landsmen and kinsmen. Although they arrived without the kinds of social connections that won young men of pedigreed backgrounds clerkships in commercial firms of the first rank, they could cash in ethnic, religious, familial, and hometown ties when seeking employment.

Those who had already spent time peddling may have enjoyed an advantage when competing for clerical positions. Given that competition for business was intense, firms were eager to hire those who had already formed relationships with potential suppliers and customers elsewhere, hoping that rural storekeepers would prefer to purchase their stock from a familiar source.[10] The willingness of business owners to employ young men who shared their own ethnic identity—and were often younger brothers, nephews, or cousins—reinforced the ethnic character of the dry goods and clothing trades and ensured that familial ties often overlapped with commercial connections long after former clerks struck out on their own. A clerk who demonstrated promise might be asked to join the firm as an agent or partner or be lent money or stock so that he could strike out on his own. The latter option enabled a wholesaler to maintain a continuing commercial relationship with his former clerk, and perhaps a financial stake in his success as an investor in his enterprise.

Others clerks consummated their connections with their firm by marrying the daughter or sister of their employer. Samuel Rosenwald did exactly this when he married Augusta Hammerslough in 1857. Rosenwald had been in the United States for three years, about two of which he had spent peddling before finding employment as a clerk in a clothing store owned by the prosperous Hammerslough brothers in Baltimore. A month after marrying his employers' sister, he and his new bride were sent to Peoria, Illinois, to run the brothers' newly opened Baltimore Clothing House. Whether this marriage was arranged or an expression of genuine love, it reveals the power of an employer to advance the career of a clerk. After several more deployments managing outposts of his brothers-in-law's growing empire—Talladega, Alabama, Evansville, Indiana—Rosenwald settled in Springfield, Illinois. The latter move was made hastily in the early summer of 1861 to seize the opportunities presented by the mustering of soldiers at nearby Camp Butler.

The Civil War was good for the Hammersloughs and their brother-in-law; Rosenwald boasted of outfitting at least one locally raised cavalry regiment. In 1868, the brothers, now involved in manufacturing clothing in New York, sold their Springfield store to Rosenwald. Just as it had for his father Samuel, Julius Rosenwald's fortunes also turned after working as a clerk for the Hammerslough brothers. Julius left Springfield at age sixteen for a clerical position in his uncles' garment manufacturing business in New York City. After several false starts in the clothing business, he and his brother-in-law purchased Sears, Roebuck and Company in 1895.[11]

Clerking prepared young men for American business in other ways as well. Much as non-Jewish clerks joined mechanics institutes, subscribed to library societies, started debating clubs, and purchased manuals, newspapers, and other edificatory literature that promised to aid their striving toward social and material advancement, unmarried young Jewish men created an equivalent culture of self-improvement.[12] This enabled members of the community to participate in central institutions of the new bourgeois culture, and to do so in a manner that reinforced their Jewish identity.

Yet for the most part these new social venues supplied little Jewish content. Instead the clubroom nourished a Jewish secular identity rooted in friendship and fraternity rather than religious tradition. The literary society provided a space for aspirant members of the bourgeoisie to audition and primp the cloak of gentlemanly behavior well away from the critical eye of the Christian public. Substantial numbers of young men were attracted by the opportunity to cultivate the literary tastes and modes of polite behavior regarded as essential for gentlemanly status; many more perhaps by the camaraderie, fashionable fellowship, and idle leisure of the clubroom.

This zeal for joining does not appear to have extended to the religious realm. Isaac Mayer Wise complained that in Cincinnati, single men—"clerks, bookkeepers, apprentices, [and] journeymen"—remained unaffiliated with the city's synagogues.[13] If peddling imposed limits on the practice of Judaism—a peddler's lonely wanderings took him from the company of fellow Jews, sometimes for weeks at a time—many of the young Jewish men who found work as clerks appear to have chosen alternative outlets for forming and expressing their identities.

Wise's lament reveals the importance of clerical work and of clerks in the eyes of their contemporaries. This group was too important to ignore. This article could not agree more.

NOTES

[1] For examples of Jewish involvement in the clothing trade in the medieval and early modern periods, see Todd Endelman, *The Jews of Georgian England, 1714–1830* (Ann Arbor: University of Michigan Press, 1999), 178; Salo W. Baron, Arcadius Kahan, et al., *Economic History of the Jews* (New York: Schocken Books, 1975), 191, 266–78; Mark Wischnitzer, *A History of Jewish Crafts and Guilds* (New York: Jonathan David, 1965), 45, 98–100, 143–45, 147, 161, 174, 180, 225, 227.

[2] John Higham, *Send These to Me: Immigrants in Urban America* (Baltimore: Johns Hopkins University Press, 1975), 123.

[3] See Hasia Diner, "Entering the Mainstream of Modern Jewish History," in *Jewish Roots in Southern Soil* (ed. Marcie Cohen Ferris and Mark Greenberg; Lebanon: University Press of New England, 2006), 86–108, as well as Avraham Barkai, *Branching Out: German-Jewish Immigration to the United States, 1820–1914* (New York: Holmes & Meier, 1994); Hasia Diner, *A Time for Gathering: The Second Migration, 1820–1880* (Baltimore: Johns Hopkins University Press 1992); Maxwell Whiteman, "Notions, Dry Goods, and Clothing: An Introduction to the Study of the Cincinnati Peddler," *Jewish Quarterly Review* 53:4 (1863); Lee Friedman, "The Problems of Nineteenth Century American Jewish Peddlers," *AJHS* (1955).

[4] Brian Luskey, *On the Make: Clerks and the Quest for Capital in Nineteenth-Century America* (New York: New York University Press, 2010); and Michael Zakim, "Producing Capitalism: The Clerk at Work," in *Capitalism Takes Command* (ed. Michael Zakim and Gary J. Kornblith; Chicago: University of Chicago Press, 2011), argue that clerking played a hitherto neglected central role in the creation of a modern capitalist system in America.

[5] The same is true in biographies. See, for example, Leon Harris, *Merchant Princes: An Intimate History of Jewish Families Who Built Great Department Stores* (New York: Harper & Row, 1994).

[6] Zakim, "Producing Capitalism," 224–31. Luskey calculates that close to fourteen thousand clerks—a broad category—lived in New York in 1855. Luskey, *On the Make*, 5–6.

[7] Anton Hieke, "The Transregional Mobility of Jews from Macon, Ga., 1860–1880," *American Jewish History* 97:1 (2011): 21–38.

[8] Census data is an imperfect measure of Jewish economic activity, given that census returns relied on self-reporting. As transients, peddlers may be underrepresented in census data. The numbers for Charleston and Boston are extrapolated from the large sample extracted from census data by Kenneth Roseman; those for Cincinnati, from the work of Stephen G. Mostov. See Kenneth D. Roseman, "The Jewish Population of America, 1850–1860: A Demographic Study of Four Cities" (Ph.D. diss., Hebrew Union College, 1971), table XIII; Stephen Mostov, "A 'Jerusalem' on the Ohio" (Ph.D. diss., Brandeis University, 1981), 107–8. For Charleston, see also James William Hagy, *This Happy Land: The Jews of Colonial and Antebellum Charleston* (Tuscaloosa: University of Alabama Press, 1993), 193–97. For an example from a small town, see Lee Shai Weissbach, "Disappearing Jewish Communities in the Era of Mass Migration," *American Jewish Archives Journal* 49 (1997): 43.

[9] Hieke, "Transreagional Mobility"; Zakim, "Producing Capitalism," 229.

[10] The New York state census of 1855 found that only three percent of clerks were women. This number does not include those who contributed to the family economy by working behind the counter. By contrast, Luskey found that over forty percent of clerks in his sample from the 1855 New York census were foreign-born. Luskey, *On the Make*, 2, 8, 36; Zakim, "Producing Capitalism," 227–28, 234.

[11] Jacob Rader Marcus, *United States Jewry*, vol. 2 (Detroit: Wayne State University Press, 1993), 90, 107; Peter M. Ascoli, *Julius Rosenwald* (Bloomington: University of Indiana Press, 2006), 1–3; Rowena Olegario, "Credit and business culture: the American experience in the nineteenth century" (Ph.D. diss., Harvard University 1998), 242–43. In New York, Julius boarded with his Uncle Samuel and Aunt Emelia Hammerslough; Emelia's brother was banking pioneer Samuel Sachs.

[12] This phenomenon is discussed at length in Adam D. Mendelsohn, "Tongue Ties: Religion, Culture and Commerce in the making of the Anglophone Jewish Diaspora, 1840–1870" (Ph.D. diss., Brandeis University 2008), 174–218.

[13] *Israelite* (2 October 1857): 102.

Ella Zirner-Zwieback, Madame d'Ora, and Vienna's New Woman

Lisa Silverman

Fashion remembers 1926 as the year Coco Chanel created the "little black dress." Few may remember that 1926 was also the year the studio of Madame d'Ora (the pseudonym of Vienna-born photographer Dora Kallmus) produced dozens of photographs for Ludwig Zwieback and Brothers, Vienna's renowned luxury department store. Nevertheless, these photographs, which seem to have been taken for advertising purposes, deserve our attention.[1] Evoking the emancipated, modern, androgynous New Woman, while also referencing more conventional femininities, as well as traditional Austrian motifs, their pointed images make a range of statements about contemporary Austrian women.

Some of the models wear luxurious, expensive, fur-trimmed coats, sequined dresses, and feathered headdresses [Figs. 1, 2, 3]. Others are poised to ride horses or brave winter weather in appropriately fashionable attire [Figs. 4, 5]. One model appears in a smart black waitress uniform replete with a frilly lace apron and headband, in an image clearly aimed at her employer's purchas-

Figure 1. Woman in a fur-trimmed cloak and feathered headdress. Madame d'Ora for "Zwieback-Moden," 1926. ÖNB/Wien, *204620-D.*

Figure 2. Woman in a sleeveless evening dress with feathered headdress and stole. Madame d'Ora for "Zwieback-Moden," 1926. ÖNB/Wien, *204595-D.*

Figure 3. Woman in a knee-length evening dress with feathered headdress. Madame d'Ora for "Zwieback-Moden," 1926. ÖNB/Wien, *204593-D.*

Figure 4. Two women in riding clothes with hat, horse, and whip.
Madame d'Ora for "Zwieback-Moden," 1926. ÖNB/Wien, *204555-D*.

Figure 5. Woman in a knee-length
skirt, with sweater and scarf, heads-
carf, and kneesocks. Madame d'Ora
for "Zwieback-Moden," 1926.
ÖNB/Wien, *204544-D*.

Figure 6. Woman in a waitress uniform holding a tray. Madame d'Ora
for "Zwieback-Moden," 1926.
ÖNB/Wien, *204613-D*.

ing power [Fig. 6]. Another image of a woman in a pleated skirt, V-neck shirt, jacket, and cloche targets workingwomen seeking an outfit for the office or a daytime stroll around town [Fig. 7]. Many pictures feature the pantaloons, short skirts, pants, sleeveless tops, and flapper-style shapeless dresses associated with the New Woman, while almost all of the models sport her signature short bobbed haircut, the popular *Bubikopf* [Figs. 8, 9]. But the model wearing pantaloons has an unmistakably feminine shawl, while another short-haired woman wears a frilly, flowered dress [Fig. 10].

Figure 7. Woman in a pleated skirt, V-neck shirt, jacket, and cloche. Madame d'Ora for "Zwieback-Moden," 1926. ÖNB/Wien, *204542-D.*

Figure 8. Woman in knee-length pants, long socks, and a cape. Madame d'Ora for "Zwieback-Moden," 1926. ÖNB/Wien, *204545-D.*

Figure 9. Model in a sleeveless, sheath dress with headdress and feathers. Madame d'Ora for "Zwieback-Moden," 1926. ÖNB/Wien, *204621-D.*

Figure 10. Model in a frilly dress. Madame d'Ora for "Zwieback-Moden," 1926. ÖNB/Wien, *204594-D.*

The photographs from 1926 represent only a portion of the pictures d'Ora's studio took for Zwieback's department store between 1917 and 1927, but they are distinguished both by their sheer number and by the range of styles they depict. The photos address several audiences: the traditional, wealthy, older customers of haute couture, as well as a range of more recent customers who emerged largely in the 1920s, from actresses and public figures seeking a glamorous look to more ordinary women dressing for a day at the office or an evening of dancing. Yet these were clearly no run-of-the-mill stock photographs. In interwar Central Europe, studio photographers typically worked as freelancers. They found their own models, clothing, and accessories and then sold their photographs to newspaper and magazine editors, often using *Bilderdienste* [photographic agencies] as intermediaries.[2]

A simple glance at the photographs reveals the most basic level on which their female models explicitly engage the symbolic construction of gender norms: some look traditionally feminine, while others appear androgynous. Scholars have shown how reading cultural forms in light of the symbolic construction of gender can help us understand how institutions and texts used the politics of sexuality in addressing female audiences, particular in Weimar Germany.[3] In a similar vein, I argue that the symbolic construction of Jewish difference also affected the terms of that address, though it often did so implicitly, that is, without clearly identifiable representations of either Jewish or non-Jewish elements. Reading these photographs with both gender and Jewish difference in mind, I argue, renders an essentialist reading of them through either category impossible and teaches a valuable lesson about the lasting legacy of Jews who participated in the shaping of Austrian culture.

While the involvement of Jews in the garment and fashion industry is by now recognized as an important facet of Jewish history, many scholars still refuse to recognize fashion as a significant form of culture. Instead, they read it as a superficial byproduct of modernity, less serious than active agents like architecture, film, and art.[4] Because fashion is often associated with a feminized sphere of frivolity and excess that is tightly bound to commerce, some identify it as part of a burgeoning culture industry à la Adorno: superficial, narcissistic, and wasteful.[5] However, to understand the full implications of fashion photography in interwar Central Europe, we need to examine both the role of Jews in the distribution and marketing of fashion, and the spatial, temporal, and cultural coordinates of the fashion system as a whole. In other words, we need to apply the methodologies of cultural studies. Thus, rather than trying to identify specific "Jewish" qualities in any of these photographs,

I will focus on the nature of both d'Ora and Zirner-Zwieback's work in photography and fashion, asking how their status as women born as Jews inflected their approaches to areas in which Jews—and especially Jewish women—had an influence disproportionate to their presence in the general population.

In this context, I refer to Jewish difference as a dialectical, hierarchical framework that encompasses the relationship between the socially constructed categories of "Jew" and "non-Jew," much like the term "gender" refers to the relationship between the socially constructed categories of "man" and "woman." This theoretical model allows us to avoid essentializing our understandings of what is "Jewish" and automatically implies that the definitions of "Jew" and "Jewish" are necessarily dynamic. Thus, while d'Ora's and Zirner-Zwieback's self-identification as Jews is not insignificant, it does not establish an a priori rule for determining their relevance to Jewish cultural history. Instead, I aim to show here that both fashion and photography can provide powerful evidence not just about the styles of the time and their cultural implications, but also about Jewish history, regardless of the extent to which they explicitly display "Jewish" content or can be definitively identified as created by Jews.[6]

GENDER AND JEWISH DIFFERENCE

By 1926, both d'Ora and Zirner-Zwieback had reached the pinnacles of their careers. At the age of forty-five, Madame d'Ora was not only one of Vienna's top photographers, but also she was well-known throughout Europe for her distinctive portraits and fashion photographs. Like any number of other daughters from middle-class Viennese Jewish families, Dora Kallmus achieved a successful career both because of—and in spite of—her family. She and her older sister Anna were both well educated; they learned to speak English and French, played the piano, and traveled widely through Europe. Dora was poised, it would seem, for anything. At first, she wanted to be an actress, then, a dressmaker—but her father forbade her from pursuing either profession. Only by chance did she discover her talent with the camera while on holiday in Nice and decide to pursue a career as a photographer. Her father was not exactly delighted with the news: as d'Ora recalled, he likened having his portrait taken to mundane acts like buying shoes. But, not wanting to deny his daughter yet again, he relented.[7]

D'Ora began her uphill battle of photographic training in 1904, when women were restricted to roles as studio receptionists or, at best, negative retouchers. She was the very first woman allowed to attend classes at the *Graphische Lehr- und Versuchsanstalt*; however, she said that practical tasks, like working with chemicals to develop photographs, were withheld from her as if they were dirty jokes.[8] Only with her father's financial backing and the technical support of a fully trained male assistant, Arthur Benda, whom she had met during a brief apprenticeship with portrait photographer Nicola Perscheid, could D'Ora open in 1907 what would later become one of Vienna's most successful photography studios. As suggested by Virginia Woolf's now-famous 1929 statement about a woman requiring "money and a room of her own" in order to write, it was not until she had both the means and the space to pursue her craft that d'Ora—and other women in Vienna after her—had the freedom to create.[9]

As a photographer, d'Ora became far more immersed in the worlds of her original desires—acting and fashion design—than she might ever have imagined. Like those belonging to the women for whom she paved the way, photography studios became sites of creativity, ideas, and originality, where many of them experimented with the limits of gender, class, race, and Jewish difference on their own terms. Although restrictions on women's career opportunities remained strong in many areas in the early twentieth century, photography was an open and attractive alternative career option for Jews in Central Europe. As it developed further, links to other career networks popular with Jews, such as journalism, advertising, and fashion, photography became a more serious profession for Jews in Berlin and Vienna, and for Jewish women in particular. If we approach Jewish women's photographs not only for their content, but also as the material deposits of a many-faceted social process encompassing production, consumption, and marketing, we can better understand how their work engaged both Jewish difference and gender.

Today, Madame d'Ora is best known for her photographic portraits of cultural luminaries and her use of dramatic lighting, soft focus, and heavy retouching. She rapidly became popular among the Viennese elite; in 1916, she was asked to photograph the coronation of Kaiser Karl, king of Hungary, after which other members of the imperial family visited her studio. Her portraits of celebrities such as Josephine Baker, Karl Kraus, Arthur Schnitzler, and Gustav Klimt received international acclaim, and her studios in Vienna and elsewhere became fashionable meeting places.[10] Many hailed her as a master of setting, lighting, and retouching, but these skills comprised only the technical foundation of her ability to capture the image of a woman as she wished to be seen. In 1921, she and Benda opened another studio in Karlsbad for the summer months, in order to better cater to a cadre of international, elite vacationers. Those clients convinced her to open a studio in Paris in 1923, after which date she devoted increasing amounts of time to this location.

Ultimately, Benda returned to Vienna to run the studio there after the two quarreled. Indeed, a number of the photographs taken during this period—including those taken for Zwieback's department store featured here—bear the letters "A. B." under the standard "d'Ora" logo, indicating his primary involvement in taking the photograph. However, as photography scholars have noted, it was not until 1927 that the two broke definitively, and it is difficult to say with certainty who was primarily responsible for the photographs. By Benda's own admission, it was only after he took over the studio completely at the start of 1927 that he considered himself to have complete artistic freedom—suggesting that d'Ora had remained involved in the production of the studio's photographs even while in Paris. This lack of definitive certainty regarding the provenance of the 1926 photographs makes it imperative that we set aside essentializing notions of authorship and focus on how the images themselves engage gender and Jewishness.[11]

Meanwhile, as d'Ora was gaining international acclaim, Ella Zirner-Zwieback was solidifying her reputation as a shrewd, tasteful department store owner. Zirner-Zwieback posed for d'Ora's studio in Vienna at least five times beginning in 1921, in an alliance that concurrently registered Zirner-Zwieback's celebrity and importance, while also showing that she recognized

d'Ora's photographic prowess. A portrait from 1926 testifies to Zirner-Zwieback's success. Wearing a dark fur coat, holding a flower up to her chin, and looking demurely at the camera over her fur-trimmed shoulder, Zirner-Zwieback, in soft focus, appears seductive, in control, and almost ageless [Fig. 11].

In all the portraits taken by the studio, her self-assured and, in some cases, theatrical poses suggest that she was aware of the power of

Figure 11. Portrait of Ella Zirner-Zwieback in a fur coat. Madame d'Ora for "Zwieback-Moden," 1926. ÖNB/Wien, *204626-D*.

fashion and photography to actively shape the image of women, both as society wanted to see them and as they wished to be seen. Here, Zirner-Zwieback uses her fur coat to tease the viewer by offering only a partial glimpse of the celebrity they wish to see. But the image of a temptress wrapped in black fur also specifically evokes turn-of-the-century paintings that play upon the notion of the Jewish woman as femme fatale, including, notably, Gustav Klimt's 1901 *Judith I*, in which Adele Bloch-Bauer holds the head of Holofernes.[12] Transforming Zirner-Zwieback from department store owner to seductress, the portrait also playfully utilizes the stereotype of the *belle juive* [beautiful Jewess] that figures woman's "Otherness" as the basis for her power.[13]

In contrast to these portraits, which play upon complicated images of sexuality and power, the photographs for Zwieback's fashion house present women as active participants in modern life. They use fashion as a medium that can help establish aesthetic norms rather than merely follow them.[14] But their juxtaposition of modern haircuts and clothing with more traditional accoutrements and haute couture informs us about much more than the kinds of clothes that Zwieback's department store sold. Along with the aesthetics of the photographs, it indicates that both Zirner-Zwieback and her photographer understood fashion's paradoxical ability to allow women to conform to fashion trends while at the same time fostering a sense of individuality.

Since the end of World War I, women in Austria had gained the right to vote and entered a broadening spectrum of careers in greater numbers. Their increased visibility in the public sphere raised societal concerns about changing gender norms that threatened the traditional order of things. The increasingly iconic representation of the New Woman was a visible symbol of contemporary gender destabilization; she challenged conventional notions of femininity and sexuality by appearing in public with short hair, trousers, and an abundance of intellectual and sexual curiosity. The use of this image to market books, films, and clothing became the norm in Central Europe and elsewhere. And while this trope was not always negatively coded, the New Woman was typically portrayed mythically, particularly in the popular illustrations of Ernst Dryden, as a "symbol of uniformity and cold, haughty, unattainable elegance" who responded largely to male subjectivity and desire.[15] She was thus reduced to an imposed homogeneous "femaleness": anonymous, angular, and not coincidentally, often pictured with other objects [Fig. 12].

The 1926 photographs for Zwieback's department store challenge such male-oriented images. By calling into question these increasingly standardized representations of the New Woman, they suggest that the figure encompassed

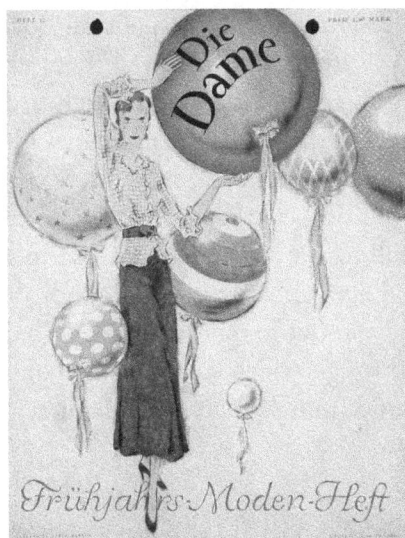

Figure 12. An illustration by Ernst Dryden for *Die Dame*, 1928. ÖNB/ Wien, 16311644.

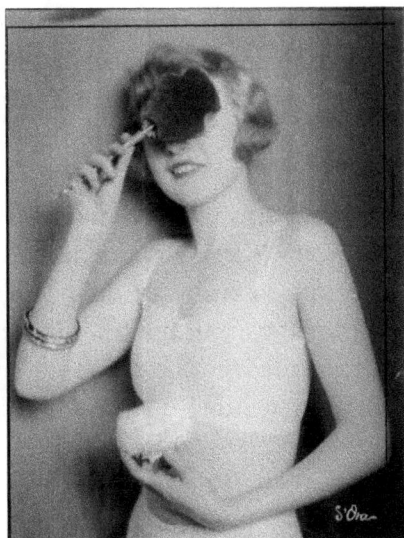

Figure 13. A model in a bra holding a hand mirror. Madame d'Ora for "Zwieback-Moden," 1926. ÖNB/ Wien, *204602-D*.

a broader range of consumer desires and gender roles.[16] Whether the photos evoke luxury, extravagance, and exclusiveness or the more practical side of life, or whether they feature cutting-edge or more traditional clothing, they encourage women to fashion themselves in keeping with their inner desires, rather than according to increasingly rigid habits based largely on what men imagined women's desires should be. Neither d'Ora nor Zirner-Zwieback were avant-garde feminists seeking to undermine established norms of femininity. But these images indicate that the combination of photography and fashion offered a powerful medium through which women could shape consumer needs without foregrounding male subjectivity and desire. The fact that these photographs address consumer desire not only by playing with gender norms, but also by engaging the socially constructed categories of Jewish difference, points to the power of Jewish difference in shaping contemporary cultural norms.

As women from Jewish backgrounds, both d'Ora and Zirner-Zwieback were keenly aware of the possibilities of both fashion and photography for the "reinvention" of the self in the modern world. Such reinvention was inescapable in interwar Austria. After the collapse of the Habsburg Monarchy, Austrians were forced to develop new self-understandings amidst political, social, and economic disarray. As all Austrians uneasily reconceptualized themselves along new national and urban lines, their self-conceptions increasingly relied upon longstanding prejudices and stereotypes of the Jew as the ultimate Other. Both Jews and non-Jews used this age-old paradigm to interpret, clarify, and critique the terms of the country's altered political, social, and economic conditions, even as Jews became leaders of political movements and rose to the forefront of social and cultural programs. Like gender, class, race, and other frames of reference through which people give order to their world, Jewish difference became a powerful cultural motif through which Austrians articulated and rearticulated their responses to their conditions—in art, architecture, and literature, as well as fashion.

THE BUSINESSWOMAN AND THE PHOTOGRAPHER

By all accounts, Ella Zirner-Zwieback maintained firm control over her business, a vertically integrated fashion system that included manufacturing, marketing, and retail distribution. Born in 1878 to Ludwig and Katharina (née Singer) Zwieback, Zirner-Zwieback originally intended to have a different career; she trained at the Vienna Conservatory and became a prizewinning pianist. But in 1899, under pressure from her family to find a suitable marriage partner, she wed Alexander Zirner, the son of the Jewish imperial court jeweler, and had two children. In 1906, she inherited Zwieback and Brothers, Vienna's eight-story premier luxury department store. Zirner officially ran the company until his death in 1924, but Zirner-Zwieback was heavily engaged in the business. When she became the store's sole proprietor in 1926, she redecorated the building (possibly by her own design).[17] She made sure the store sold the latest fashions, but also she broadened its appeal by reopening a tearoom around the corner.[18]

Zirner-Zwieback's business and fashion talents were not limited to women's clothing. She conceptualized new designs for servants, children, and men, and introduced innovative ideas for household wares like tablecloths, bed linens, and bath towels.[19] Fred Adlmüller, a leading fashion designer in Vienna in the 1930s and 40s, recalled that she gave him his start in the fashion industry by hiring him as a display arranger in 1929, when Zwieback's had already become Vienna's trendiest department store. Within three months, he had risen to head of the gentleman's department.[20] Laura Wärendorfer Zirner, who married Zirner-Zwieback's son Ludwig, attested that even when she met her, many years after her forced departure from Vienna in 1938, Zirner-Zwieback maintained the attitude of a "great lady" and possessed a "fantasy-rich but also horrific" business drive. Ludwig Hirschfeld's 1927 tourist guidebook confirms her personal investment in and effect on her work:

> Zwieback [department store]. . . . is no mere outfitter; it is a fashion-able outfitter's with a pronouncedly personal tone, a tone supplied by Frau Ella Zirner-Zwieback, the head of the house, a striking Viennese personality, at once a perfect society lady and a good business-woman, full of ambition and good taste, and a wonderful pianist to boot. The "lines and colors" noticeable on a great number of Vienna women are of Frau Zirner's composition.[21]

Zirner-Zwieback did not confine her interests to Vienna. Fluent in French, Italian, and English, she traveled widely for business and to seek out innovations for the store; at one point, she apparently imported an entire cash register system from America. According to her daughter-in-law, she bought an estate in Yugoslavia for which she hired a marmalade cook from England, a pastry chef from Budapest, and furnished a bathroom with pink marble she bought from the queen of Romania. Ludwig recalled being picked up from the train station and driven to the estate in a carriage drawn by four horses. Ludwig and Zirner-Zwieback's two children from her marriage to Alexander Zirner were raised by governesses—at one point three at once—because she was so busy with work.[22]

Madame d'Ora may have come from a less prominent background than Zirner-Zwieback, but she was similarly devoted to her career. Although she was a pioneer in her field, by the 1920s several other women operated their own photography studios, and many of them were Jews. As a free profession positioned squarely between art and craft, photography had become a popular trade for Jews in Central Europe by the end of the nineteenth century. Although the early twentieth century still saw many restrictions on women's career opportunities, photography—a new profession with relatively low start-up costs—was an open and attractive option.[23]

Early admirers of photography championed its possibilities for wide dissemination as well as its supposed ability to reproduce reality objectively. But Gisèle Freund, a Jewish photographer born in Berlin in 1908, put her finger on its appeal when she claimed that photography's illusory objectivity allowed it to express the values of the dominant social class. As Freund noted, "The importance of photography does not rest primarily in its potential as an art form, but rather in its ability to shape our ideas, to influence our behaviour, and to define our society."[24] Given the major role that clothing performs in the social construction of identity, the power of fashion photography as a potential agent of social change becomes apparent.[25] Since both Jews and women had long been excluded or marginalized from institutions of social power, fashion photography offered them unique possibilities for creating and shaping culture.

It is important to note that both Zirner-Zwieback and d'Ora's connections to their Jewish roots were tenuous at best. D'Ora converted to Catholicism in 1919, and a number of her later photographs suggest the importance of Christian iconography to her aesthetic sensibility. While Zirner-Zwieback did not deny her Jewish background, she certainly distanced herself from it; according to her daughter-in-law, she would have been "dumbfounded" to hear anyone refer to her as a Jew.[26] But, like most Jewish-born Viennese, the two were aware of the powerful stereotypes about Jews anchored in Austrian culture. In this light, their disavowals of Judaism can be seen as articulations of the terms of their own self-identification via the socially constructed categories of Jewish difference.

FRENCH CULTURE AND JEWISH DIFFERENCE

Zirner-Zwieback and d'Ora's mutual affinity for French culture and taste is perhaps the best example of how and why one could simultaneously—and paradoxically—distance oneself from Jews and Judaism while playing up tropes about Jews as Other. On one level, their intense attraction to French culture was a method of acculturation and distancing; by appearing as French as possible, they presented themselves as chic, tasteful, sophisticated, and therefore, "un-Jewish." On the other hand, the affinity between Jews and cosmopolitan French culture was highly visible, especially in the interwar period when European department stores, many of them Jewish-owned, manufactured and sold copies of French couture.[27] Given their involvement in fashion and photography, d'Ora and Zirner-Zwieback must have been especially attuned to traditional antisemitic accusations that Jews mimicked non-Jewish culture and customs, which furthered their associations with rootlessness and inauthenticity.[28]

Ironically, however, affiliating with French culture enabled the women to turn their status as Other into something desirable, as they reframed Otherness as an aspirational quality for women seeking to be sophisticated, tasteful, and worldly. Along with her Paris studio and her clear preference for French designers, the complexities of d'Ora's French self-fashioning are best reflected in her name: calling herself Madame d'Ora, she sounded not only French, but also aristocratic. Yet by not completely masking her original name, the title also hints at her non-French roots. Zirner-Zwieback, like many other department store owners, recognized that promoting haute couture required a deep association with Paris, which was not only the world center of fashion, but also the site of the first department store, Le Bon Marché.[29] Due to her efforts, Zwieback and Brothers gained a reputation as "the most Parisian department store in the world," according to the 1926 *Handbook of Viennese Society*.[30] Hirschfeld's 1927 guidebook not only compliments Zirner-Zwieback on the store's Parisian reputation, but also tells readers which stores are truly French and which are only trying to "pass," thus emphasizing her achievement.[31] Of course Jewish women were not the only ones wont to reinvent themselves along the lines of French couture. But the intensity of d'Ora and Zirner-Zwieback's drive toward this reinvention suggests that French self-fashioning boosted their appeal as it addressed their status as Other.

D'Ora revealed her belief in the transformative possibilities of French couture in an article about a visit to Josephine Baker's home, published in *Die Dame* in 1926. Like her portrait photograph of Zirner-Zwieback, d'Ora's text teases her audience with a tantalizing glimpse of the celebrity's body. She explains that, contrary to expectations, she gained easy access to the star. "Everyone warned me," d'Ora writes, "You won't be able to go to Baker! She won't let you in! She won't be able to understand at all what you want from her!" But d'Ora even managed to enter her boudoir, where she found a small figure huddled in bed, very different from the outgoing image Baker projected on stage. D'Ora tells readers that she admonished Baker for not dressing in French couture: "Poor little Josefine! You should wear clothes from Poiret and Callot, you should put on evening shoes that scare you, you should wear hats that seem superfluous to you and jewelry from Dunan that you won't like as well as glass beads."[32] In essence, she argues that adopting French fashion would highlight, rather than mask, Baker's Otherness to her own advantage.

In the heavily politicized context of interwar Vienna, fashion, too, became fair ground for expressing national feelings and contempt for outsiders. Many Viennese fashion houses found themselves in crisis. In addition to the poor overall economy, their usual contacts with the fashion capital of Paris were cut off, limiting the international items and influences they could offer.[33] Fashion houses coped in two ways. Some abandoned international ties, using the restricted conditions to foster an independent *Wiener Mode* [Viennese fashion], turning isolation and postwar inflation into an opportunity for the Austrian-based fashion industry, which could now sell its designs domestically without competition.[34] In particular, the *Tracht* [Austrian folk dress] and sports clothing industries expanded as demand grew for "authentic" Austrian-Alpenland dress.[35]

Stores that relied heavily upon fashion from abroad clearly could not switch gears as easily, since many consumers still wanted French couture. To compensate for their lack of actual Parisian fashions, these stores sent couriers to attend fashion shows in Paris, where they would either sketch the designs or buy single pieces. The stores would then use these templates to produce copies to sell in Austria with the label "Original Paris model."[36] French couture items were also copied in Brussels, where trade associations worked hard to develop closer ties to France through trade agreements. Zirner-Zwieback often traveled to Rome, Paris, and London searching for the latest designs,[37] while Madame d'Ora was involved in photographing French couture copies in Belgium. One photograph from 1931 shows a model in a copy of a design from House of Worth that was featured in the spring collection of the Belgian dressmaker Natan.[38]

In a 1928 article in *Die Moderne Frau*, Viennese opera singer Alfred Jerger made light of this practice. He poked fun at Jewish women who copied French haute couture while describing a trip to Paris he took with a friend in the fashion industry. Jerger watched his friend carefully carry out his mission, noting:

> . . . one remembers all the subtleties of every detail in these works of art and copies it, possibly making small changes. Because, first of all, not all "original Parisian models" are appropriate for the individuality of the beautiful, graceful Viennese woman, which is an equally attractive type as the full-blooded Frenchwoman. And then all women—not only the Chosen of Fifth Avenue—should be given the opportunity to make themselves as beautiful as humanly possible for us, the lords of creation.[39]

Deploying the common trope of wealthy Jewish women as the most demanding consumers of foreign luxury goods, Jerger refers to the "Chosen of Fifth Avenue," referencing the coding of New York as Jewish and Fifth Avenue as a wealthy, upscale, showy thoroughfare (he may also be evoking the Jewish-owned Saks Fifth Avenue, which opened in 1924). These women clearly take the lead in the marketing and consuming of luxury items, as copying becomes another association with an industry already overdetermined as "Jewish."[40] That Zirner-Zwieback was a direct target of such stereotypes is clear from Hugo Bettauer's best-selling satirical 1923 novel *Die Stadt ohne Juden* [*The City without Jews*], in which she is the only figure mentioned by name in conjunction with the fictional downfall of fashion in Vienna after the expulsion of the Jews.[41]

Despite her love of French couture, however, Zirner-Zwieback knew very well the limits of the financially strapped public and was too shrewd a businesswoman to sacrifice the economic needs of the company. While some of Zwieback's advertisements and posters from this period glorified France, others emphasized tradition and low prices in an attempt to attract customers interested in mass-produced, ready-to-wear items like the sporty knitted sweaters, narrow knee-length skirts, and loose hanging dresses with low waistlines typical of the 1920s.[42] Advertisements for inexpensive clothing could also be used to lure women into the store, where they would find the expensive luxury items they "really" desired. Such savvy consumer practices indicate that Zirner-Zwieback was purposefully fine-tuning the association of Zwieback's with haute couture to draw in a diverse customer base.

The photographs from 1926 suggest an atypical New Woman who incorporated elements not only of the androgynous "garçonnière," as she was sometimes referred to, in yet another French reference, but also the feminine tradition of haute couture, and even provincial Austrian styles. In creating this mix, they challenged standard representations that were implicitly associated with Jews to serve marketing interests. According to Atina Grossmann, contemporary rhetoric about the New Woman as a danger to society linked her to Jewishness via her sexuality, consumerism, and financial greed.[43] Kerry Wallach suggests that the "Jewish" values of the New Woman in Weimar Germany often remained subtly below the surface. Jewish women who participated in Weimar culture were often "uniquely and discernibly Jewish," even if their outer appearance and modes of self-presentation did not appear on the surface to differ from other women.[44]

Periodical articles and advertisements featured positive representations of independent New Women who, as Darcy Buerkle notes, are often coded in Weimar-era publications as just "Jewish enough" to evoke the desired effect on potential consumers. For example, cover art and advertisements often showed figures with dark or curly hair, engaging codings that would generate consumer desire without going too far.[45] Such images, predicated on negatively casting Jewish women as the "ultimate" consumers, could entice Jewish women who recognized themselves or lure other women who respected the Jewish woman's mark of approval. However, as Buerkle points out, advertising in Central Europe between the wars alternately included and excluded certain kinds of women. At first, it evoked Jewish women as ultimate consumers, but eventually, it effaced them as the image of the "Aryan" woman became the ideal and Jews were forced out of the industry.

THE PHOTOGRAPHER'S SALON

If photographs themselves were a powerful vehicle for Jewish women in fashion and advertising, so too were the photography studios in which they were produced. As such, it is worth considering how the space of the photography studio resembled another form of social interaction that provided similar possibilities for Jewish women: the salon. These informal get-togethers, typically made up of Jews and non-Jews and often held in the homes of upper-class Jewish women, played a significant role in the development of European literature, art, and politics from the late eighteenth century on, as women hosted not only discussions, but also musical and theater performances, and literary readings.

Emily Bilski, Emily Braun, and Deborah Hertz have noted that the women who hosted salons did much more than merely provide backdrops for the creative endeavors of others. In the eighteenth century, salons such as Rahel Varnhagen's were the site of serious study and a base for Enlightenment ideals. By the nineteenth and twentieth centuries, salons fostered the introduction of art movements like modernism, the Secession, and the avant-garde, and enabled women to become engaged with political movements, social reform, and organized dissent. According to Bilski and Braun, in salons women did not merely serve men, but served themselves, by "speaking and writing, creating erudite identities, holding their own." By fostering conversation and ideas at the salon, they argue, politically disadvantaged women barred from professional spheres could become agents in cultural exchange.[46]

Barbara Hahn maintains a less romanticized view of these gatherings. She notes that, because of our limited sources for understanding what actually happened in salons, it is difficult to pinpoint exactly what made a gathering a "salon" or the exact nature of women's roles. The letters of nineteenth-century participants idealized salons by construing them as clearly defined phenomena that set active agendas to create ideal societies. But since the conversations that took place in salons were not recorded and salons produced no lasting cultural products, they cannot be described as much more than ephemeral and unbounded spaces that left little or no traces. As Hahn notes, "'Salon,' one could say, is the sign of an inaccessible ideal, an irreplaceable loss."[47]

Still, the similarities between what these salons offered to elite Jewish women and the possibilities provided by the photography studio are apparent. D'Ora's studio, like others, also served as a site of intellectual and creative stimulation, where people commingled according to the desire of the host, who not only surrounded herself with the leading cultural figures of the day, but also actively participated in discussion. Both the salon and the studio offered women a chance to expand upon global ideas and foster extended social networks among Jews and non-Jews in a site located somewhere between the public and the private. For many, a commitment to French culture was also an important part of the salon experience.[48]

Bilski and Braun point out that the salon provided women with a ticket to enter mainstream culture through individual associations with the upper class and intelligentsia (rather than lineage or marriage) that many considered "the swiftest means of arriving, of mastering Western European high culture, and the finest forum for achievement."[49] For some, this may have meant leaving associations with Jewishness behind. But for d'Ora and Zirner-Zwieback, the studio offered a chance to transform their status as Other into a more appealing, desirable quality. As Jennifer Craik has pointed out, commercial photography revolutionized the representation of fashion, not just through technical advances that depicted clothes more accurately (than in illustrations), but also by changing how people viewed relationships among clothes, those who dressed in them, and the contexts in which they were worn.[50] In the photography studio, women could actively and collaboratively decide what clothes would be seen and how they would be viewed, thus helping to shape consumer habits of seeing. The studio let them explore how clothing and appearance could work to advance women's status, and it allowed them the opportunity to leave behind a visual legacy.

Unlike women who participated in salons, both photographer and subject left physical traces of their interactions for audiences to appreciate and interpret. But to comprehend the deeper range of references to power, sexuality, and consumer desire of those traces, we must understand these photographs as the deposit of the social relationships between women and men, Jews and non-Jews, who lived in a time and place where both gender and Jewish difference mattered a great deal. As Mila Ganeva argues, the imagined world conjured up by textual and visual images of clothing was as essential to the experience of Central European fashion as the act of actually wearing it.[51] Both Zirner-Zwieback and d'Ora channeled their creative energies into this imagined world. Reading their photographs for gender and for Jewish difference reveals how deeply these women understood the power of fashion to address the socially constructed boundaries that separated men and women, Jews and non-Jews, and how aware they were of knowing exactly how to bend but not break them.

ACKNOWLEDGMENTS

I am deeply grateful to Daniel H. Magilow and Elana Shapira, whose expertise and insight greatly improved this article.

NOTES

[1] I have not yet been able to locate these photographs in Austrian and German newspapers, nor have experts been able to direct me to additional sources where they might be located.

[2] On the fashion industry in Vienna during World War I and interwar period, see Gerda Buxbaum, *Mode aus Wien, 1815–1938* (Vienna: Residenz, 1986), 101–2.

[3] For excellent and thorough discussions of this topic, see Patrice Petro, *Joyless Streets: Women and Melodramatic Representation in Weimar Germany* (Princeton: Princeton University Press, 1989); and Richard W. McCormick, *Gender and Sexuality in Weimar Modernity: Film, Literature, and "New Objectivity"* (New York: Palgrave, 2001).

[4] Christopher Breward, *Fashioning London* (London: Berg, 2004), 11.

[5] Stella Bruzzi and Pamela Church Gibson, eds., *Fashion Cultures: Theories, Explorations, and Analysis* (London: Routledge, 2000), 2.

[6] I explore Jewishness as a category of critical analysis further in Lisa Silverman, "Beyond Antisemitism: A Critical Approach to German Jewish Cultural History," *Nexus: The Duke Journal of German Jewish Studies* 1 (2011): 27–45.

[7] Madame d'Ora, "Wie ich Photografin wurde und wie ich aufhörte es zu sein." Typescript. Preus Photography Museum, Norway.

[8] Madame d'Ora, "Wie ich Photografin wurde."

[9] Virginia Woolf, *A Room of One's Own*, (Peterborough: Broadview Press, 2001), 6 [orig. 1929].

[10] In 1925, d'Ora and Benda opened a studio in Paris together. However, the two quarrelled, and in 1927, Benda returned to Vienna and took over the studio there, operating it under the name "d'Ora-Benda-Wien." After this break, d'Ora and Benda never spoke to each other again. After 1940, d'Ora was forced to sell her Paris studio; she survived the war in hiding in Lalouvesc, a village in the Ardèche in the south of France. Both the subject and style of d'Ora's photographs changed radically after the war, though she also continued with portrait photography. In 1945, she photographed displaced persons camps in Austria, and in 1956, at the age of seventy-five, she completed a series vividly depicting the Paris slaughterhouses. She spent her final years in Frohnleiten, Austria, in her family's house (named *Haus Doranna* after the two sisters), which was returned to her after a legal battle with the city over its restitution. She died there in 1963.

[11] In 1928, d'Ora even filed a lawsuit against Benda over his inappropriate use of her name in some of the photographs. After their definitive split in 1927, after which Benda took over the Vienna studio, his photographs all bear the logo "D'ora-Benda." See Monika Faber, *Madame d'Ora, Wien-Paris. Portraits aus Kunst und Gesellschaft 1907–1957* (Vienna: Brandstätter, 1983), 15.

[12] On the representation of Jewish women as femme fatales, see Janis Bergman-Carton, "Negotiating the Categories: Sarah Bernhardt and the Possibilities of Jewishness," *Art

Journal, vol. 55, no. 2 (Summer 1996): 55–64; and Bram Dijkstra, *Idols of Perversity: Fantasies of Feminine Evil in Fin-de-siècle Culture* (New York: Oxford University Press, 1986).
[13] On the figure of the seductive and destructive *belle juive* in the culture of the time, see Sander L. Gilman, "Salome, Syphilis, Sarah Bernhardt, and the Modern Jewess," in *The Jew in the Text: Modernity and the Construction of Identity* (ed. Linda Nochlin and Tamar Garb; London: Thames & Hudson, 1995), 97–120. The association of black fur with seduction also evokes Austrian author Leopold Sacher-Masoch's *Venus im Pelz* (Venus in Furs), first published in 1869, in which the author describes the ability of fur to spur arousal. See Elana Shapira, "'Assimilating with Style': Jewish Assimilation and Modern Architecture and Design: The Case of the 'Outfitters' Adolf Loos and Leopold Goldman and the Making of the Goldman & Salatsch Building" (Ph.D. diss., University of Applied Arts, Vienna, 2004).
[14] For an examination of writing on women's fashion that achieved similar ends, see Mila Ganeva, *Women in Weimar Fashion: Discourses and Displays in German Culture, 1918–1933* (Rochester: Camden House, 2008), 51.
[15] Ganeva, *Women in Weimar Fashion*, 66. Ernst Dryden, born Ernst Deutsch in 1887 in Vienna, was Jewish. His choice of an English-sounding pseudonym is in keeping with the association of men's high fashion with England. For a gendered reading and critique of Dryden's illustrations and essays reinforcing the myth of the New Woman, see Ganeva, *Women in Weimar Fashion*, 66–68.
[16] As Elizabeth Otto and Vanessa Rocco note, the New Woman was actually an abstract concept and set of ideals across various nations that represented an entire range of female forms, rather than any one in particular. See "Introduction: Imagining and Embodying New Womanhood" in *The New Woman International: Representations in Photography and Film from the 1870s through the 1960s* (Ann Arbor: University of Michigan Press, 2011), 1–17; 1. See also Matthew S. Witkovsky, *Foto: Modernity in Central Europe, 1918–1945* (New York: Thames & Hudson, 2007), 71–74.
[17] Laura Wärndorfer, unpublished autobiography, 41. I am grateful to August Zirner for allowing me access to this source.
[18] The tearoom was located on the corner of Weihburggasse 4 and was until recently the restaurant "Drei Husaren."
[19] Wärndorfer, autobiography, 40–41, 43.
[20] Fred Adlmüller, "Was mich interessiert, ist die Mode," in *Vom Dritten Reich zum Dritten Mann. Helmut Qualtingers Welt der vierzigen Jahren,* (ed. Wolfgang Kudrnofsky; Vienna: Verlag Fritz Molden, 1973), 99–111,102–3.
[21] Ludwig Hirschfeld, *The Vienna that's not in the Baedeker* (trans. T. W. Maccallum; Munich: R. Piper & Co. Verlag, 1929), 188.
[22] Though it was not known to him at the time, Ludwig was the son of composer Franz Schmidt, with whom Zirner-Zwieback had had an affair during the early years of her marriage. In 1938, she fled Austria, living first in France and finally in New York, where she died in 1970. The department store was Aryanized soon after she fled; in addition to the store, she was forced to sell at auction the other real estate associated with the store, her apartment on the Kärntnerstrasse, and her house in the village of Mauer, at auction. Ludwig, who died in 1971, became a music professor at the University of Illinois-Cham-

paign Urbana. Wärndorfer, autobiography, 40–41. Many thanks to Dieter Hecht for his help with this information.

[23] See Tim Gidal, *Deutschland: Beginn des modernen Photojournalismus* (Lucerne: Bucher, 1972).

[24] Gisèle Freund, *Photography and Society* (London: Gordon Fraser, 1980), 4–5.

[25] Diana Crane, *Fashion and its Social Agendas: Class, Gender, and Identity in Clothing* (Chicago: University of Chicago Press, 2000), 1.

[26] Wärndorfer, autobiography, 42.

[27] Being cut off from Paris's fashion networks in the immediate postwar years had a lasting effect on fashion houses in Vienna, Brussels, and other European cities in the interwar period. For details, see Buxbaum, *Mode aus Wien*, 203, and Véronique Pouillard, "In the Shadow of Paris? French Haute Couture and Belgian Fashion Between the Wars," in *Producing Fashion: Commerce, Culture, and Consumers* (ed. Regina Lee Blaszczyk; Philadelphia: University of Pennsylvania Press, 2008), 62–81.

[28] Many salonières maintained strong bonds with their fathers, depended upon their financial support, and were well aware of negative stereotypes about Jews. Emily D. Bilski and Emily Braun, eds., *The Power of Conversation: Jewish Women and their Salons* (New Haven: Yale University Press, 2005), 18–19.

[29] A number of Jewish fashion houses had French departments in lavish salon rooms for their aristocratic and wealthy clients. Ingrid Loscheck, "Contributions of Jewish Fashion Designers in Berlin," in *Broken Threads: The Destruction of the Jewish Fashion Industry in Germany and Austria* (ed. Roberta S. Kremer; Oxford: Berg, 2007), 55. On department stores in Paris, see Philip G. Nord, *The Politics of Resentment: Shopkeeper Protest in Nineteenth-Century Paris* (New Brunswick: Transaction, 2005).

[30] "Vienne Oblige. Eine Eintragung im Handbuch der Wiener Gesellschaft," cited in the exhibition catalogue *Wien. Stadt der Juden—Die Welt der Tante Jolesch* (ed. Joachim Riedl Vienna: Zsolnay, 2004), 34–35.

[31] Hirschfeld, *The Vienna that's not in the Baedeker*, 184–85.

[32] Madame d'Ora, "Josefine Baker," *Die Dame* (August, 1926), 261. "Arme, kleine Josefine! Du sollst Kleider von Poiret und Callot tragen, du sollst evening shoes anziehen, vor denen du solche Angst hast, du sollst Hüte tragen, die dir überflüssig erscheinen und Schmucksachen von Dunan, die dir weit weniger gut gefallen als bunte Glasperlen." Paul Poiret and Callot Soeurs were well-known fashion design houses in Paris.

[33] See n. 21.

[34] Buxbaum, *Mode aus Wien*, 103. A similar development occurred in Weimar Germany in the world of fashion, according to which some critics lauded the cutoff from France and French fashion as a chance to focus on "national" German fashion. See Maria Makela, "The Rise and Fall of the Flapper Dress: Nationalism and Anti-Semitism in Early-Twentieth-Century Discourses on German Fashion," *Journal of Popular Culture* 34:3 (Winter, 2000):183–208, 195.

[35] At this time, Austria developed an international reputation for knit sportswear and undergarments. Buxbaum, *Mode aus Wien*, 103. A 1926 article on dirndls [traditional dress] in a Viennese women's magazine clarifies the nature of "Austrian"—as opposed to trendy—clothes as follows: "A made-up face and lipstick do not suit the dirndl. The

color that goes best with it is to be obtained for free from the sun. It is the ideal dress for summer visits to the Alps, the garden and parties in the Wienerwald [Vienna woods]. It cannot bear the stony streets of the big city. It seems out of place there." Cecile Spitzer, "Dirndl!," *Die Moderne Frau*, Heft 2, 1926.

[36] Not all foreign buyers were allowed to enter French fashion houses; those who did were subjected to strict regulations. Jewish-owned firms like Hirsch & Cie in Brussels set up collaborative networks between Belgium and France to facilitate importing French designs and manufacturing reproductions. Pouillard, "In the Shadow of Paris?," 65–66.

[37] Wärndorfer, autobiography, 41.

[38] Archives Générales du Roayaume de Belgique, I288, Folder 2268, cited in Pouillard, "In the Shadow of Paris?," 76.

[39] Alfred Jerger, *Die Moderne Frau*, Nr. 4 (1928), 7. "Das heißt man merkt sich bis ins kleinste Detail hinein alle Finessen dieser Kunstwerke und kopiert sie dann, macht eventuell kleine Aenderungen. Denn erstens eignen sich nicht alle Original Pariser Modelle für die Individualität der schönen, anmutigen Wienerin, die ein nicht minder reizvollerer Typ ist, als die Vollblutfranzösin. Und dann soll doch allen Frauen—nicht nur den Auserwählten der Fifth Avenue Gelegenheit geboten werden, sich für uns, die Herren der Schöpfung, so schön als nur irgend möglich zu machen."

[40] See Georg Simmel, Philosophie der Mode, Berlin 1905, 9. See also Elana Shapira, "Jewish Patronage and the Avant-Garde in Vienna," in *Patronage and Collecting—A Tribute to Western Culture. Jewish Patronage and Modernism* (ed. Annette Weber, forthcoming).

[41] For more on depictions of Jewish women as the ultimate consumers of luxury items, see Lisa Silverman, *Becoming Austrians: Jews and Culture between the World Wars* (New York: Oxford University Press, 2012), 79–87.

[42] Posters dated 1927 feature Paris, balls, fur, pearls, evening clothes, mirrors, beauty, and the words *"Pariser Mode"* [Paris fashion]. Other posters emphasize the good quality and low prices of linens and undergarments, and feature the Zwieback store's logo with the words *"Tradition Verpflichtet"* [committed to tradition]. By 1930, low prices are promoted with even more urgency: one poster advertising a half-price sale features a graphic of a man in a black suit with an enormous pair of scissors cutting a large ten schilling note in half. Wienbibliothek, Plakatensammlung.

[43] Atina Grossmann, "The New Woman and the Rationalization of Sexuality in Weimar Germany" in *Powers of Desire: The Politics of Sexuality* (ed. Ann Snitow, et al.; New York: Monthly Review Press, 1983), 167.

[44] See Kerry Wallach, "Observable Type: Jewish Women and the Jewish Press in Weimar Germany," (Ph.D. diss., University of Pennsylvania, 2011), 2, 5.

[45] Darcy Buerkle, "Gendered Spectatorship, Jewish Women, and Psychological Advertising in Weimar Germany," *Women's History Review* 15:4 (2006): 631.

[46] Bilski and Braun, *The Power of Conversation*, 5–7.

[47] Barbara Hahn, *The Jewess Pallas Athena* (trans. James McFarland; Princeton: Princeton University Press, 2005), 70.

[48] Some Jewish salonières emulated traditions of French sociability, "adopting its customs, language (most were fluent in French), and attributes." Bilski and Braun, *The Power of Conversation*, 17. In addition to supporting Austrian artists, Berta Zuckerkandl also

remained committed to French culture by translating many works of French literature into German or arranging for the translations, and introducing the designs of Paul Poiret to the city. Elana Shapira "Berta Zuckerkandl," *Jewish Women: A Comprehensive Historical Encyclopedia.* 1 March 2009. Jewish Women's Archive. July 7, 2012. http://jwa.org/encyclopedia/article/zuckerkandl-berta.

[49] Bilski and Braun, *The Power of Conversation*, 16.

[50] Jennifer Craik, *The Face of Fashion: Cultural Studies in Fashion* (London: Routledge, 1994), 93.

[51] Ganeva, *Women in Weimar Fashion*, 50.

Photographers, Jews, and the Fashioning of Women in the Weimar Republic

Nils Roemer

The Weimar Republic created a new visual culture that permeated the arts and consumer culture, heralding a new way of seeing. Illustrated journals and newspapers as well as the affordability of new cameras transformed the photograph into a central facet of the newly emerging Weimar culture.[1] Men like Erwin Blumenfeld and Martin Munkácsi, but particularly women such as Grete Stern, Ellen Auerbach, Ilse Bing, Else Ernestine Neuländer-Simon, Florence Henri, and Germaine Krull, excelled professionally in photography. Much of their fashion photography is to this day largely unexplored. Forced exile shortened their careers, gender bias placed them into less visible positions, and their photography's association with commerce made them less desirable collectables. Even the recent rediscovery of some of the celebrated Weimar female photographers reclaimed their artistic production, yet continued to neglect more often their fashion photography.[2]

The pioneering development in fashion photography of this period was inextricably linked to Jewish female photographers. Jews were as disproportionately overrepresented in photography as in almost any other realm of visual culture. As Mila Ganeva commented, most fashion photographers came from ". . . conventional, bourgeois Jewish families."[3] Yet ethnicity, class, and gender overlapped and often interacted in complicated ways that easily defy crafted ideas about a "Jewish eye."[4] Indeed, many Jewish photographers who engaged visual culture were shaped less by their cultural and religious background and more by their class and gender. Their Jewish identity does not seem to have mattered to their aesthetic vision. "Jewishness," as Jonathan Karp and Barbara Kirshenblatt-Gimblett have argued, appears "as contingent and contextual rather than definitive and presumptive."[5]

Aesthetic concepts and techniques of the avant-garde entered advertisement and the realms of commerce. Else Neuländer-Simon, known as Yva (1900–1942), Ilse Bing (1899–1998), as well as Grete Stern (1904–1999) and Ellen Auerbach (1906–2004), who together founded *ringl + pit* studio, all initially collaborated with avant-garde artists. Yva worked with the photographer Heinz Hajek-Halke, Stern and Auerbach with photographer Walter Peterhans, who also had taught at the Bauhaus in Dessau. Kurt Schwitters, Paul Klee, and the Dutch architect Mart Stam inspired Bing, who maintained a critical distance from Bauhaus photography without, however, disregarding Bauhaus technical and aesthetics ideals. Moreover, in 1930, Bing befriended Ella Bergmann-Michel, who with her husband was known for hosting avant-garde artists in Frankfurt, like El Lissitkzy and Kurt Schwitters, with whom Bing interacted.[6]

Fashion photography, in which art and consumerism often became intertwined, promoted new ideals of beauty. Beginning in the 1920s, mass publications placed photographs of beautiful women on their covers to stimulate sales. The rapid development of photographic and printing technologies and their widespread application in all spheres of public life had made this possible. Taking pictures and producing photographs for mass periodicals was no longer a costly and complicated adventure. In his famous 1927 essay "Photography," Siegfried Kracauer, the Weimar film theorist, cultural critic, and sociologist, highlighted the proliferation of visual material produced to appeal to and shape the taste of female consumers:

> The most striking proof of photography's extraordinary validity today is the increase in the number of illustrated newspapers. In them one finds assembled everything from the film diva to whatever is within reach of the camera and the audience. . . . The new fashions also must be disseminated, or else in the summer the beautiful girls will not know who they are.[7]

Women's fashion, like other forms of consumerism during the Weimar Republic, did not seek to fulfill needs, but rather aimed to satisfy desires.[8] Regardless of whether fashion advertisement offered ready-made ideals of self or the individuals generated their own new identities, purchasing entailed more than the simple acquisition of a product. For the British artist and director of a BBC documentary on fashion in 1972, John Berger, advertisement produced a feeling of desire for the displayed product, creating "envy for herself as she will become if she buys the product."[9] The purchase of a product engaged the individual buyer in a comprehensive process of self-fashioning, collapsing the boundaries between the image and her.[10] To acquire as well as to peruse products or advertisement represented a "longing to experience those pleasures created and enjoyed in the imagination, a longing which results in the ceaseless consumption of novelty."[11]

The desire to design an individual's identity had become intrinsic to a time that was often associated with loss of identity. In his essay "The Metropolis and Mental Life," the German philosopher and sociologist Georg Simmel argued that the modern city threatened individuality by reducing humans to their respective economic and functional roles.[12] In the same essay, Simmel contemplated ways in which the individual could reassert himself or herself. In an essay on fashion, he analyzed the individual and class-signifying role of fashion. He detected a desire of the middle and lower class to adopt the newest fashion in an effort to appear as a member of a higher class, along with an impulse to shape one's own identity. He posited the existence of two conflicting impulses in the consumption of fashion: the desire to create oneself and the social wish to belong to higher social class.[13] Born into a prosperous Jewish business family, but baptized as a child, Simmel also reflected on the meaning of the Stranger, who sought to assimilate and become like everyone else, but would invariably remain marked as Other by the act of assimilation itself.[14] In these three essays, Simmel noticed contradictory forces that provide an instructive framework to think about Jewish female fashion photography and the varied subject position female photographers shaped for themselves with and in their photography.

Fashion photography promised products that stirred the desire to belong to a particular class and culture, but therefore often excluded specific ethnic markers.[15] Moreover, without an existing Jewish visual culture and a tradition of women's representation, there existed no model for Jewish female photography. If there existed a specific Jewish visual culture around the turn of the century, it featured men, not women. The German Jewish artist Hermann Struck repeatedly cast older men as the representatives of Jewish traditions, a tendency that was even further strengthened in his later collaboration with Arnold Zweig. Men, rather than women, became the visual icons of the Jewish tradition.[16] Jewish visual culture had created ideals of Jewish masculinity, whereas women appeared simply as an embodiment of beauty ideals. Jewish photography otherwise existed only in its infancy in photojournalism and largely in the private and semiprivate realm of Jewish families and communities.

Fashion promised even to overcome existing social, cultural, or ethnic differences. This is probably most obvious in the case of Lisl Goldarbeiter, who became Miss Austria in 1929, came in second place in the Miss Europe competition, and won the title of Miss Universe in Galveston, Texas, the same year. The success of Goldarbeiter only highlights the absence of racial barriers, not of racism per se. She also faced antisemitic rejections of her status as beauty queen.[17] Similarly, Josephine Baker was widely heralded and celebrated in Paris and in Berlin, but her admirers never failed to racialize her as the embodiment of untainted African beauty and sex. Gender and race thus often became intertwined in the public domain.[18]

Sociologically speaking, Jewish women became representatives of the new professional women, entering the workforce. Often maligned as childless, oversexed, career-oriented threats to the Weimar gendered order, fashion photographers represented and produced images of the New Women. Their new visibility cast them as harbingers of the widely debated New Women, who defied traditional gender roles that had relegated women to the private sphere. Female photographers like Auerbach, Irene Bayer, Bing, Marianne Breslauer, Gisèle Freund, Lotte Jacobi, Florence Henri, Krull, and Lucia Moholy excelled professionally in the realm of photography. They were part of a wave of innovation in European design and photography that today is referred to as the New Vision, which temporarily erased distinctions between commercial and artistic motives in photography.[19]

The highly charged, conflicted, and contested image of the New Woman in the Weimar Republic was often coded as foreign and alien. The New Woman was cast not only as adamant consumer, but also as dangerous, as Darcy Buerkle has argued.[20] The fashion photography of the celebrated Jewish female photographers, however, remained silent on their identity as Jews. To the newly emerging professional Jewish photographers, their identity as artists, women, and photographers mattered more than their Jewish ethnicity.

Auerbach, who was born as Ellen Rosenberg on May 20, 1906, in Karlsruhe, moved to Berlin, where she met Grete Stern. In their commercial photography studio in Berlin, *ringl + pit*, they explored new ways of portraying women and promoting visions of the New Woman.[21] The award-winning "Komol" (1932), which advertised a hair dye, took first place in the Deuxième Exposition Internationale de la Photographie et du Cinéma in Brussels. Instead of an appeal to glamorized beauty, the photo opts for simplicity. Two women's profiles in cardboard are layered with mesh screen and white and dark hairpieces. The mesh and hairpieces add texture to the flat silhouettes, thereby creating dimensionality for women. The advertisement speaks to women's familiarity with the product and its process. Beauty appears as the result of an artistic and creative endeavor and not as reflection of male gazes. The simple silhouettes address any woman—their contours do not reveal their complexion or eye color, while the side view further obstructs any attempt to identify them. The appeal of "Komol" resided in the product's ability to transform hair into white or dark without, however, idealizing either or coding them as different ethnic identities.[22]

Their "Pétrole Hahn" (1931) was a comical take on the image of the New Woman portrayed in advertisement. The advertisement shows a young, blonde-haired, dark-eyed female mannequin, wearing an old-fashioned nightgown and holding up the product. A closer look reveals that the hand belongs to a real woman, thereby fusing the doll-like mannequin with a living woman. The creativeness and artificiality of beauty are being investigated while the advertisement promotes it.[23] Similarly, their advertisements "The Corset" (1929) and "Head and Gloves" (1930) critically dissected traditional views of women. "The Corset" showcases a woman tying the corset's back. She is turned away from the camera; she doesn't turn around to engage the viewer as her head and legs are cut off from the photo. The potential for sexually provocative photos is mitigated by its reduction and the nonengagement of the model. In "Head and Gloves" (1930), a mannequin's head, with knitted hat over a bobbed hairstyle, stares across a folded pair of silk top-stitched gloves at an empty property. The hat's cabled lines, the mesh's geometric patterns, and the gloves' stitches against the wire screen make overture to Bauhaus photography instead of beauty ideals. The photo shot from above shows the mannequin looking at the gloves, but the photo's perspective and her empty gaze veil her identity from the viewer.[24]

In 1933 after Hitler had come to power, Auerbach immigrated to Palestine, where she made, in Tel Aviv, a 16mm black-and-white film about the growing city for the World International Zionist Organization, as well as photos of everyday life in Palestine. They are images of what the artist encountered in her new environment, managing to catch them in the spur of the moment. If the *ringl+pit* pictures could for the most part be considered studio work, focused on representations of identities, with her immigration, such criteria took on a secondary importance in Auerbach's photos in the Yishuv [community of Jewish residents].[25] She captured the modernity of the country in photos that feature, for example, two painters hanging from the side of a building by ropes, but refrained from producing stereotypical views of the Jewish pioneers.

In 1935, the Arab revolts caused the recently opened Ishon, the child photography studio founded by Auerbach and her partner, to falter. As a result, the couple decided to leave the country for London to meet up again with Stern. In 1937, she married Walter, who had long been her companion, as a prerequisite for immigration to the United States. In New York, she earned a living by continuing her work as a child photographer. At this juncture, some of her photos betray the sensibilities of exile, loss, and dislocation. Her "Statue of Liberty" (1939) does not show the towering statue as a welcoming beacon to the new world, but captures a framed photo of the statue on the floor of a thrift shop surrounded by other discarded objects. A wire wrapped around the picture frame, seemingly confining her, undermines her status as the symbol of freedom.[26]

Born in 1899 into a comfortable Jewish family in Frankfurt, Germany, Ilse Bing enrolled first at the University of Vienna, then in 1920 at the University of Frankfurt for a degree in mathematics and physics, only to switch in 1922 to art history.[27] In 1929, while still pursuing her academic studies, Bing gained photojournalism commissions for *Das Illustrierte Blatt,* a monthly supplement of the illustrated magazine *Frankfurter Illustrierte,* for which she continued to provide regular picture stories until 1931. She also started collaborating with the architect Mart Stam, a prominent modernist who taught at the Bauhaus school of design from 1928–1929 and was appointed chief architect of the major urban renewal of Frankfurt in 1929.[28] With her artistic horizons expanded and finding some commercial success, Bing finally gave up her thesis in the summer of 1929 to exclusively concentrate on photography. In 1929, she acquired a Leica, which had become available since it was exhibited in 1925 at the Leipzig Spring Fair. The new 35mm point-and-shoot camera technology increased photographers' mobility.

Greatly impressed by an exhibition of modern photography in Frankfurt, particularly the work of Paris-based American photographer Florence Henri, Bing decided in 1930 to move to Paris, the capital of the avant-garde and modern photography, where female photographers like Krull and Henri (along with Bing) came to even greater prominence than in Weimar Berlin. For the first couple of years in Paris, Bing published her work regularly with German newspapers, continuing her association with *Das Illustrierte Blatt,* publishing numerous photo-essays. Gradually, her work appeared in leading French illustrated newspapers such as *L'Illustration, Le Monde Illustré,* and *Regards.* From about 1932, she increasingly worked for fashion magazines like *Vogue, Adam,* and *Marchal,* and from 1933–1934 for the American *Harper's Bazaar.* Additionally, she covered Parisian fashion for the *Frankfurter Zeitung* and contributed photos to her Frankfurt contact, Käthe von Porada's *Mode in Paris* [Fashion in Paris] in 1932.[29]

In recognition of her pivotal accomplishments, a solo exhibition at the June Rhodes Gallery in New York honored her work in 1936 and brought her to America, where she stayed for three months, during which time she made photographs in New York and Connecticut. Bing returned to Paris, but in 1940 she was confined to the infamous Vélodrome d'hiver before she was interned in Gurs. With the support of the fashion editor of *Harper's Bazaar,* she and her husband Konrad were able to leave for America in June 1941.

In her photos, she experimented with prisms, multiple exposures, and mirrors, cropping fragments and enlarging them many times their size. The

French photographer Emmanuel Sougez aptly called her the "Queen of the Leica" in 1932.[30] Her "House of Worth," from Paris 1933, shows a woman's black silk dress; there is no mannequin visible and the photo aims solely to capture the pooling of fabric from the drape of the dress. The dress appears almost liquid with differing reflections of light.[31] Recommended by a celebrity of Parisian high society, Daisy Fellowes, Bing commenced to work for *Harper's Bazaar* in November 1933, continuously producing photos of shoes, jewelry, handbags, and belts. Like all her work for *Harper's Bazaar*, her "Shoes" (1935) was done entirely in the studio. It displays extreme reduction and focuses entirely on the silk shoes in front of a black background. Neither a body, legs, nor face are visible, but the object acquires an almost sensual texture. The pointing of the right foot gives the picture a distinctly feminine touch. Her "The Honorable Daisy Fellowes' Gloves by Dent, London," for *Harper's Bazaar*, 1933, simply shows on a metal surface two white gloves. Like with *ringl + pit*, new aesthetics and gender politics exclude a woman from the photo. Yet the casual placement of the gloves appear as if they have just been cast aside, reflecting a new feminine confidence.

Lucia Moholy's striking close-up portrait of Bing at the Bauhaus in 1927 is a contrast to Bing's own self-portraits, which advertise and showcase her as an artist and photographer. Moholy's aimed to capture and reveal Bing in a close-up, which had become popular with Sergei Eisenstein's film *Battleship Potemkin* (1925). This photo mirrors similar portraits of Auerbach and Stern. Auerbach's "Ringl (Stern) with Glasses" (1929) captures her friend in a close-up with a tilted head. Despite the closeness of the viewer and the subject, Stern's eyes are looking down and do not interact with the viewer. Her expression is equally removed, leaving the impression of both distance and proximity. Similarly, Stern's "Portrait of Ellen Auerbach" (c. 1930) captures her friend lying with her right hand under her head on a patterned surface with a black hat and sweater. Her white face elevates her from the patterned background to highlight her identity and sense of herself. Yet she, too, remains distant.[32]

Bing's early "Self-Portrait" (1925) shows her in her private room behind her camera on a tripod. She looks into closet's mirror captured by the camera, appearing to present herself, if however tentatively, in the private realm as a photographer. Her appearance and that of the interior of the room with framed pictures and paintings on the wall are both enabled by the mirror's reflection and constricted by its frame.[33] Years later, her self-portraits acquired a more artful and professional appearance. "Self-Portrait in Mirrors" (1931) stages a complex mise-en-scène between two reflections: one in the mirror and the other in the camera.[34] Unlike many other Weimar self-portraits of photographers, her face remains visible and is not hidden behind the camera. She appears as the artist and photographer, who uses the Leica, but her vision is not limited by the camera's lens that captures what she chooses. Whereas her earlier self-portrait was more hesitant, here she looks seriously and confidently from behind her camera into her reflection.

Her famous "Self-Portrait with Leica" (1931), shot in her room at the Hotel de Londres, highlights the creative aspect of photography and the illusionary quality of all representations. Her self-portrait becomes an artful, subjective enacting and staging of herself and not a portrait. Almost reminiscent of Dziga Vertov's Soviet avant-garde movie *Man with a Movie Camera* (1929) that foregrounds the camera as the maker of images, Bing's photo shows her staring intently at a mirror, thereby portraying as much herself as the act of taking pictures. Her camera is focused on the reflection, while a second mirror on the side returns her back profile.[35]

Her photos from New York offer distant views of the city, which appears as an object of her camera but not as an inhabited space. Both mesmerized by the cityscape and its architecture and attuned to the gloomier side of its inhabitants, her photos displace the artful constructor of images with the view of displaced person in exile.[36] "Dead End I, Queensborough Bridge, NY" (1936) shows two men in conversation, who are turned away from us, while a third one sleeps on the wooden piers in front of the East River. The steamboats in the distance are set on their journey, and the men appear immobile. The location of the river does not conjure mobility, but at best distant and unreachable homes.[37] "Dead End II" (1936) shows the New York skyline from a bridge. While the bridge is cut off with only the narrow walkway visible, not giving view to the city at the end, New York itself is looming, yet inaccessible.[38] Even more revealing is Bing's "The Elevated and Me" (1936).[39] On the train station of New York's El that went from Chatham Square to 149th Street in the Bronx, no train is in sight, but the city of New York fills the left side of the photo. The train station is less a place of movement than an observation spot for panoramic views of the city's landscape. The panoramic scope that aims to bring the city into closer view underscores this sense, but instead simply captures the reflection of the photographer. The photographer Bing thereby becomes the observer of a distant city, but not the traveler who takes the train.

Probably best known as the teacher of Helmut Newton, Yva was born in Berlin in 1900. In 1925, she opened her own studio in Berlin with about ten employees. With the help of her brother, Ernst Neuländer, a co-owner of the famous Berlin fashion salon, Kuhnen, she established herself as one of the city's most acclaimed fashion photographers.[40] Her breakthrough came in 1927 with ten photographs in *Die Dame;* from then on she was constantly present on the pages of the top-circulation women's magazines. From 1929 on, Yva's *Fotoserien* [photographic stories] appeared in the pages of the popular Ullstein's magazine, *Der Uhu*.[41] Her works were included in landmark exhibitions of the period, such as the 1929 *Film and Foto* in Stuttgart and the 1930 *Das Lichtbild* in Munich. Yva, who grew up in an assimilated Jewish family, was forced to close her atelier in 1938 due to the Nazi work prohibition. She then worked as an X-ray assistant in the Jewish hospital before she and her husband, Alfred Hermann Simon, were arrested, deported to Majdanek concentration camp, and murdered in 1942.

Like Auerbach, Stern, and Bing, Yva responded to new trends in advertising, such as manipulating the female body as a display medium. Yva embraced the promised modernist antidote to sexualization and feminization of women in art by emphasizing the ungendered image. Her series of photographs bordered genres—fashion photography, advertising, and portrait—outlining Yva's unique critical rejoinder to the conventions of the visual representation of women's images for women's audiences in the 1920s and 1930s. The pervasive use of the female body in fashion photography accelerated the emergence of a new sexualized commercial language. Women's bodies were reduced to an erotic commodity that obliterated the appearance of individual identities.[42] Yet her fashion photography displayed a great range of technical composition and varied representations of women.

As Ganeva observed, Yva's "huge photographic opus covers a wide thematic and stylistic spectrum—from fashion photography to advertisement to daring act photos and avant-garde images."[43] She is therefore difficult to classify. Her short-lived collaboration with Hajek-Halke, an experimental photographer in Berlin, places Yva with the avant-garde, her act photos place her with the sexual revolution of the period, and her fashion photography places her squarely with the powerful consumer culture and debates about the New Woman.

Yva's "Bathing Suit, Modell Schenk" shows two women facing each other wearing identical swimsuits. At first glance, the photo seems to capture one woman and her reflection. Looking closer, the photo captures two blonde women. One woman has her back turned toward us, whereas the other, who appears to be signaling, is faced toward the camera, eyes averted. The doubling is contradicted by the askance gazes; there is no center point of interaction confronting the viewer with two separate and yet almost identical looks. Her slightly more conventional "Elegant Hat in Blue Silk with White Flap and Shawl," 1932, displays classic lines in black and white that highlight the model's three-quarter face, showing her lips, nose, and almost her eyes under the brim of the hat, giving her a mysterious and sophisticated appearance.

In her photograph titled "Schmuck," Yva focused on the model's hands and lower arms. The arms' position invokes embrace, adding to the sensual atmosphere generated by the soft focus and the base of the arms. [44] Yva endowed her images of women with an invisible mask. Her emphasis on the artifice then could be read as exercising control over any impulses of uncritical identification with the fashion model.[45] Similarly, Yva's self-portraits represent a conscious self-fashioning. Her 1926 "Selbstbildnis der Photographin" [Self-Portrait of a Photographer] intentionally presents her as a female photographer and artist.

The photo, which shows a cubist painting by Hajek-Halke in the background, effectively merges two images into one. Art, skills, and technology are enabled in this photo, as well as the new position of Yva as photographer, who appears without a camera. It is only the title that inscribes her as a photographer, representing herself as a female artist first, while her short hair gives her almost an androgynous appearance. Contrary to the logic of the German grammar that engenders her, she presents herself as an artist, whose gender is secondary. Her crossed hands over her chest invoke confidence rather than humility and modesty as Carmel Finnan suggests, while also offering glimpses of herself to the public.[46] The emphasis on the professional public identity effectively veiled private identity, including her Jewishness, from the viewer's gaze.

The female Jewish photographer's biographies mirror the social profile of the German Jewish community. Their orientation toward higher education, the arts, and fashion photography was the result of their socioeconomic status and ethnicity. Within their photography, however, is articulated the varied subject positions they inhabited as women, artist, Jews, and exiles. They engaged ideals of beauty and femininity in their fashion photography, their photos offering them as New Women partaking in the debates over the newly emerging visual culture of the Weimar Republic. Further, their self-portraits foreground their professional and artistic identity as photographers sans gender or ethnicity. Yva and *ringl +pit* even adopted professional pseudonyms. Is the absence of ethnic identifications a sign of the status as Other? Many were outsiders who became the true insiders of Weimar's new culture, as the historian Peter Gay famously claimed in 1968.[47] Yet the complex interplay between avant-garde, photography, and fashion, and the varied ways they commingled, became invented, adopted, and reshaped by women, Jews, and other Germans who defy any simple classification.

NOTES

[1] Hanno Hardt, "Pictures for the Masses: Photography and the Rise of Popular Magazines in Weimar Germany," *Journal of Communication Inquiry* 13:1 (1989): 7–29.

[2] See, for example, Nancy C. Barrett, *Ilse Bing: Three Decades of Photography* (New Orleans: New Orleans Museum of Art, 1985). Barnett reclaims Bing first and foremost as artistic photographer, paying barely any attention to her fashion photography.

[3] Mila Ganeva, "Fashion Photography and Women's Modernity in Weimar Germany: The Case of YVA," *NWSA Journal* 15:3 (2003): 1–25, here 3.

[4] The publication of Max Kozloff, New York: Capital of Photography (New York and New Haven: Jewish Museum and Yale University Press, 2002) triggered an intense debate about the idea of Jewish photography.

[5] Barbara Kirshenblatt-Gimblett and Jonathan Karp, eds., "Introduction," *The Art of Being Jewish in Modern Times* (Philadelphia: University of Pennsylvania Press, 2008), 1–19, here 3.

[6] See, for example, Barrett, *Ilse Bing*, 17.

[7] Siegfried Kracauer, "Photography," in *The Mass Ornament: Weimar Essays* (trans. and ed. Thomas Y. Levin; Cambridge: Harvard University Press, 1995), 47–63, here 57.

[8] Mila Ganeva, *Women in Weimar Fashion: Discourses and Displays in German Culture, 1918–1933* (London: Camden House, 2011).

[9] John Berger, *Ways of Seeing* (Harmondsworth: Penguin Books, 1972), 135.

[10] Ibid., 46.

[11] Colin Campbell, *The Romantic Ethic and the Spirit of Modern Consumerism* (Oxford: Blackwell, 1989), 205.

[12] Georg Simmel, "The Metropolis and Mental Life," in *The City Cultures Reader* (ed. Malcolm Miles, Tim Hall, and Iain Borden; 2nd ed.; London: Routledge, 2003), 12–19.

[13] Georg Simmel "Fashion," *International Quarterly* 10 (Oct. 1904): 130–55. See also Sabine Hake, "In the Mirror of Fashion," in *Women in the Metropolis* (ed. Katharina von Ankum; Berkeley: University of California Press, 1997), 185–201, who makes a similar point, arguing that fashion did not provide models of individuality, but rather created ideals that women felt compelled to embrace.

[14] Georg Simmel "Stranger," in *The Sociology of Georg Simmel* (trans. and ed. Kurt H. Wolf; New York: Free Press, 1950), 402–8.

[15] Yet exceptions did exist and ethnicity too shaped the new visual culture in which ideals of beauty, gender, and race were constructed. Stars encapsulated new racial ideals, like Hans Albers, Josephine Baker, and Anna May Wong. See Pablo Dominguez, "Film Stars as Embodiments of Gender, Nation and Race, 1918–1939" (Ph.D. diss., University of Heidelberg, 2012).

[16] Arnold Zweig, *The Face of East European Jewry. With Fifty-Two Drawings by Hermann Struck* (ed. and trans. Noah Isenberg; Berkeley: University of California Press, 2004).

[17] "Miss Austria: Off for Galveston," *New York Times* (12 May 1929): E2, and "Miss Universe Jeered in Rumania as Too Thin: Austrian Jewish Beauty Seeks Refuge in Cathedral and Police Rescue Her," *New York Times* (30 August 1929): E2. See also Kerry Wallach, "'Recognition for the Beautiful Jewess.' Beauty Queens Crowned by Modern Jewish Print Media," in *Globalizing Beauty: Aesthetics in the Twentieth Century* (ed. Hartmut Berghoff and Thomas Kühne; Washington, DC: German Historical Institute, forthcoming).

[18] Nancy Nenno, "Femininity, the Primitive, and Modern Urban Space: Josephine Baker in Berlin," in *Women in the Metropolis*, 145–61.

[19] See Julia Silvia Feldhaus, "Between Commodification and Emancipation: Image Formation of the New Woman through the Illustrated Magazine of the Weimar Republic" (Ph.D. diss., Rutgers University, 2010).

[20] Darcy Buerkle, "Gendered Spectatorship, Jewish Women, and Psychological Advertisement in Weimar Germany," *Women's History Review* 14:4 (September 2006): 625–36; and Sharon Gillermann, *Germans into Jews: Remaking the Jewish Social Body in the Weimar Republic* (Stanford: Stanford University Press, 2009), 30–32, on the internal Jewish debates over the New Women.

[21] Ute Eskildsen and Susanne Baumann, *ringl+pit: Grete Stern, Ellen Auerbach* (Essen: Fotografisches Kabinett, Museum Folkwang, 1993); and Ute Eskildsen, ed., *Ellen Auerbach, Berlin, Tel Aviv, London, New York* (Prestel: Munich, 1998).

[22] Ute Eskildsen, *Ellen Auerbach*, 21.

[23] Ibid., 20.

[24] Ibid., 24 and 18.

[25] Ibid., 31–41.

[26] Ibid., 54.

[27] On Bing, see Barrett, *Ilse Bing*, 9–30.

[28] Stam commissioned Bing to record all of his housing projects in Frankfurt. He also introduced her to Frankfurt's avant-garde artistic circles.

[29] Käthe von Porada, *Mode in Paris* (Frankfurt am Main, Societäts-Verlag, 1932).

[30] Emmanuel Saugez, "XXIX-Salon international d'art photographique," *Bulletin de la Société Française de Photographie et de Cinématographie* 3:21 (September 1932): 182.

[31] Larisa Dryansky, *Ilse Bing: Photography Through the Looking Glass* (New York: H. N. Abrams, 2006), 115.

[32] http://bauhaus-online.de/en/atlas/werke/portrait-ellen-auerbach

[33] Dryansky, *Ilse Bing*, 10 and 73.

[34] http://broadwayworld.com/article_/index.php?article=MOMA_Presents_PICTURES_BY_WOMEN_A_HISTORY_OF_MODERN_PHOTOGRAPHY_57_20100503#ixzz1b0FhO1jL

[35] Dryansky, *Ilse Bing*, 45–46 and 109.

[36] See, for example, Barrett, *Ilse Bing*, 82–89; and Dryansky, *Ilse Bing*, 39.

[37] Ilse Bing, "Dead End I, Queensborough Bridge, NY" (1936), The Metropolitan Museum of Art, New York. http://www.metmuseum.org/Collections/search-the-collections/190038424?rpp=20&pg=1&ft=*&where=Germany&who=Ilse+Bing&pos=1.

[38] Ilse Bing, "Dead End II" (1936), The Metropolitan Museum of Art, New York. http://www.metmuseum.org/Collections/search-the-collections/190038435.

[39] See, for example, Barrett, *Ilse Bing*, 83; and Dryansky, *Ilse Bing*, 209.

[40] Yva has received considerable attention. See Marion Beckers and Elisabeth Moortgat, *Yva. Photographien 1925–1938* (Ausstellungskatalog *Das Verborgene Museum 2001*; Berlin: Ernst Wasmuth Verlag, Berlin 2001); Ernst Wasmuth, *Yva: Photographies 1925–1938* (Tübingen: Ernst Wasmuth, 2002); Carmel Finnan, "Between Challenge and Conformity: Yva's Photographic Career and Oeuvre," in, *Practicing Modernity: Female Creativity in the Weimar Republic* (ed. Christiane Schönfeld; Würzburg: Königshausen & Neumann, 2006), 120–38; Ganeva, "Fashion Photography and Women's Modernity in Weimar Germany," 1–25.

[41] Marion Beckert and Elisabeth Moortgat, "Ihr Gaten Eden is das Magazin: Zu den Bildergeschichte von Yva im UHU, 1930-1033," in *Fotografieren hieß teilnehmen: Fotographinnen der Weimarer Republik* (ed. Ute Eskildsen; Dusseldorf: Richter, 1994), 239–49, here 239.

[42] Finnan, "Between Challenge and Conformity," 129.

[43] Ganeva, "Fashion Photography and Women's Modernity in Weimar Germany," 5.

[44] Finnan, "Between Challenge and Conformity," 130.

[45] See the similar argument by Mary Ann Doane, "Film and Masquerade: Theorizing the Female Spectator," *Screen* 23: 3–4 (1982): 74–87

[46] Finnan, "Between Challenge and Conformity," 120 and 123–24.

[47] Peter Gay, *Weimar Culture: The Outsider as Insider* (New York: Harper and Row, 1968).

Weimar Jewish Chic: Jewish Women and Fashion in 1920s Germany

Kerry Wallach

"Judaism has literally come into fashion: everyone's wearing it again!" This claim was made by German Jewish author Sammy Gronemann in a book of satirical anecdotes from 1927.[1] His assertion hints at the complex relationship between self-fashioning and Jewishness, suggesting that Jewishness itself was worn and displayed on the body in 1920s Germany. Indeed, the Weimar Republic (1919–1933) witnessed renewed interest in Jewish culture as well as significant contributions by Jews to the creation of general Weimar culture, and many of the best-known styles were created or promoted at least in part by Jewish women. Yet it was also a time during which growing antisemitism prompted the need for caution among Jews in public, a topic that recurred in contemporaneous debates in Jewish circles. This essay considers the fashioning of Jews from different angles: what, if anything, was Jewish about fashion in Germany in the 1920s and early 1930s, and was it possible to distinguish distinctive Jewish styles? To what extent was being Jewish considered fashionable in Germany during this time, and what effects did the popularity of Jewishness—or lack thereof—have on styles worn by Jews?

Broadly speaking, Jewish women played a significant role in creating and popularizing mainstream fashion trends of Weimar Germany; they were substantially overrepresented among fashion journalists and had a strong presence among designers, to say nothing of fashion photographers.[2] Further, Jews were among the consumers who shopped for fashionable and luxury goods, often in Jewish-owned stores; their tastes helped guide the fashion market in a variety of ways. The first part of this essay examines several key ways in which Jewish Germans shaped fashion-related industries in Weimar Germany, with a range of inquiry extending from clothing designers to those who helped make styles fashionable, to fashion journalists, graphic artists and illustrators, as well as major distributors of clothing such as department stores.

Whereas some fashion historians have argued that there was no connection between the Jewish identities of many people involved in the creation of Weimar fashion and the actual fashions they produced or promoted, I argue that there existed numerous contexts in which Jewishness directly impacted fashion in Germany during the 1920s and early 1930s. In choosing to wear certain items of clothing or accessories, Jewish women often had to navigate the tensions between modernity and tradition, between opulence and restraint, and between austerity and luxury. In the second part of this essay, I consider what was at stake for Jews in Weimar Germany who grappled with the dangers of visibly displaying Jewishness on their persons. Here I return to Gronemann's humorous comment that people were wearing Jewishness to suggest that when displayed on the body via clothing or accessories, signifiers of Jewishness were often highly subtle and difficult to detect.

PARTICIPATION OF JEWISH WOMEN IN FASHION-RELATED INDUSTRIES

Historically, Jews occupied such a prominent place in German fashion that they often were accused of controlling nearly all industries pertaining to the creation of garments; with the growing numbers of women in the workforce in the early twentieth century, Jewish women, too, came to be associated with fashion. It is widely accepted that a disproportionate number of fashion-related businesses were Jewish-owned, though exact statistics differ greatly (Jews made up no more than four percent of the German population even in Berlin, which was home to roughly 160,000 Jews in the 1920s, or one-third of all Jews in Germany).[3] Jewish men such as Valentin Manheimer and Herrmann Gerson, many of them immigrants from Eastern Europe, are credited with launching Berlin's *Konfektion* [ready-to-wear] industry: their salons and department stores sold mass-produced clothing at fixed prices already in the late nineteenth century.[4] Beginning in the 1930s, antisemitic groups and others alleged that prior to 1933, eighty percent (or more) of retail stores, department stores, and chain clothing businesses in Germany were under Jewish ownership. In his important work on Berlin *Konfektion* and fashion, historian Uwe Westphal sets out to debunk this myth, maintaining that only about forty-nine percent of German *Konfektion* businesses belonged to Jews.[5] Today, most scholars agree that eighty percent is a vastly inflated number and that the percentage of Jewish-owned clothing design and manufacturing businesses is closer to fifty percent.[6] Historian Irene Guenther, whose work on German fashion in the 1930s is among the recent and most extensive studies on the subject, corroborates and builds on Westphal's estimates.[7]

Although the fact that Jews owned many fashion-related businesses placed them at the center of Weimar style, it was by no means only through business ownership that Jewish women made their mark on fashion. Jewish women were known trendsetters in Germany, particularly those writing for mainstream fashion magazines such as *Die Dame* [The Lady, 1912–43], *Styl*

[Style, 1922–24], and *Elegante Welt* [Elegant World, 1912–62]. In fact, Jewish women of the nineteenth and early twentieth centuries are often regarded as cultural forecasters or even as agents of modernity—not only for fashion trends, but also for culture more broadly. Their impact on German fashion intersected with other arenas on many levels, from food and art to shopping and entertainment venues. Some Jewish women displayed great self-awareness about the fact that they were in a strong position to usher in cutting-edge modern concepts. In one 1926 contribution to a best-selling Jewish newspaper, Emmy Broido reminded readers that the Jewish woman of the day "leads fashion trends; serves as a strict judge of taste; and she functions as a critical barometer for the up and coming."[8] To be sure, not all Jewish women working in fashion would have been interested in the inner-Jewish perspective on their capabilities, but members of the Jewish community such as Broido nevertheless took pride in women's accomplishments.

Throughout the 1920s and early 1930s, women with varying degrees of Jewish self-identification continued to drive mainstream German fashions and tastes through their work for noteworthy fashion publications. As Weimar scholar Mila Ganeva details at length in her book, *Women in Weimar Fashion: Discourses and Displays in German Culture, 1918–1933,* Jewish women such as Johanna Thal, Julie Elias, Ola Alsen, Ruth Goetz, and Elsa Herzog numbered among the leading fashion journalists of the day.[9] The images of graphic illustrators including Alice Newman, Dodo (Dörte Clara Wolff), and Lieselotte Friedlaender, many of whom trained at Berlin's Reimann-Schule, appeared in advertising brochures, fashion magazines, supplements to widely circulated daily newspapers such as the *Berliner Tageblatt* [Berlin Daily] and the *BZ am Mittag* [Berlin Journal at Noon], and elsewhere.[10] Though they rarely brought Jewish identity into dialogue with their work for the fashion world, these journalists and graphic artists emphasized values such as individuality and modern forms of self-expression, topics that were also central to the discourse on Jewish self-representation.

Jewish fashion journalists introduced many of these discussions into the general sphere by way of their regular fashion columns. For example, fashion journalist Johanna Thal (1886–1944, born Martha Johanna Wulkan) served as a central contributor and as editor of the fashion section of *Die Dame* from approximately 1916 to 1934 [see Fig. 1].[11] Her concise lead articles provided an initial source of information about new fashions; it was often Thal who announced what the German fashions for the coming season would be. As Ganeva has noted, Thal's contributions often underscored the pursuit of individuality and the agency of female practitioners of fashion.[12] Although we have no evidence that Thal's writings about fashion referenced or were informed by her Jewish identity, her work—and the fact that it ceased abruptly in the mid-1930s, when she as a Jewish writer was banned from general German magazines, after which Thal subsequently left Berlin for Vienna—reminds us that fashion was a subjective endeavor determined by both wearer and observer, and that fashion is very much contingent on the era during which it is produced.

Fashion journalist Julie Elias was a notable exception among Jewish fashion writers insofar as her work appeared not only in general publications, but also sometimes was aimed at Weimar Jewish readerships. On occasion, Elias (1866–1943, born Levi) brought mainstream fashion to the Jewish masses.[13] One article about the new, longer silhouettes of 1929 appeared in *Das jüdische Magazin* [The Jewish Magazine], a short-lived Berlin publication; an image of Elias reinforced the connections between the current styles, which may have appealed to Jewish readerships insofar as they were somewhat more conservative, and the fact that a Jewish woman was describing them in a Jewish publication.[14] Still, Elias is better known for her contributions to the mainstream fashion magazines *Die Dame*

Figure 1. Johanna Thal, fashion editor of *Die Dame*, no. 4 (November 1920), 8. Courtesy of the Kunstbibliothek, Staatliche Museen zu Berlin.

and *Styl*, and to the *Berliner Tageblatt*. Though her articles for general periodicals rarely touched on topics pertaining to Jewish fashion, they sometimes alluded to subjects that Elias inflected with Jewishness in other ways, perhaps the most significant of which was food.[15]

For Elias, who enjoyed entertaining at home in Berlin with her husband, art historian Julius Elias, food was not only of great cultural significance, but also provided a way of subtly inserting Jewishness into general discussions. In the introduction to her acclaimed cookbook from 1925, *Das neue Kochbuch* [The New Cookbook], Elias describes her interest in keeping cuisine—which she explicitly relates to fashion—in line with current research in hygiene and health.[16] Further, she includes distinctively Jewish recipes in this cookbook, such as recipes for matzah balls and matzah soup nuts, both Passover favorites. According to other recipe titles, several were borrowed from prominent Jewish figures such as painter Max Liebermann's wife, Martha, and fashion writer Elsa Herzog (1876–1964).[17] References to Jewish cuisine also appeared on occasion in Elias's contributions to *Die Dame*, for example, *Schalet* [cholent], a long-simmering stew commonly eaten on the Sabbath.[18]

Indeed, Elias found ways to connect fashion and Jewish culture in a number of other works aimed at young women. Her book, *Die junge Frau* [The Young Woman, 1921], makes overt references to the Talmud as an authority on matters such as being a good household manager.[19] Another slightly more literary work, *Taschenbuch für Damen* [Paperback for Ladies, 1924], addresses her own experiences studying fashion; it also features illustrations by Jewish artist Emil Orlik (1870–1932), another regular contributor to *Die Dame*. One particularly illuminating quote from *Taschenbuch für Damen* reveals an awareness of the possibilities of dually encoding one's self-presentation: "In fashion-related things it is often that which is hidden, which is precisely that, which one wants to display."[20] Like many other Jews in Germany, Elias herself was a master of finding the right moments to reveal Jewishness; for the most part, however, she focused on mainstream fashion advice and recipes.

The works of graphic designers and illustrators can be read somewhat differently than those of journalists; although Jewish illustrators such as Dodo and Alice Newman made no overt references to Jewish themes in their fashion sketches and paintings, one might interpret some of their subjects as encoded with traits commonly associated with Jewish women.[21] The dominant female image of 1920s Germany was that of the New Woman [*Neue Frau*], a subject who, particularly during the years of Nazi rule, was retrospectively conflated with stereotypes about Jewish women: the New Woman was understood to be modern, emancipated, and she was often depicted with bobbed, dark hair. For Dodo (1907–1998, Dörte Clara Wolff), who often portrayed female figures in line with prototypical images of the New Woman, these drawings also reflected Dodo's self-image of a "dark-haired Jewish girl."[22] Like many other Jewish cultural figures who faced unemployment after the Nazi takeover of the German press in 1933–34, Dodo opted to publish in a variety of Jewish magazines and newspapers between 1933 and her emigration from Germany in 1936. It was not unusual that a number of her works from this period took up Jewish themes, though these images generally were not connected to fashion.[23]

As journalists and illustrators, but also as fashion designers renowned for their creative and artistic talents, Jewish women made their mark on the world of Weimar fashion. High-fashion milliner and designer Regina Friedländer is perhaps the best example of a Jewish woman whose work was significant for many different groups of the 1920s, including readers of women's fashion magazines, well-attired Berlin consumers, costume designers who worked in theater and film, people interested in architecture and design, and those who perceived a connection between art and fashion. Very little biographical information is available for Regina Friedländer (also known as Regina Heller); her designs were in wide circulation from roughly 1914 to 1931, though her first salon likely opened around 1900. Her main salon near Potsdamer Platz remained open through 1936, after which it likely was forced to close.[24]

Figure 2. Regina Friedländer hat designs, *Die Dame*, no. 7 (January 1921), 11. Courtesy of the Kunstbibliothek, Staatliche Museen zu Berlin.

Figure 3. Regina Friedländer hats and furs. Plate from *Styl* magazine; drawing by Annie Offter-dinger. Courtesy of the C. Jahnke Collection, Vancouver, Canada.

Whereas Friedländer's relationship to Jewish contexts was not made explicit in any of her work, scholars consistently list her among the Jewish fashion designers of Weimar Berlin, and the surname Friedländer also would have been construed as Jewish by her contemporaries, thus inflecting her work with a sense of Jewish artistry.[25] Friedländer's fashion designs, and particularly her hats and other forms of headpieces, appeared with great regularity in *Die Dame* and *Styl*, both in photographs and in drawings [see Fig. 2 and Fig. 3].[26] She often held fashion shows in her salons, and she took part in other social events such as a theatrical pantomime and a fashion show featuring as a model the Jewish actress Maria Orska (1893–1930, born Rahel Blinder-mann).[27] Further, Elsa Herzog organized a fashion show supplement to the Berlin art exhibition titled *Die Frau von heute* [The Woman of Today, 1929], which featured Friedländer on November 21, 1929. Julie Elias and Ola Alsen, too, helped coordinate the exhibition, which, while not explicitly Jewish in any way, was organized and attended by numerous Jewish women.[28]

Together with several other designers, Regina Friedländer set the tone in high-fashion headgear for over a decade, and her work was renowned for its artistic value as well as its fashionability. Her designs were featured as costumes in early films such as *Aus Liebe gefehlt* [Absent from Love, 1917].[29] In 1921, Adolph Donath's art journal *Der Kunstwanderer* [The Art Wayfarer] termed Friedländer "an Artist of Fashion"; several of her pieces were depicted in contemporary paintings by Charlotte Berend and Wolf Röhricht, the latter of which was displayed in the Akademie der Künste in Berlin, thereby merg-

ing with the art world on several levels.[30] Additionally, Friedländer's salon
near Potsdamer Platz was featured at length in an article in the architecture
and design journal *Innendekoration* [Interior Design] in 1922. In this article,
journalist Johanna Thal terms Friedländer a *Meister-Modistin* [Master Mil-
liner] whose work seamlessly blends fashion with art.[31] The detailed, even
ornate wall decorations in Friedländer's salon were painted by the Berlin-based
Jewish artist Lene Schneider-Kainer, who at that time was best known for her
portraits of women.

Artist Schneider-Kainer's body of work, too, represents a nexus of
fashion and art, though the fact that she likely entered the fashion world in
part out of financial necessity reminds us that some Jewish women may have
been involved in fashion simply to make a living. Originally from Vienna,
Schneider-Kainer (1885–1971) took painting courses in Vienna, Munich,
and Paris before landing in Berlin. Until 1926, she was married to Ludwig
Kainer (1885–1967), a painter and graphic artist who regularly contributed
to fashion magazines and other illustrated volumes, including Julie Elias's *Die
junge Frau*. In January 1925, Schneider-Kainer herself opened a Mode-Kunst-
Salon, a fashion and art salon not far from Berlin's Kurfürstendamm, where
she simultaneously displayed handcrafted clothing and her watercolor paintings. Among the works sold in this salon were handmade ladies' undergarments [*Damenwäsche*], which she embroidered with artistic designs.[32] Adolph
Donath described Schneider-Kainer in *Der Kunstwanderer* as an artist who
found a practical solution to the hard times of the inflation years by taking it
upon herself to make and sell clothing alongside art.[33] Berlin newspapers and
fashion magazines, too, hailed the opening of Schneider-Kainer's store and
featured photographs of her and her work. Yet her salon did not remain open
for very long, and she gave it up by December 1926 when she departed on a
work trip to Asia; it is possible that her store did not achieve great success. For
Schneider-Kainer, as for Friedländer, Jewishness did not make itself evident
in fashion creations, although the lives and work of both women were closely
intertwined with those of other Jewish figures.

On the distribution end, Jewish women played numerous roles within
the spaces of Jewish-owned department stores, salons, and boutiques. As historian Paul Lerner discusses at length in his work on department stores, many
of the major German department stores were founded by Jewish families, a
great number of which were of East European origin: Hermann Tietz, Nathan
Israel, Salman Schocken, and others.[34] Jewish women played several pivotal
roles vis-à-vis department stores: many worked behind the scenes as in-house

graphic designers, salesgirls, consultants, and coordinators of fashion shows, roles which fashion historian Regina Blaszczyk has classified as "fashion inter- mediaries."[35] In fact, there is some evidence that the Jewish press encouraged talented young women to seek out jobs in department stores and houses of *Konfektion*, particularly in the early 1930s when good jobs were scarce.[36] Other women influenced taste and styles through the act of consuming or simply by window shopping or observing wares on display.

Through seasonal placement and subtle imagery, retail stores, includ- ing fashion houses and department stores, reached out to Jewish consumers in inventive ways to help them achieve the status of fashionable, modern women.[37] Ganeva has argued that it was fashion house Herrmann Gerson's participation in the "'theatricalization' of fashion marketing" that helped popularize fashion teas, and later fashion shows—fashion as a form of enter- tainment—beginning as early as the 1890s.[38] Indeed, store owners and man- agers often served as initiators of new fashion trends: for example, department store owner Georg Tietz writes of his early inspiration to purchase heron feathers, which he bleached and packaged; he then offered his *Lehrmädchen- Verkäuferinnen* [saleswomen in training] a premium to sell off 10,000 Marks worth of feathers within five days.[39] Advertisements published in August and September encouraged shopping in advance of the high holidays, when even relatively unobservant, liberal Jews might have been more likely to purchase expensive new outfits or luxury products in order to appear fashionable at this festive time of year. In contrast to mainstream Weimar fashion, which was perceptibly Jewish only in the most subtle ways, the fashion of Jewish women was not only a hotly debated topic, but also one that was profoundly Jewish.

FASHION AS A MEANS OF DISPLAYING (AND DISGUISING) JEWISHNESS

As we have seen, the majority of Jewish women who were intensively involved with the creation and promotion of Weimar fashion did so in a manner that did not obviously address Jewishness; most of their designs and writings about fashion appeared in general contexts. Yet the claim made by fashion historian Ingrid Loschek that "no stylistic difference between the fashion creations of Jewish and non-Jewish fashion houses existed" speaks only to the styles created for mainstream consumers.[40] Although accurate with respect to gen- eral German designs, Loschek's position does not consider contexts in which distinctively Jewish garments or accessories were purchased and worn or in which general fashions were deployed on Jewish occasions. Even though most of the fashions of the 1920s had little to do with Jewishness, there were some notable exceptions to this rule. Indeed, historians such as Leora Auslander have argued that Jews in Weimar Germany created "subtle and complex" subcultures in which Jewishness was deeply relevant to taste and aesthetics.[41] In the following, I build on this notion to demonstrate that Weimar Jewish subcultures encompassed fashion in a variety of ways related to personal style, religious observance, Jewish customs, and acute sensitivity to the dangers of Jewish visibility.

Among Jews in Weimar Germany, fashion was an extremely gendered undertaking. Gender also was closely linked to the public visibility of Jews, which was a matter of great concern during this era of growing antisemitism. Religiously observant Jewish men, particularly new immigrants to Germany from Eastern Europe, but also others who wore visible markers such as head coverings or long black coats, remained easy targets even in metropolitan areas such as Berlin, which otherwise provided a significant degree of anonymity to its four million residents. Outbreaks of antisemitic riots that targeted easily identifiable Jews took place on multiple occasions in the 1920s, often in the Scheunenviertel district near Berlin's Alexanderplatz, which at that time was home to many East European immigrants.[42] In contrast to their male counterparts, Jewish women took advantage of contemporary styles to modernize and update their appearance. Already in the late eighteenth century, religiously observant women began replacing their caps and cloth head coverings with wigs designed to imitate women's own hair. As a general rule, the more modern Jewish women became, the less overtly Jewish they appeared.

Jewish dress in Weimar Germany incorporated aspects from contemporary German fashion as well as inner-Jewish perspectives on appropriate attire. Not surprisingly, conservative male members of Jewish communities objected to any drastic changes to the Jewish female aesthetic, and fashion trends thus spread more slowly among Jewish consumers, often lagging approximately two to three years behind. In the early 1920s, a wave of articles about the controversial topic of Jewish women and fashion appeared in several different German-Jewish periodicals. Whereas many of these articles supported a movement to convince Jewish women to dress in a less visible or ostentatious way so as not to draw attention to themselves as Jews, others assessed the role of women's dress in relation to Jewish law.

In addition to mainstream fashions worn by both Jewish and non-Jewish women, a distinct set of stylish looks was promoted specifically to Jewish women, though most were not perceptibly Jewish. The custom of wearing new clothes on Jewish holidays inspired Jewish fashion in a cyclical manner: Jewish styles often took the form of special new outfits purchased to wear to synagogue on the Jewish New Year, for Passover, or to balls held on festive occasions such as Purim and Hanukkah. For Jews in Germany, as well as elsewhere in Europe and in the United States, it was very common to purchase luxury goods in advance of upcoming holidays and other public ritual occasions.[43] It is possible that fashionable hats by designers such as Regina Friedländer were worn to synagogue or for other Jewish purposes; hats figured as updated versions of religious head coverings for many women.[44] In addition to annual events, wedding fashion, too, was given a Jewish spin; a few articles in the Jewish press actively cultivated a kind of "Jewish wedding chic" by tailoring general fashion to suit the needs of brides invested in Jewish wedding traditions, such as fasting or wearing solid gold wedding rings.[45]

Guidelines for women's fashion in the 1920s were influenced by contemporary attitudes toward Jews, many of which were intertwined with a fear of the repercussions for appearing well off and fashionable. Women who displayed expensive tastes or dressed in a flashy way, particularly on Jewish holidays or in proximity to synagogues, were accused of incurring unnecessary attention that could prompt antisemitic acts. Upper-class travel destinations, such as summer vacation resorts, were considered especially dangerous; already in 1922, Jewish travelers were warned in the *C.V.-Zeitung*, the newspaper of the *Centralverein deutscher Staatsbürger jüdischen Glaubens* [Central Association of German Citizens of the Jewish Faith], to avoid summer vacation spots known to be antisemitic, including nearly every Bavarian bath and resort.[46]

Whether women were at liberty to choose what to wear—and whether to display certain highly visible items such as jewelry—was also a matter of contention. The president of the Centralverein, Ludwig Holländer, acknowledged that the *Schönheitsgefühl* [feeling of beauty] of Jewish women might be in jeopardy if they were compelled to make drastic changes to their aesthetics. Still he posed difficult questions concerning public visibility: "Should women stop putting on jewelry, should everything fashionable be banned? . . . Where is the boundary of jewelry, of striving toward a compliance with looking modern?"[47] For Holländer and others, the problem lay not in owning or wearing luxury objects, but in flaunting them publicly and attracting unwarranted attention. In a similar vein, Berlin attorney Adolf Asch founded an organization in 1922 that issued warnings "to guard the dignity customary before and after the divine services on the High Holidays, and especially to ask Jewish women to avoid all showy luxury in clothing and jewelry."[48]

Precisely because they often embraced so-called "sinful" or luxurious modern styles, Jewish women were at times more susceptible to critique than their male counterparts. In fact, extensive debates about what styles were appropriate for Jewish women took place in the Weimar Jewish press. Discussants such as Holländer wrote of their desire for women to appear less conspicuous in public; rabbinic councils and others advocated for Jewish women to dress modestly and to eschew the latest styles by avoiding short skirts, revealing clothing, and high heels. That some Jewish women supposedly showed too much skin led the editors of the Orthodox Jewish newspaper *Der Israelit* [The Israelite] to claim that these women were engaged in "gedankenloser Nachäffung unjüdischer Mode" [thoughtless mimicry of un-Jewish fashion]. In the same front-page lead article, *Der Israelit* encouraged Jewish women to reject modern, degenerate styles and resist the notion of "Ethisierung der Eitelkeit" [ethically justifying vanity]. To combat this practice, *Der Israelit* supported recovering the ancient Jewish traditions of *tznius* [modest dress]; only through modesty would the Jewish people become worthy of redemption.[49]

When Jewish women added their voices to the inner-Jewish debate about fashion in the mid-1920s, they represented a variety of viewpoints: some reiterated the importance of cultivating inner, moral values, whereas others made a strong case for being permitted to take part in current trends. Contributing to a non-partisan newspaper, Else Fuchs-Hes (1889–1978; later Else Rabin) argued in favor of a more conservative perspective, namely that Jewish women needed to be true to themselves and could do so by resisting the superlative clothing fashion of the day: skirts that were potentially too short, stockings that were too gaudy, heels that were too high, hair that was too short.[50] Journalist Doris Wittner (1880–1937), in contrast, took up the cause of liberal Jewish women, arguing that they should be granted the freedom to wear the latest fashions. Barring them from doing so, she boldly claimed, would be tantamount to imposing Christian or antisemitic restrictions on Jewish expression. Wittner further sardonically equated the arguments of the Union for Traditional and Ritually Adherent Rabbis with those used by traditional Christian, Muslim, and antisemitic regulatory practices, thereby underscoring the point that Jewish women should be permitted to take part in mainstream fashions.[51]

In accordance with the suggestion that Jewish women should avoid appearing too conspicuous in public, the Jewish press advertised items designed to help their wearers look no different from the average German woman. Perhaps the best example is the way in which married Orthodox women

Figure 4. Advertisement for pageboy wigs, *Der Israelit*, no. 10 (7 March 1929), 8. This same ad appeared regularly in *Der Israelit* from March 1929 to March 1931.

participated in the extremely popular 1920s hairstyle known as the *Bubikopf* [pageboy bob]. Indeed, what author Sammy Gronemann termed the "Orthodox *Bubikopf*"—women's wigs or *sheitels* in the style of the pageboy bob—was advertised most widely from the late 1920s until 1931, in both Orthodox and other Jewish publications [see Fig. 4]. In his 1927 book of satirical anecdotes that also was serialized in the best-selling Jewish newspaper, the *Israelitisches Familienblatt* [Israelite Family Pages], Gronemann described the phenomenon of the Orthodox *Bubikopf* as barely detectable: "the impeccable pageboy would hardly lead one to suspect that it is a wig worn in the interest of protecting an ancient Jewish tradition."[52] He also made fun of the hypocritical nature in which many religiously observant Jewish women donned fashionable short wigs in order to adhere to Jewish laws about covering one's hair, yet did so in the most stylish way possible, complete with ostentatious jewelry and low-cut dresses. It is not difficult to grasp why the trend of *Bubikopf* wigs became popular so quickly; many nineteenth- and early twentieth-century wigs were likely heavy and unmistakable, visibly marking the wearer as possibly Jewish, even from a distance. Smaller, updated *sheitels* enabled observant women to blend in better with their surroundings and to perceive themselves as more in line with modern styles.

But *Bubikopf* wigs were about more than just navigating the tensions between traditional and modern hairstyles; they also provided Jewish women with a highly subtle way of signifying Jewishness. Even random passersby on the street potentially could identify Jews by way of these hairpieces, particularly if worn in combination with modest clothing. Within Weimar Jewish circles, women further worried about the sensitive issue of being discovered wearing a bad wig—in this case, bad wigs signified not only a poor sense of style, but also made the wearers more of a target for antisemitism. One 1932 ad in *Der Israelit* featured Florian Elzer's Frankfurt beauty salon and boasted that an assistant from the Berlin store of beauty specialist Elise Bock (known as "the German Helena Rubinstein") soon would visit to make clients' *sheitels* fit perfectly.[53] Elzer's ad reminded female customers, who presumably knew all too well what he meant: "Nothing is worse than when someone can tell that you're wearing a wig."[54] This line carries with it another implication: if they know how to identify it, people can always spot who is wearing a wig; even hidden signifiers of Jewishness can be made recognizable.

This line sums up the message about women's fashion conveyed by advertisers, but also by other contributors to the Jewish press: cultivate a Jewish identity, but find a way to wear Jewishness such that it is barely detectable in public. For women in the Weimar period, "Jewish chic" meant appearing fashionable and German on the surface—even setting the trends in mainstream German fashions—but displaying Jewishness in only the most subtle ways, if at all. As journalists, artists, designers, distributors, and consumers, Jewish women made a remarkable impact on Weimar tastes and fashion trends. At the same time, some also found a way to incorporate Jewishness into their versions of these styles, albeit in a manner that was practically invisible to the untrained eye.

POSTSCRIPT: JEWS AND FASHION AFTER 1933

Many German Jews maintained strong ties to the fashion industry after 1933 despite restrictions placed upon them by the Nazi government. Although there were countless fashion shows, balls, and other social events organized by Jewish women during the 1920s, it was only after 1933 that major fashion events were aimed at exclusively Jewish audiences.[55] As Jewish women were shut out of German fashion with the gradual "Aryanization" (forced transfer of Jewish-owned businesses to "Aryan" owners) of all fashion-related businesses between

Fig. 5. Audience and model at a fashion show of the artists' relief organization [*Künstlerhilfe*] of the Jewish community, Berlin (4 September 1934). Berlin Jewish Community Collection AR 88. Courtesy of the Leo Baeck Institute, New York.

1933 and 1938, they found other specifically Jewish outlets for their interests. Further, fashion came to symbolize a lighthearted and enjoyable comfort for Jewish women, an age-old pleasure that distracted them from difficult times. In 1934, an event of the artists' relief organization titled *Ein Tag für die jüdische Frau* [A Day for the Jewish Woman] aimed to bring Jewish women into contact with Jewish-owned firms, which they as consumers were encouraged to support. A further goal of the event was "to satisfy women's desire for exhibitions and to stimulate feminine, and, if present, masculine purchasing desires."[56] This Day for the Jewish Woman, which was held between Rosh Hashanah and Yom Kippur in 1934, included a show of coming winter fashions supposedly organized by Elsa Herzog [see Fig. 5].[57]

Also around this time, Jewish writer and journalist Clementine Krämer (1873–1942), an amateur fashion expert who had worked in retail, proclaimed in a public lecture to Jewish women that fashion always had been, and continued to be, of great interest to women, noting that fashion in itself was always changing and thus was inherently modern. The notes for her lecture, which she likely presented in 1935 to members of the Jüdischer Frauenbund, titled *Modeplauderei* [Musings on Fashion], can be found among her papers.[58] These notes contain a close analysis of decades of fashion magazines, as well as different fabrics, colors, and styles, though in an initial outline she writes that she intentionally avoided a discussion of what constituted ethical attire for Jewish women during such a precarious time.[59] The styles themselves were likely more interesting—or simply more fun—for Krämer and her audience than a debate about propriety and modesty.

For Krämer and others in the mid-1930s, there was a clear distinction between *Mode* [fashion] and *Tracht* [traditional folk costume], the latter of which frequently was associated with so-called "Aryan" attire. According to Krämer, *Tracht* was static and unchanging, and perhaps more conservative, whereas the newest *Mode* styles were captivating but bound to die out quickly. Her words echo earlier writings of Johanna Thal, who often emphasized the ephemeral nature of *Mode*. Historian Irene Guenther has written extensively about the evolution of fashionable styles in the Third Reich and the predominant shift away from *Mode*, which was negatively deemed foreign, American, and also Jewish.[60]

Indeed, the strongest ties between Jewish women and current fashions arguably existed during the Weimar years, when their participation in various fashion-related industries reached its peak. In the early years of Nazi rule, Jewish women continued to create, discuss, and showcase fashions among themselves, but their contributions to general German fashions were constricted greatly by a clear separation between Jewish and German cultural spheres. After 1938, there were no longer any Jewish-owned fashion houses or department stores to be found in Germany; only the most fortunate Jewish designers, illustrators, and journalists were able to escape and bring their work to other centers of fashion such as London and New York.

ACKNOWLEDGMENTS

I would like to thank Mila Ganeva (Miami University of Ohio), Adelheid Rasche (Kunstbibliothek Berlin, Sammlung Modebild-Lipperheidesche Kostümbibliothek), Heike-Katrin Remus (Stadtmuseum Berlin), and Christine Waidenschlager (Kunstgewerbemuseum Berlin) for sharing their knowledge about Regina Friedländer, among other references; and fashion historian Claus Jahnke (Vancouver, Canada), who generously permitted me to work with his collection.

NOTES

[1] "Das Judentum ist geradezu Mode geworden: man trägt es wieder!" Sammy Gronemann, *Schalet: Beiträge zur Philosophie des "Wenn Schon!"* (afterword by Joachim Schlör; Leipzig: Reclam Verlag, 1998), 48. Sammy Gronemann (1875–1952) was an attorney, a well-known author, and an important Jewish public figure; he was especially active in Zionist circles and emigrated to Tel Aviv in the 1930s.

[2] On Jewish women as fashion photographers, see Nils Roemer's contribution to this volume.

[3] On Jewish populations in Weimar Germany, see Marion A. Kaplan, ed., *Jewish Daily Life in Germany, 1618–1945* (Oxford: Oxford University Press, 2005), 273–74.

[4] On Jewish founding roles and participation in Berlin *Konfektion* in the nineteenth and early twentieth centuries, see Mila Ganeva, *Women in Weimar Fashion: Discourses and Displays in German Culture, 1918–1933* (Rochester: Boydell & Brewer, 2008); Erika Ehlerding, "Mihu Jehudi: Jüdische Konfektionäre in Styl," in *Styl: Das Berliner Modejournal der frühen 1920er Jahre* (ed. Adelheid Rasche and Anna Zika; Stuttgart: Arnoldsche, 2009), 176–81; Roberta S. Kremer, ed., *Broken Threads: The Destruction of the Jewish Fashion Industry in Germany and Austria* (Oxford: Berg, 2007); Uwe Westphal, *Berliner Konfektion und Mode: Die Zerstörung einer Tradition, 1836–1939* (Berlin: Edition Hentrich Berlin, 1992); and Brunhilde Dähn, *Berlin Hausvogteiplatz: Über 100 Jahre am Laufsteg der Mode* (Göttingen: Musterschmidt-Verlag, 1968). On 1920s fashion more broadly, see also Nora Fiege, *Berliner Konfektion und Mode in den 1920er Jahren: Neue Kleider für Neue Frauen?* (Hamburg: Diplomica Verlag, GmbH, 2009; Berlin: Kunsthochschule Berlin-Weißensee Diplomarbeit, 2008); Christine Waidenschlager and Christa Gustavus, *Mode der 20er Jahre* (Tübingen: Ernst Wasmuth Verlag, 1993); and Christine Waidenschlager and Christa Gustavus, *Berliner Chic: Mode aus den Jahren 1820–1990* (Berlin: Stiftung Stadtmuseum Berlin, 2001).

[5] Westphal, *Berliner Konfektion und Mode*, 90.

[6] One nonscholarly article published online in 2010, which supposedly draws on the expertise of journalist Ruth Haber (who contributed to Waidenschlager, *Berliner Chic*), goes so far as to claim that 90 percent of Berlin *Konfektion* was under Jewish ownership. Wolfgang Altmann, "Berlin—Stadt der Mode," *Tip Berlin* (1 July 2010). Retrieved from http://www.tip-berlin.de/kultur-und-freizeit-shopping-und-stil/berlin-stadt-der-mode. In addition, Roberta Kremer's 2007 book, which grew out of a 1999 Vancouver Holocaust Education Centre exhibition by the same name, suggests that higher statistics might be more accurate in some cases, namely that 80 percent of department and chain-store businesses were Jewish-owned and that 60 percent of wholesale and retail clothing businesses were Jewish-owned. See Kremer, *Broken Threads*, 14. No evidence in support of these figures is cited in either case.

[7] See Irene Guenther, *Nazi Chic? Fashioning Women in the Third Reich* (Oxford: Berg, 2004), 84. For an in-depth discussion of scholarly positions on statistics pertaining to Jews in German fashion industries, see Susan Ingram and Katrina Sark, *Berliner Chic: A Locational History of Berlin Fashion* (Chicago: Intellect, The University of Chicago Press, 2011), 67–76.

[8] Broido writes that the Jewish woman is "tonangebend für die Mode; strenge Richterin des Geschmacks, sie ist Kritikerin mit einer Witterung für das Neue und Kommende." Emmy Broido, "Die Jüdin von heute," *Israelitisches Familienblatt*, 1926, no. 47 (25 November 1926): 13.

[9] Ganeva, *Women in Weimar Fashion*, 66.

[10] Lieselotte Friedlaender descended from a formerly Jewish family that had converted to Protestantism. Although she likely did not self-identify as a Jew during the Weimar period, she is often considered as a Jewish artist because she was not permitted to work under her own name after 1933. See, for example, Ingrid Loschek, "Contributions of Jewish Fashion Designers in Berlin," 49–75, here 63 and 75 n.27. On Lieselotte Friedlaender, see Burcu Dogramaci, *Lieselotte Friedlaender (1898–1973)—eine Künstlerin der Weimarer Republik. Ein Beitrag zur Pressegraphik der 20er Jahre* (Tübingen: Ernst Wasmuth Verlag, 2001). For additional information about fashion illustrators, see also Burcu Dogramaci, "Fenster zur Welt: Künstlerische Modegraphik der Weimarer Republik aus dem Bestand der Kunstbibliothek zu Berlin," *Jahrbuch der Berliner Museen*, vol. 45 (2003): 201–33.

[11] Though little is known about Johanna Thal's fate, my research suggests that she emigrated from Berlin to Vienna in 1935, and was deported from Austria to Theresienstadt in 1942 and later to Auschwitz, where she likely met her death in 1944. This biographical information is taken from an entry on Johanna Thal's husband, journalist (Friedrich) Julius Hirsch (1874–1942), in Hannah Caplan, et al., eds., *International Biographical Dictionary of Central European Emigrés 1933–1945*, Vol. 2.1 (Munich: K. G. Saur, 1983), 514. There is also a short entry for Johanna Thal in the Berlin Jewish address book, suggesting that she lived at Grolmanstr. 55 in Berlin in the early 1930s. See *Jüdisches Adressbuch für Groß-Berlin. Ausgabe 1931* (foreword by Hermann Simon; Berlin: arani-Verlag, 1994), 409.

[12] According to Ganeva, Thal likely contributed to *Die Dame* from 1916 to 1934. See Johanna Thal, "Kritisches über die Mode," *Die Dame*, November 1921, no. 4: 13; cited in Ganeva, *Women in Weimar Fashion*, 39.

[13] Although Julie Elias's date of death is usually listed as 1945, an obituary published in *Aufbau* [Reconstruction] in 1943 suggests that she died two years earlier than was previously thought. See Max Osborn, "Julie Elias," *Aufbau* (24 December 1943): 7.

[14] Julie Elias, "Die veränderte Silhouette," *Das jüdische Magazin*, vol. 1, no. 4 (November 1929): 53–55.

[15] See Julie Elias, "Mode und Küche," *Berliner Tageblatt*, no. 96 (26 February 1929): 2.

[16] Julie Elias, *Das neue Kochbuch: Ein Führer durch die feine Küche* (Berlin: Ullstein Verlag, 1925), xi.

[17] Elias, *Das neue Kochbuch*, 22 [*Mazzeklöße*; *Mazzeschwämmchen*]; "Gänseleber nach Elsa Herzog," 35; and "Parfait von Kaffee. Nach Martha Liebermann," 231.

[18] Julie Elias, "Festgerichte," *Die Dame*, December 1929, no. 6: 113.

[19] Julie Elias, *Die junge Frau: Ein Buch der Lebensführung* (Berlin: Rudolf Mosse Buchverlag, 1921), 108.

[20] "In Modedingen ist oft das, was man verbirgt, gerade das, was man zeigen möchte." Julie Elias, *Taschenbuch für Damen* (Berlin: Ullstein Verlag, 1924), 108.

[21] Several works by Alice (Lissi) Newman (née Edler) were acquired recently by the Jewish Museum Berlin. On Alice Newman, see Westphal, *Berliner Konfektion und Mode*, 161–66 and 216–17; and Andreas Nachama, *Jüdische Lebenswelten* (exhibition catalog; Berliner Festspiele; Frankfurt am Main: Jüdischer Verlag, 1991), 216–18.

[22] Renate Krümmer, ed., *Dodo: Leben und Werk / Life and Work 1907–1998* (Ostfildern: Hatje Cantz Verlag, 2012), 17. On correlations between Jewishness and the dark hair of the New Woman, see Darcy Buerkle, "Gendered Spectatorship, Jewish Women and Psychological Advertising in Weimar Germany," *Women's History Review* 15:4 (September 2006): 625–36.

[23] After 1933, Dodo contributed illustrations to the *Jüdische Rundschau, Israelitisches Familienblatt, C.V.-Zeitung,* and the Berlin *Gemeindeblatt.* See Krümmer, *Dodo*, 25 and 115–19.

[24] Based on information available in Berlin address books, it would seem that Regina Friedländer first began selling women's hats [*Damenputz*] around 1900; the first time her store is listed as a "Salon" was in 1903. (To complicate matters, there are two entries for women named Regina Friedländer who worked in Berlin fashion in 1900.) Regina Friedländer's hat salon existed at several different locations on Linkstraße through 1910. After a brief stint at Potsdamer Straße 20/21 circa 1911–1913, the primary Regina Friedländer salon opened in 1914 at Königgrätzerstraße 2-3 near Potsdamer Platz and likely remained open continuously through 1936 (this street was later renamed Budapester Straße, Friedrich-Ebert-Straße, and Hermann-Göring-Straße, and is today Ebertstraße). In 1928 and 1929, Friedländer opened a second salon at Kurfürstendamm 48; it is possible that she closed this second store after 1929 due to economic circumstances. Unfortunately, I have not been able to verify any information about the birth or fate of the renowned fashion designer. My current theory is that hat designer Regina Friedländer opened her salons in her maiden name (or perhaps under another family name or the name of a first husband, as she is never referred to as "Fräulein"); in Berlin address books prior to 1906, the name of the salon *Inhaberin* [owner/proprietor] is listed as "Frau Regina Friedländer," whereas beginning in 1907, the proprietor's name is given as "Frau Regina Heller," suggesting that Regina Friedländer might have (re-)married and taken her husband's name in 1906 or 1907. (It is also possible that the business transferred hands from Regina Friedländer to a different woman, Regina Heller, in 1907, though the consistency of the first name makes this less plausible.) The 1907 address book entry for "Regina Heller" confirms that she is the owner of the label "Regina Friedländer" and lists her home address as Güntzelstr. 19; by 1920, this same Regina Heller lived at Von-der-Heydt-Str. 4. Online: http://adressbuch.zlb.de/. The 1931 Jüdisches Adressbuch für Groß-Berlin lists a woman by the name of Regina Heller living at the same address on Von-der-Heydt-Str., which confirms that the designer Regina Heller/Friedländer self-identified as Jewish. *Jüdisches Adressbuch für Groß-Berlin*, 153.

[25] My research confirms that Regina Friedländer considered herself Jewish; see above note. In addition, Ingrid Loschek and Erika Ehlerding have counted Regina Friedländer among Berlin's leading Jewish salon owners. See Ingrid Loschek, "Contributions of Jewish Fashion Designers in Berlin," 61; and Erika Ehlerding, "Mihu Jehudi," 178. The illustra-

tor Lieselotte Friedlaender, who was not related to Regina Friedländer and who did not identify as Jewish, was forced to work under pseudonyms after 1933 because her last name was perceived as Jewish (see note 10).

[26] The extensive collection of fashion historian Claus Jahnke in Vancouver, Canada, contains dozens of original garments, periodicals, and other fashion memorabilia from the early twentieth century, including several images of work by Regina Friedländer. Many images from his collection appear in Kremer, *Broken Threads*; numerous labels from garments can be viewed online at: http://www.giselamueller.info/threadlagged/threadlagged/jahnke.htm. Additional images of Friedländer's work can be found at the Kunstbibliothek in Berlin.

[27] Dähn, *Berlin Hausvogteiplatz*, 207.

[28] See Verein der Künstlerinnen zu Berlin, *Die Frau von heute: Gemälde, Graphik, Plastik* (exhibition catalog; Berlin, November–December 1929).

[29] Dähn, *Berlin Hausvogteiplatz*, 208.

[30] See "Kunst und Mode. Mit einer Zeichnung von Charlotte Berend," *Der Kunstwanderer*, November 1921: 129. One painting was reproduced in *Die Dame*; see "Aus der Ausstellung 'Farbe und Mode' in der Berliner Akademie der Künste," *Die Dame*, March 1921, no. 12: 2.

[31] Johanna Thal, "Der Salon Regina Friedländer: Ein neuzeitlicher Geschäfts-Raum," *Innen-Dekoration*, 1922, vol. 33, no. 2: 336–49. Online: http://www.digizeitschriften.de/dms/img/?PPN=urn%3Anbn%3Ade%3Absz%3A16-diglit-104562&DMDID=dmd00150. Several of Lene Schneider-Kainer's decorative wall paintings are clearly visible in illustrations for this *Innendekoration* article.

[32] Sabine Dahmen, *Leben und Werk der jüdischen Künstlerin Lene Schneider-Kainer im Berlin der zwanziger Jahre* (Dortmund: edition ebersbach, 1999), 118–22.

[33] Adolph Donath, *Der Kunstwanderer*, 1925: 204. Cited in Dahmen, *Leben und Werk der jüdischen Künstlerin Lene Schneider-Kainer*, 119.

[34] See Paul Lerner, "Circulation and Representation: Jews, Department Stores and Cosmopolitan Consumption in Germany, c. 1880s–1930s," *European Review of History*, 17.3 (2010): 395–413; and Paul Lerner, "Consuming Powers: The 'Jewish Department Store' in German Politics and Culture," in *The Economy in Jewish History: New Perspectives on the Interrelationship between Ethnicity and Economic Life* (ed. Gideon Reuveni and Sarah Wobick-Segev; New York: Berghahn Books, 2011), 135–54.

[35] See Regina Lee Blaszczyk, "Rethinking Fashion," in *Producing Fashion: Commerce, Culture, and Consumers* (ed. Regina Lee Blaszczyk; Philadelphia: University of Pennsylvania Press, 2008), 1–18.

[36] See, for example, Katharina Feige-Straßburger, "Was lernen unsere Töchter?," *C.V.-Zeitung*, no. 16 (15 April 1932): 153–54.

[37] On the marketing strategies of German department stores, see Kerry Wallach, "Kosher Seductions: Jewish Women as Employees and Consumers in German Department Stores," in *Das Berliner Warenhaus: Geschichte und Diskurse / The Berlin Department Store: History and Discourse* (ed. Godela Weiss-Sussex and Ulrike Zitzlsperger; Frankfurt a.M.: Peter Lang, 2013), 117–37.

[38] Mila Ganeva, "Elegance and Spectacle in Berlin: The Gerson Fashion Store and the Rise of the Modern Fashion Show," in *The Places and Spaces of Fashion, 1800–2007* (ed. John Potvin; New York: Routledge, 2009), 121–38, here 124.

[39] Georg Tietz, *Hermann Tietz: Geschichte einer Familie und ihrer Warenhäuser* (Stuttgart: Deutsche Verlags-Anstalt, 1965), 86–87. On Jews and the distribution of feathers, see Sarah Stein, *Plumes: Ostrich Feathers, Jews, and a Lost World of Global Commerce* (New Haven: Yale University Press, 2008).

[40] Ingrid Loschek, "Contributions of Jewish Fashion Designers in Berlin," 71.

[41] Leora Auslander, "The Boundaries of Jewishness, or When is a Cultural Practice Jewish?," *Journal of Modern Jewish Studies* 8:1 (2009): 47–64, here 55. See also Leora Auslander, "'Jewish Taste?' Jews and the Aesthetics of Everyday Life in Paris and Berlin, 1920–1942," in *Histories of Leisure* (ed. Rudy Koshar; Oxford: Berg Press, 2002), 299–318.

[42] On antisemitic violence against Jews in Weimar Germany, see David Clay Large, "'Out with the Ostjuden': The Scheunenviertel Riots in Berlin, November 1923," in *Exclusionary Violence: Antisemitic Riots in Modern German History* (ed. Christhard Hoffmann, Werner Bergmann, and Helmut Walser Smith; Ann Arbor: University of Michigan Press, 2002), 123–40; and Trude Maurer, *Ostjuden in Deutschland, 1918–1933* (Hamburg: H. Christians Verlag, 1986).

[43] On traditional associations of specific Jewish holidays with the use of luxury goods and the many ways in which advertisers in the United States took advantage of these connections, see Andrew R. Heinze, *Adapting to Abundance: Jewish Immigrants, Mass Consumption, and the Search for American Identity* (New York: Columbia University Press, 1990). See also Jenna Weissman Joselit, *New York's Jewish Jews: The Orthodox Community in the Interwar Years* (Bloomington: Indiana University Press, 1990), 102.

[44] In their everyday dress, many American Jewish women, for example, replaced "old-fashioned" head coverings (such as wigs) with fashionable hats. See Barbara A. Schreier, *Becoming American Women: Clothing and the Jewish Immigrant Experience, 1880–1920* (exhibition catalog; Chicago Historical Society, 1994), 49–83.

[45] See, for example, these two articles in a Yiddish-language Berlin magazine and a Frankfurt-based Orthodox Jewish newspaper, respectively: "In London iz letstens fargekumen a mode-oysshtelung," *Yidishe ilustrirte tsaytung*, 1924, no. 2 (30 May 1924): 25; and Felix Kanter, "Etwas vom Eheringe," *Der Israelit*, 1920, no. 20 (20 May 1920): 11.

[46] The Centralverein was a liberal Jewish self-defense organization founded in 1893. See, for example, Hans Guggenheimer, "Bayerische Sommerfrischen! Ein Mahnwort an jüdische Reisende," *C.V.- Zeitung*, 1922, no. 4 (26 May 1922): 49. On resort antisemitism in the Weimar Republic, see Frank Bajohr, *"Unser Hotel ist judenfrei": Bäder-Antisemitismus im 19. und 20. Jahrhundert* (Frankfurt a.M.: Fischer Taschenbuch Verlag, 2003), 53–115; and Inbal Steinitz, *Der Kampf jüdischer Anwälte gegen den Antisemitismus: Rechtsschutz durch den Centralverein deutscher Staatsbürger jüdischen Glaubens (1893–1933)* (Berlin: Metropol, 2007).

[47] "Sollen die Damen keinen Schmuck mehr anlegen, soll alles Modische verbannt sein? . . . Wo findet der Schmuck, wann findet das Streben nach modern-gefälligem Aussehen

seine Grenze ?" (ellipsis added). Ludwig Holländer, "Selbstwürde," *C.V.-Zeitung*, 1922, no. 14 (10 August 1922): 173–74. For a discussion of Holländer's article and other articles in this newspaper, see Avraham Barkai, *"Wehr Dich!" Der Centralverein deutscher Staatsbürger jüdischen Glaubens (C.V.) 1893–1938* (Munich: C. H. Beck Verlag, 2002), 108–9.

[48] Cited in Peter Gay, *Freud, Jews and Other Germans: Masters and Victims in Modernist Culture* (New York: Oxford University Press, 1978), 183. Original: "Die positive Arbeit der Organisation bestand vor allem in der Ermahnung der Glaubensgenossen, an den hohen Feiertagen die gewohnte Würde auch vor und nach dem Gottesdienst auf der Strasse zu wahren, und die jüdischen Frauen insbesondere zu bitten, allen auffälligen Luxus in Kleidung und Schmuck zu vermeiden." Adolf Asch, *Auszug aus Memoiren von Dr. Adolf Asch (Die Inflationsjahre 1919–1928)*, 3. Courtesy of the archives of the Leo Baeck Institute Jerusalem, file no. 2 (Adolf Asch).

[49] "Frauenmoden," *Der Israelit*, 1925, no. 3 (15 January 1925): 1–2.

[50] Else Fuchs-Hes, "Frauenpsyche und Mode," *Israelitisches Familienblatt*, no. 26 (25 June 1925): 17. On Else Fuchs-Hes, see Claudia Prestel, "Frauenpolitik oder Parteipolitik? Jüdische Frauen in innerjüdischer Politik in der Weimarer Republik," *Archiv für Sozialgeschichte* 37 (1997): 121–55, here 124–45.

[51] Doris Wittner, "Frauenmode," *C.V.-Zeitung*, no. 28 (9 July 1926): 373–74. See also the short article to which this piece was a response: "Gegen die Auswüchse der Frauenmode," *C.V.-Zeitung*, no. 26 (25 June 1926): 350. On journalist Doris Wittner, see Kerry Wallach, "Front-Page Jews: Doris Wittner's Berlin Feuilletons," in *Discovering Women's History: German-speaking Journalists 1900-1950* (ed. Christa Spreizer; Oxford: Lang, forthcoming 2014).

[52] "Der tadellose Bubikopf lässt kaum ahnen, das es sich um eine im Interesse der Wahrung altjüdischer Zucht getragene Perücke handelt." Gronemann, *Schalet* (1998), 113. See also Sammy Gronemann, "Schalet: 20. Der orthodoxe Bubikopf," *Israelitisches Familienblatt*, no. 10 (8 March 1928): 998.

[53] It is highly unlikely that Elise Bock (1864/1866–circa 1945) was Jewish, although the Elise Bock Company may have been purchased by a family of Jewish descent in the early 1930s. See Dorit Kupka, *Kosmetik—Domäne der Frau? Zur Verberuflichung weiblicher Tätigkeiten* (Straelen: Peter Keuck, 2005), 129–36.

[54] "Nichts ist schlimmer, [als] wenn man sieht, daß Sie eine Perücke tragen." "Florian Elzer Eleganter Schönheitssalon," advertisement, *Der Israelit*, no. 29 (14 July 1932): 12.

[55] Though it is possible that synagogues or Jewish women's groups organized fashion events in the Weimar period, I have found no evidence of fashion events exclusively for Jewish audiences prior to 1933. However, several beauty pageants—which sometimes were paired with fashion shows—were organized in order to select Jewish beauty queens. See, for example, "Bar Kochba-Hakoah Ball," *Gemeindeblatt der jüdischen Gemeinde zu Berlin*, no. 12 (December 1931): 360.

[56] "Das Brüdervereinshaus hatte sich in ein Warenhaus im kleinen verwandelt, zur Befriedigung weiblicher Schaugier und zum Anreiz femininer und, falls vorhanden, maskuliner Kauflust." E. Ta., "Sommerlüfte—Wintermode," *Jüdisch-liberale Zeitung*, no. 72 (7 September 1934): 3–4.

[57] The Leo Baeck Institute New York is in possession of several images of this fashion show, a few of which depict items of clothing hanging along the walls of the venue, waiting to be purchased.

[58] "*Modeplauderei*" was a common title for fashion columns in Weimar fashion magazines. As a child, Clementine Krämer grew up among the fabrics of her father's retail store in Karlsruhe. She worked as a saleslady for the S. Eichengrün & Co. firm after her husband's business went bankrupt in 1929. See Werner J. Cahnman, "The Life of Clementine Kraemer," *Leo Baeck Institute Yearbook* 8 (1964): 267–91, here 290.

[59] Clementine Krämer Collection. AR 2402. Leo Baeck Institute, New York and Berlin. Reel 1, Folder 7. Though undated, these lecture notes contain a clear reference to fashion magazines "from 1905 to 1935," suggesting that the lecture was held in 1935 or shortly thereafter. The document is located in a folder of materials created in conjunction with Krämer's work for the Jüdischer Frauenbund.

[60] See Guenther, *Nazi Chic?*, 91–141.

Unbuttoned: Clothing as a Theme in American Jewish Comedy

Ted Merwin

Without the massive influx of Jews from Eastern Europe at the turn of the twentieth century, two major industries might never have taken root in New York. One was the manufacture of clothing, especially ladies' ready-to-wear garments. The other was show business, from vaudeville and Broadway to silent film. While these fields might seem related merely in terms of the design and manufacture of costumes for the entertainment industry, they ended up being deeply connected on a metaphoric level.

Indeed, clothing took on a symbolic dimension in comedy created by Jewish entertainers. These comedy routines helped to refashion Jewish identity in America by both celebrating the rapid success of Jews and tapping into profound anxieties that Jews had about their role in a competitive, capitalistic society. Many of these very routines about clothing helped to catapult Jewish entertainers into prominence, defining American Jewish humor and weaving it into the very warp and woof of American popular culture.

Jews arrived in New York in the 1880s just as the ready-made clothing industry, especially for women's apparel, was taking off. A third of the Jewish workers in Eastern Europe had been tailors; as a common Yiddish saying went, *Ver geyt keyn Amerika?* [Who goes to America?] *Die shnayders, shusters, un ferdganovim.* [The tailors, shoemakers, and horse thieves.] They slipped naturally into the garment trade in New York, taking on a wide variety of occupations: cutters, pressers, basters, button-makers, dressmakers, cap-makers, fur-trimmers, and so on. By 1905, the entire industrial output of only three American cities was larger than the value of New York's garment industry. Nor were Jews only involved in manufacturing clothing; as in London, where the "Old Clo'es" street vendor plying his wares was a fixture of the East End Jewish neighborhood, Jews on the Lower East Side sold secondhand apparel to immigrants who could not afford to outfit themselves with new raiments.[1]

As Burton Hendrick put it in an influential essay on the "invasion" of New York by the Jews, their "greatest triumph has been [their] absolute control of the clothing trades." Claiming that fully one-half of all the apparel worn in the country was made by Jews on the Lower East Side, Hendrick noted that "they have turned the whole East Side into one huge workshop." Through their rapid ascent in the garment industry, Hendrick averred, immigrant Jews had displaced the "Knickerbocker aristocracy" of the city by moving uptown and taking over the steel skyscrapers on Fifth Avenue for their offices.[2]

At the same time that Jews achieved success through clothing manufacture, they also became dominant in the field of entertainment.[3] Indeed, historian Neal Gabler has suggested that one reason that Jews ended up owning most of the Hollywood film studios is that they had learned how to gauge popular taste from their experience in selling clothing.[4] The overall urbanization of the American population and the influx of millions of immigrants, mostly from Southern and Eastern Europe, led to a great demand for amusement, from blackface minstrel routines (mostly popular, of course, among working-class ethnic whites) to Yiddish theater. Partly because show business still had a centuries-old tinge of immorality—being associated, in many people's minds, with prostitution and with the inherent duplicity of playing a role on stage or screen[5]—it was relatively open to Jews and other societal outcasts. Jews soon became active in every branch of the industry, from writing plays (whether in Yiddish or English), to acting, directing, producing, and ultimately owning both legitimate theaters and nickelodeons. By the turn of the twentieth century, according to theater scholar Harley Erdman, half of the entertainment business in New York was in Jewish hands.[6]

Clothing was especially ripe for comedic treatment. Immigrants' anxieties and insecurities about their garb encapsulated their uncertainties about fitting into America. Over the course of the twentieth century, as Jews became more ensconced in America, their relationship to clothing changed; they became retailers, wholesalers, and eventually—in remarkably large numbers—fashion designers. But clothing also remained highly symbolic to Jews as an index of their visibility in American culture. As one nineteenth-century etiquette manual advised those who wished to move up in society, "Your clothes are your visiting cards, your cards of admission."[7]

Given the popularity of "racial" comedy on the vaudeville stage, in which both European immigrants and African Americans were mercilessly lampooned, it is no surprise that Jewish clothing makers and dealers made a frequent appearance. Some of the actors who performed these skits were Jewish themselves, like Willie and Eugene Howard, but they were also frequently performed by non-Jewish actors such as Frank Bush, Joe Welch, and David Warfield.[8] Many of these skits were published to enable amateur actors to perform the ethnic caricatures, either in public or domestic settings. These booklets often contained a description of the suggested costume, which could include a black coat and white vest, a worn coat, a red tie, striped trousers that were too short and showed off garishly colored stockings, large shoes, a black wig with lots of black facial hair, and a silk hat pushed down on the back of the head. In addition, actors were expected to elongate their noses with putty and to adopt an exaggerated Yiddish accent (which often ended up sounding more like German).

In one turn-of-the-century routine, "The Troubles of Rozinski," written by Harry Lee Newton and A. S. Hoffman, a Jewish buttonhole maker is forced, under threat of physical violence, to join the coatmakers' union. Rozinski is then visited by various union representatives who induce him to "cough up" additional sums. Then the union calls a strike and Rozinski is out of work. While walking the picket line, Rozinski is clobbered by a scab and ends up in the hospital. When he is released from the hospital, he gets into a series of fights with a bartender in a saloon, which Rozinski always loses. Finally, he goes to a graveyard to mourn for his deceased wife, Becky, but he keeps crying at the wrong grave and having to start all over again. The skit ends with Rozinski getting angry at a friend for whistling and being happy in the cemetery; the friend explains his behavior by saying that he has two wives buried there.[9]

This "Jew monologue," as it was called, is a catalogue of negative Jewish stereotypes. The audience is supposed to laugh at Rozinski, not sympathize with him. The character is a complaining, penny-pinching, over-sentimental, ignorant, weak, and thoroughly ridiculous fellow who seems ill-suited for membership in a society that values strength and self-reliance. All the anxieties that mainstream Americans had about failing to succeed are embodied in Rozinski, who just cannot seem to get anything right. Even his occupation—making holes—can be seen as a joke on the vacuity of his life and career.[10]

These stereotypes began to change with the work of Montague Glass, the son of an English linen merchant who immigrated to New York with his family in 1890. Glass started writing comic pieces during his time as a law student at New York University. Upon becoming an attorney and gaining Jewish clients, Glass frequently came into contact with immigrants who worked in the garment industry. He invented a pair of good-natured, Yiddish-accented Jewish clothing manufacturers, Abe Potash and Morris ("Mawruss") Perlmutter, whose clothing firm became the setting for his fiction.

After establishing the two characters in stories like "The Striped Tourists" and "A Cloak and Suit Comedy," Glass was picked up by the *Saturday Evening Post*, and he published close to seventy stories in that publication over the course of five and a half years. These stories became the basis for Glass's plays and films. His first play, titled simply *Potash and Perlmutter*, was a runaway hit in New York, London, and even—eight years later—in Berlin (where it, translated into German, was the first American play performed in the city after World War I). Glass followed it with a series of other plays; by the 1920s, the two partners moved out of the clothing business and into selling cars and, eventually, running a detective agency.

Glass was notable for combatting stereotypes of Jews as frightening and unassimilable; he departed from the usual depictions of immigrant Jews on the vaudeville and Broadway stages. Part of the appeal of the Potash and Perlmutter series was the inside look that it offered into the highly competitive cloak and suit trade, much as the novels of Scott Turow were to do for the legal profession at the end of the twentieth century. In a way that would be familiar to vaudeville audiences, the short, stocky Morris Potash (played by Barney Bernard) quarreled incessantly with the tall, blond Abe Perlmutter (played by Alexander Carr), trying to top each other with pointed one-liners.

Both actors told interviewers that they believed that they were helping to break down Jewish stereotypes and advance the cause of Jewish acceptance in America. "I think the day of the ultra-comic Jew on the stage, the Jew with the exaggerated nose and splay feet t'is gone," Bernard pointedly told the *Chicago Tribune*, expressing the hope that his portrayal afforded the audience "an idea of the real Hebrew as he lives, breathes, and exists today."[11] Carr, for his part, put himself forward as the one responsible for enhancing the image of the Jew, suggesting that the stark contrast between his character and Bernard's "marks the rapid progress of the Jew in advancing himself in culture as well as in wealth"[12] [Fig. 1].

Figure 1. Potash and Perlmutter. Courtesy of National Museum of American Jewish History, Philadelphia.

In the first play, advertised in the theater program as an "up-to-date garment in three pieces,"[13] the firm tries to overcome steep losses on striped tourist suits and plum-colored empire gowns by marketing a women's dress called the Rockaway Sackerine, which is a knock-off of a top-selling dress called the Arverne Saque. After their book-keeper, Boris, is arrested as a Russian anarchist, trouble seems to be descending from all sides. The partners hire a top designer away from another firm only to discover that the other company had been attempting to get rid of him without breaking his contract; they trick the other firm into rehiring him by presenting some of Perlmutter's designs as his. Along the way, Potash and Perl-mutter foil the plans of various criminals, including their own salesman, Mark Pasinsky, who is in the simultaneous employ of a number of clothing firm; he betrays himself when he mixes up his various samples. All ends happily when Boris is freed and marries Abe's daughter, Irma.

In a review of the original London production, the critic for *Current Opinion* claimed that the play was groundbreaking in its depictions of Jew-ish characters. While it "deals with a phase of life peculiar to New York," he conceded, "the atmosphere of 'local color' which saturates this comedy empha-sizes the essential and elemental humanity of its central characters." The play was notable, he opined, as a "psychological study of the mingled enterprize [sic] and caution, astuteness and rashness, of the Semitic temperament." At a time when Jews were still objects of curiosity, this reviewer fell back on long-standing racial stereotypes of the Jew as "hustler," while at the same time he emphasized the Jewish characters' "essential . . . humanity."[14]

That the play was about Jewish characters helping to set the standard for American fashion resonated on many levels with critics and audiences alike, both at home and abroad. At the same time, there was something patently comical about Jews being the arbiters of fashion; in the minds of the majority, Jews still appeared to be uncouth and ill-mannered. As the radical Reform Rabbi Joseph Krauskopf (who held Sabbath services on Sundays to speed Jewish acculturation) saw it, Jews often became ostentatious and pushy in their efforts to win accep-tance by high-class Americans.[15] The celebrated Jewish writer Anzia Yezierska wrote that Glass "turned out his caricatures of Jews like sausage meat for the pop-ular weekly and monthly magazines. Americans reading his Potash and Perlmut-ter stories thought those clowning cloak and suiters were the Jewish people."[16]

Yet for one prominent non-Jewish writer, the two hapless Jewish clothing manufacturers emblematized the ceaseless drive and energy of the metropolis itself. Willa Cather (who was, within the decade, to write *O Pioneers, My Anto-nia* and other major novels about life on the Great Plains) opined that *Potash and Perlmutter* was "the most successful—and the best—play now running in New York," despite the fact that "there is not an American in the piece and the only character who speaks conventional English is a Russian refugee."

Jews had become so dominant in New York, Cather said, that "the apartment-houses are built for—and usually owned by—Potash or Perlmutter; the restaurants are run for them; the shops are governed by the taste of Mrs. Potash and Mrs. Perlmutter; and, whether one likes it or not, one has to buy garments fundamentally designed to enhance the charms of those ladies." Cather conceded that all immigrants are not Jewish. But, she insisted, "our flavoring extract is Potash and Perlmutter." The characters in the play, she concluded, "are weaving the visible garment of New York, creating the color, the language, the 'style.'"[17]

With a mix of admiration and envy, Cather picked up on the metaphorical aspects of the Jewish involvement in the clothing industry—the ways in which Jews were not just fabricating the actual garments that all New Yorkers (and all Americans) were wearing, but the ways in which they were also determining the city's very image of itself. Non-Jews were obliged, in symbolic terms, to wear "Jewish" clothes—to adapt themselves to a Jewish pattern or to fit themselves to a Jewish mold. As Lisa Marcus has written, "Cather's claim that one cannot escape Jewish influence reflects a paranoid over-inflation of Jewish affluence. . . . Jews are highly successful, woven into (and weaving) the fabric of the nation, but at the same time, they are pushy, gaudy, and imposing—unwanted, obtrusive outsiders."[18]

In writing about Jewish influence, Cather joined the debate over immigration that was raging in the second decade of the twentieth century. Her focus on apparel was to be turned inside out in the rhetoric of Madison Grant, who in a highly influential 1918 tract observed that new immigrants from Europe "adopt the language of the native American, *they wear his clothes,* they steal his name and they are beginning to take his women, but they seldom adopt his religion or understand his ideals"[19] (emphasis added). Such rhetoric picked up speed in the 1920s and helped to justify the passage of stringent immigration laws that essentially cut off the flow of new arrivals from both Southern and Eastern Europe. The most powerful antisemite of the period, auto manufacturer Henry Ford, used the pages of his newspaper, the *Dearborn Independent,* to rail against what he perceived as the debasement by Jews of every aspect of American society and culture.

Ford accused Jews of profiteering by raising the price of clothing after World War I; he called the garment industry "exclusively Jewish," speculating, bizarrely, that the Jew was drawn to that occupation because of his

> aversion to manual labor, his abhorrence of agricultural life, and his
> desire to arrange his own affairs. . . . Thus, preferring any kind of
> a life in the city, and not taking to the trades which involve much

bodily effort, the Jew gravitates to the needle, not in the capacity of a creative artist, as is the commercial tailor, but in the production of quantities of ready-made goods.[20]

This kind of rhetoric was not new; since the turn of the century, Jews had been viewed stereotypically as having been so beaten down by centuries of persecution that they lacked physical strength and thus found themselves in occupations that depended more on manual dexterity.[21]

With increasing Jewish prosperity in the years following World War I came movement from the lower class into the lower middle class and relocation from the Lower East Side to the newer Jewish neighborhoods in Upper Manhattan (mostly Harlem), the Bronx, and Brooklyn. This rapid process of acculturation was reflected in the work of the next generation of Jewish comedians. While moving away from some of the most overt and pernicious stereotypes that characterized turn-of-the-century portrayals of Jews (by both Jewish and non-Jewish performers) on the vaudeville stage, these entertainers presented a more up-to-date appearance but still often retained a Yiddish accent and other Jewish mannerisms. They continued to trade on the Jewish involvement in the garment industry as a source of humor—their stage "business," as it were, echoing the trade in which so many Jews continued to be occupied, albeit increasingly in wholesale and retail rather than garment manufacture.

Figure 2. Fanny Brice.

Among the most successful of this new breed of entertainers was Fanny Brice, the daughter of successful Hungarian Jewish saloon keepers in New York. In 1910 and 1911, she initially headlined impresario Florenz Ziegfeld's *Ziegfeld Follies*, which were opulent Broadway revues. A decade later, beginning in 1921, she again starred in the *Follies*, with which she found great success well into the 1930s. Among her signature songs was "Second Hand Rose," the heavily Yiddish-accented lament of a daughter of Jewish immigrants on the Lower East Side, whose entire wardrobe, along with everything else that belongs to her, consists of hand-me-downs [Fig. 2].

Written by the Irish songwriting team of Grant Clarke and James F. Hanley, "Second Hand Rose" was to become one of the most famous songs of the twentieth century, recorded by dozens of artists. Indeed, it became an all-purpose parody of the down and out; First Lady Nancy Reagan, costumed as a "bag lady" (homeless person), sang a version of it at a major political dinner as a way of disarming her critics, who had accused her of improperly accepting extravagant gifts from fashion designers.[22]

The lyrics go like this:

> Father has a business, strictly second-hand.
> Everything from toothpicks to a baby grand.
> Stuff in our apartment came from Father's store,
> Even things I'm wearing, someone wore before.
> It's no wonder that I feel abused.
> I never get a thing that ain't been used.
>
> I'm wearing second-hand hats, second-hand clothes.
> That's why they call me Second Hand Rose.
> Even our piano in the parlor,
> Father bought for ten cents on the dollar.
> Second-hand pearls, I'm wearing second-hand curls,
> I never get a single thing that's new.
> Even Jakie Cohen, he's the man I adore,
> Had the nerve to tell me he's been married before.
> Everyone knows that I'm just Second Hand Rose,
> From Second Avenue.
>
> I'm wearing second-hand shoes, second-hand hose,
> All the girls hand me their second-hand beaus.
> Even my pajamas, when I don 'em,
> Have somebody else's 'nitials on 'em.
> Second-hand rings, I'm sick of second-hand things,
> I never get what other girlies do.
> Once while strolling through the Ritz, a woman got my goat,
> She nudged her friend and said, "Oh, look, there goes my last year's coat!"
> Everyone knows that I'm just Second Hand Rose,
> From Second Avenue.[23]

Because the singer's clothes, jewelry, and even hair curls are "second hand," she feels like a second-class citizen. It is as if her clothes, which define her identity, do not quite belong to her; they have not yet shed the aura of their former owners. Even her pajamas, which are presumably among her most intimate apparel, are monogrammed with someone else's initials. And so she questions if she has an authentic self or if she is merely a collection of the rags and patches of others.[24] There is something truly wearing, in the sense of fatiguing and wearying, about her situation, a sense that is conveyed by her need to go through an exhaustive catalog of all of her used possessions, the possession of which make her feel abused.

Yet it is not just her possessions that are inferior; she is herself, as her sobriquet implies, not quite pure—for a woman to be "second hand" suggests that she is no longer a virgin. Given the sexual double standard that obtained at the time, it is much more socially acceptable that her boyfriend has been married previously than it is for her to carry the connotation of damaged goods. Little wonder that she calls herself "just" Second Hand Rose in a plainly self-deprecating way.

Nevertheless, the singer is clearly not impoverished. She has some relatively pricey things, including her pearls, her baby grand piano in the parlor (both of which, the instrument and the room in which to install it, were important symbols of respectability in Victorian England and America), and even a fur coat. That these things were all obtained cheaply by her father seems to rankle her; her father makes it his "business," she seems to feel, to humiliate her. She concludes the song by recounting a mortifying episode in which she is "strolling" through the lobby of the fashionable Ritz-Carlton Hotel—the verb is quite significant; one "strolls" not just to see, but to be seen—and she is exposed as a fraud. Again, her very subjectivity is eclipsed; the obnoxious onlooker cries out that "there goes" her discarded, no longer fashionable coat, not that she sees a person who is wearing her coat.

Rose's heavy Yiddish accent, her low-rent status as a denizen of Second Avenue (the part of the Lower East Side that was famous for its Yiddish theaters and kosher restaurants), her father's occupation, even perhaps her Jewish boyfriend—all these mark Rose as an outsider in American society. Her Jewishness is a crushing liability, a source of stigma. And it is a religious and cultural identity that she has inherited against her will, just like all the pre-owned possessions that make her feel so cheap and tawdry. If only she could make herself new and thrust off all the baggage of her history. If only she could escape the metaphorical pawn shop of the past in which her very spirit is imprisoned.

Nevertheless, the humor of the song is inescapable. It is a jaunty, tuneful piece of music to which audiences, even today, love to sing along. The character is satirizing herself, kvetching with the kind of zest that characterizes so much of Jewish humor. As Michael Wex, in the introduction to his book *Born to Kvetch*, puts it, kvetching is "not only a pastime, not only a response to adverse or imperfect circumstance, but a *way of life* that has nothing to do with the fulfillment or frustration of desire . . . kvetching becomes a way of exercising some small measure of control over an otherwise hostile environment"[25] (emphasis added).

By kvetching, Rose finally gets some attention. Instead of laughing at her, we laugh alongside her at the ludicrousness of her situation. And there is something terribly familiar in her plight, the universal feeling of not belonging, of not fitting in, of being judged negatively because we are not well-dressed or confident enough to be accepted. Perhaps that is how two Irish songwriters composed lyrics that have resonated for generations of Americans of all religious and ethnic backgrounds.

This theme of trying to acculturate into American society through clothing was also memorably encapsulated in an extended routine by one of Brice's costars in the *Follies*, vaudeville comedian Eddie Cantor. Cantor, a short, slight fellow with highly expressive features (his nickname was "banjo eyes"), was born Israel Iskovitz on the Lower East Side. He started as a blackface comedian, then began appearing in Broadway revues, and ultimately in film and television; like Brice, he was one of the country's most beloved and highly paid performers. One of his early sketches, "A Belt in the Back," first performed in the touring version of a Broadway show called *The Midnight Rounders*, became one of his signature routines. In the sketch, he played one half of a pair of unscrupulous salesmen in a clothing store on the Lower East Side (the other is played by Louis Sorin) who use high-pressure tactics to induce a short, squeaky-voiced customer (played by Lew Hearn) to buy a suit. The routine is preserved in *Glorifying the American Girl*, a film about the *Ziegfeld Follies* that was released in 1929[26] [Fig. 3].

In the routine, the salesmen alternatively try to coerce, cajole, and clobber the customer into buying one of the many ensembles that he tries on, even as he fruitlessly searches for a fashionable one that is cinched in the rear with a belt. Nothing suits him; the jackets are all ridiculously ill-fitting, but his protests are unavailing—the salesmen have an answer to everything. If the jacket sports too many buttons for the customer's taste, Cantor simply rips one off. When the customer complains that the jacket is too tight, Cantor simply tears a seam in the back, telling him that this is a new "cooling system, the new Frigidaire." When the customer says that prefers stripes, the salesmen take out pieces of chalk and draw the lines. And in an inspired moment,

Figure 3. Eddie Cantor in *Glorifying the American Girl.* Courtesy of Billy Rose Theatre Division, The New York Public Library for the Performing Arts, Astor, Lenox and Tilden Foundations.

the salesmen call out measurements to each other in the sing-song tune that is used by rabbis while elucidating passages from the Talmud; the customer, thinking that he has found himself in a barbershop "quartet," bursts out with "Sweet Adeline."[27]

The overall theme of the routine is the customer's desperate desire to be and feel like a true American.[28] The suits that he tries on—a college-boy suit, a Prince Albert, even a sailor suit—would likely look ridiculous on him even if they fit correctly. Cantor appeals to the customer's fantasies by telling him that, if he only wears the right suit (the store has supposedly just received a mistaken shipment of Kuppenheimer suits[29] that were intended for a more upscale establishment), he can go to a baseball game, or a dance, or even the presidential inauguration and be the "talk of the town" for his stylish appearance.

The customer first tries to play along with the salesmen by agreeing that the fabric of one of the suits is of high quality, then makes a number of desperate attempts to escape, and finally expostulates that he will buy anything just to get out of the store. But the salesmen, who seem like gangster wannabes (at one point Cantor asks the customer if anyone saw him entering the store), are having too much fun attacking him; the "belt" that they want to give him is quite different from the one that he is expecting. They belittle him as if they are getting revenge on an America that has kept them, as Jews, from fitting in no matter how they look or what they do.[30]

Jewish involvement in the clothing industry led, of course, to heavy Jewish participation in the unions that fought for the rights of workers. Perhaps the most powerful and visible of these organizations was the International Ladies' Garment Workers' Union (ILGWU), founded in 1900. While it devoted most of its energy to fighting for better wages and working conditions for its members, the union leadership (the majority of which was male) also provided social and cultural programs for its members, including sponsoring radio stations and athletic teams, running a resort, and offering university classes. But its most ambitious effort was the production of an original musical, *Pins and Needles*, staged by the garment workers themselves, who rehearsed in the evenings and on weekends [Fig. 4].

Figure 4. *Pins and Needles.* Courtesy of Billy Rose Theatre Division, The New York Public Library for the Performing Arts, Astor, Lenox and Tilden Foundations.

With music and lyrics by Harold Rome, and book by a number of different writers including Marc Blitzstein (the creator of *The Cradle Will Rock*, a musical about union organizing that was being presented by the Federal Theatre Project), *Pins and Needles* spoofed everyone from Fascist dictators in Europe to callous New York millionaires. While it began with a two-week run intended for the entertainment of the ILGWU membership, it was so popular that the performers quit their day jobs and mounted a Broadway production; the show ran for three years and more than 1,100 performances. (It was the longest running Broadway musical until *Oklahoma*, which opened in 1943.) Critics praised the use of satire to deal with serious labor issues; as Richard Lockridge of the *New York Sun* put it, "They can also laugh. And probably for the first time in labor stage history, they can laugh at themselves as well at their antagonists."[31]

Most of the songs in *Pins and Needles*, which changed on an annual basis, were performed by women and highlighted women's concerns. The revue's best-known tune, "Sing Me a Song with Social Significance," parodied both the genre of Tin Pan Alley love songs and the leftist types who never stop thinking about politics, even in bed. But other songs also scored with audiences. "Nobody Makes a Pass at Me," a sex-starved garment worker's lament, was originally performed by Millie Weitz, a felling-machine operator who had performed in another ILGWU show, *So It Didn't Work*, a comedy set in a garment factory. In "Nobody Makes a Pass at Me," she catalogues all the consumer products that she has purchased in a fruitless attempt to attract male attention. And in "Chain Store Daisy," performed by brassiere operator Ruth Rubinstein, a recent college graduate struggles to succeed as a saleswoman in a department store. "I'm selling things to fit the figure," she warbles. "Make the big things small and the small things bigger."

As historian Michael Denning has written, Rome's songs "proved to be a powerful vehicle for the young garment workers, resonating with their urban working-class audiences," noting that they "make up a witty, satirical, and realistic conversation about love songs, romance, and working class life." Denning calls them the "folk songs" of the garment workers in New York, comparing them to Southern mill songs and Kentucky mining ballads.[32]

After World War II, Jews increasingly moved out of blue-collar employment and into business and the professions. Jews left the actual making of clothes to African Americans and to newer immigrant groups like Puerto Ricans. But Jews found many opportunities in owning garment factories and in the distribution of clothing through both wholesale and retail operations. One of the most famous comedy routines about Jewish clothing was a commercial on Yiddish radio for Joe and Paul's clothing store, the so-called "aristocrats of clothing," which was opened by Paul Kofsky on Pitkin Avenue in Brooklyn in 1912 [Fig. 5]. (There was no "Joe"—Kofsky thought that customers would trust him more if they thought that he had a partner.)

By the mid-1930s, Kofsky had opened additional locations in Manhattan and the Bronx. He hired the well-known composer Sholem Secunda, famous for his ballad, *"Bay Mir Bist Du Sheyn"* [You are Beautiful to Me], to write a jingle for his radio ads, which Kofsky performed himself. The resulting melody, inspired by Yiddish theater composer Joseph Rumshinsky's *"In Mayne Oygn Bist Du Sheyn"* [You are Beautiful in My Eyes], was so infectious that it quickly caught on with the listeners to WEVD, the radio station of the socialist Yiddish newspaper *The Forward*.[33]

Among the fans of the commercial was a young comedian named Aaron Chwatt (later Red Buttons), who told an interviewer that he and his friends used to sit around Kellogg's Cafeteria on West 49th Street, where comedians gathered to buy and sell jokes, and tap out the tune on the table. Chwatt eventually did a parody of the commercial in the Catskills, the mountain

Figure 5. Joe and Paul's clothing store on Delancey Street. Courtesy of Brian Merlis Collection.

hotels in upstate New York where Jews summered and where Chwatt and other comedians entertained the guests [Fig. 6].

When Chwatt was called into service in World War II, the routine was picked up the Barton Brothers, a duo known for good-natured, naughty Yiddish songs about such subjects as loose women, booze, and the growing vogue among Jews for Chinese food. They recorded it in 1947 for Apollo Records, and in just a few months, it sold three-quarters of a million records. Indeed, it became such a staple of Jewish humor that the Puerto Rican bandleader Tito Puente performed it at Grossinger's Hotel in 1959 as part of what historian Josh Kun calls a "cross-cultural, mid-century relationship between Latinos and American Jews."[34]

The Barton Brothers version goes like this:

Figure 6. Red Buttons.

Joe un Paul's a fargenign
Joe un Paul's, men ken a bargn krign

A sut, a koyt, a gabardine.
Brengt arayn dayn klaynem zin.
Cut, speech [and then a pitchman's huckstering voice]
A gite fri morgn aykh, mayne libe radio tsuherers
Mir brengn yetsts a program fun Joe un Paul's vos hobn dray stores,
Der erster store is located in Stanton and Delancey in donton Manhattan.
Der tsvayte stor is located in Hunts Poynt, Sudern Bulevard in der Bronx.
Un der driter stor is located in Pitkin Avenyu, Brwonsvil, Bruklin.
Hot ir a bar mitsve yingele vos darf hoben a slak-suit, a two-tone, a reversible slicker,
a herringbone, a djaket, a por hoyzn, a Miami charvette, a Bronx sharpie, a Bruklin droop.
Brengt im arayn tsi.
Joe un Paul's a fargenign…
Mames, hot ir a yungere boy in der heym, a yor fertsn, fuftsn yor alt, vos s'glaykht im tsu zenen
a burlesk show. Er koyft shoyn French postel karts. Er kimt ahaym, gayt arayn in der bat-rum,
makht tsi di tir un makht awww, awww, ahwww. Mames, tit mir a toyve un git dem boy a por tuler
un shikt im arayn tsu kokay-Djeni (Cockeyed Jenny). Un a' tomer vayst ir nisht vi doz iz, iz fraygt
iz fraygt ayer man. Er ken shoyn dos plats zeyer git.[35]

The translation is as follows:

Joe and Paul's is a pleasure
Joe and Paul's, you can get a bargain:
A suit, a coat, a gabardine
Bring in your small son.
Good morning to you, my dear radio listeners.
We are now bringing you a program from Joe and Paul's who have three stores. The first store is located in Stanton and Delancey in downtown Manhattan. The second store is located in Hunts Point, Southern Boulevard, in the Bronx. And the third store is located in Pitkin Avenue, Brownsville, Brooklyn.
Do you have a bar mitzvah-age boy who needs a slack suit, a two-tone, a reversible slicker, a herringbone, a jacket, a pair of pants, a Miami charvette, a Bronx sharpie, a Brooklyn-droop?
Bring him around.
Mothers, do you have a young boy at home, around 14-15 years old, who likes to see burlesque? He's already buying French post cards. He comes home, goes into the bathroom, closes the door, and goes ahwww ahwww. Mothers, do me a favor and give that boy a few

dollars and send him to Cockeyed Jennie. And if you don't know
where that is, ask your husband. He knows that place really well.[36]

Jewish listeners at the time would have been familiar with the Jewish custom
of buying a new suit for a boy for his bar mitzvah, the religious rite of passage
into adulthood. The trip to the men's clothing store, often the first shopping
trip that a Jewish boy ever took, became a ritual in and of itself.[37] Historian
Jenna Weissman Joselit calls the bar mitzvah suit a "secular counterpart of the
tallis and tefillin the bar mitzvah boy was ritually enjoined to wear," and the
"first full-length, grown-up piece of modern clothing he ever owned." When
the boy was dressed up in his new suit and an accompanying fedora or yarmulke, Joselit notes, his parents took him to a studio photographer so that his
mature look could be captured for posterity.[38] But the commercial for Joe and
Paul's, at least as adapted by the Barton Brothers, picks up on what for most
boys was a much more profound aspect of their adolescent coming-of-age,
which was their first experiences of sex. Buying new clothes for their teenage
son forced parents to confront the rapidly changing body of their child, a body
that was beginning to be governed more by its raging hormones than by its
parents' rules.

Historian Irv Saposnik dubs "Joe and Paul" a "touchstone of Jewish
memory" and "the last hurrah of Yiddish-American culture." The Barton
Brothers, he writes,

> captured a moment in Yiddish-American culture when that culture
> was more than ever a *pastiche*, when its popular expression was often
> a synthesis of Yiddish and English. With this post-war redesigned
> Yiddish, Jewish Americans helped develop a new language best
> expressed in comedy, a language that moved away from its insular
> Jewish origins to become American speech.[39]

Perhaps it is no accident that a commercial for new clothing styles spoke to
the desire of American Jews to update their image, to shed the stereotypes that
had held them back for so long, and to make a new impression on American
society. Perhaps this was the true *fargenign* [pleasure] that the commercial celebrates, the joy that Jews took in dressing for success—and refashioning their
self-image in the process.

Little surprise, then, that as Jewish comedians increasingly worked in
English and as the Jewish involvement in the clothing trade continued to
evolve, clothing remained a central component of Jewish humor. One of the
most prominent stand-up comics in the postwar era, Myron Cohen, had started as a silk salesman, and many of his jests revolved around clothing. In one,
a rich girl from Park Avenue arrives in Miami Beach wearing her mink coat.

Figure 7. Myron Cohen.

When she gets out of the car into the blazing heat, she promptly faints. A crowd of men quickly gathers around her. "Get a glass of water!" one shouts. "Find a doctor!" another yells. "Open up the mink!" screams the third. In another joke, Cohen claimed to know a salesman who has a hundred suits— all of which are pending. And in a third joke, Cohen tells of a fur company whose business is failing; one partner tries to encourage the other by saying, "Don't worry—the only thing we have to fear is fur itself"[40] [Fig. 7].

One of the most popular television shows of the postwar era, *The Goldbergs*, featured Gertrude Berg as an immigrant Jewish mother, Molly Goldberg, whose husband, Jake, played by Philip Loeb, owns a small dressmaking factory. Many of the episodes of the show revolve around clothing, including one in which Molly's husband insists that his young female foreperson create a new hat for her; the implication is that she is not sufficiently Americanized because her clothing is too old-fashioned.[41] And Jerome Weidman's bestselling 1937 novel, *I Can Get It for You Wholesale*, centers around a young Jewish garment industry executive, Harry Bogen, who betrays his friends, family, and business partners to make it to the top; it was turned into a Broadway musical in 1962, costarring the Jewish performers Elliot Gould and Barbra Streisand, who got married two years later [Fig. 8].[42]

As Jews moved out of the northeast in the years following World War II, Miami and Los Angeles both grew exponentially in their Jewish population. As historian Deborah Dash Moore has written, these "golden cities" offered a new, more relaxed lifestyle that was especially attractive to Jews who had served in tropical locales during their military service. Jewish clothing manufacturers promoted new lines of leisure clothing, such as sportswear, bathing suits, and even clothes for driving, which profoundly influenced American fashion. Moreover, the film industry, in which Jews played an extraordinarily active role, helped to popularize this new approach to dressing for recreational activity.

Figure 8. *I Can Get it For You Wholesale.*

Los Angeles-based clothing manufacturer Phil Rose embodied these new trends. Rose, who was known as the "Jack Benny of the rag business" for his jokes and aphorisms, hired Milt Larsen, a longtime writer for the NBC quiz show *Truth or Consequences* (and founder of The Magic Castle, a famous club for magicians in Hollywood) to write parodies for an album of promotional songs. These songs included "I Am the Very Model of a Modern Manufacturer" to the tune of "I Am the Very Model of a Modern Major General" (from Gilbert and Sullivan's *The Pirates of Penzance*) and "Twelve Days of Market" to the tune of "Twelve Days of Christmas."

In "Model's Lament," to the tune of "The Streets of Laredo" (an oft-recorded cowboy song about a dying boy, thought to be based on a late-eighteenth-century English folk tune, "The Unfortunate Rake"), a famished New York model cannot stop dreaming of eating in a Jewish deli. "When I get off work, I'll go straight to the deli," she warbles. "I'll order pastrami and corned beef on rye." She decides that her career will eventually have to be sacrificed to her physical and emotional need for nourishment. "Some day I'll give up my career and my diet/I'll grow plump and fat, I'll eat twelve times a day/Whatever I eat you can bet that I'll fry it!/Instead of a model I'll be a gourmet!"[43]

But the all-time king of Jewish song parodies was Allan Sherman, the comedy writer and television producer who burst into prominence in 1962 with his first album, *My Son, the Folk Singer* [Fig. 9]. Among the songs on that album was "Hello Muddah, Hello Fadduh," a boy's complaints about summer camp, sung to the tune of Amilcare Ponchielli's ballet music from his opera, *Dance of the Hours*, a piece of classical music that became familiar through its use in the Disney movie *Fantasia*. Another clever Sherman parody was "Harvey and Sheila," about a Jewish couple who move to the suburbs and adopt conservative politics; it was sung to the tune of the Jewish folk song "Hava Nagila." In Sherman's world, a man's wife runs off with his tailor ("My Zelda she found her big romance/When I broke the zipper in my pants") and Brooklyn Jews go shopping for discount clothing ("Grab those bargains off the racks/Who needs Bergdorf, who needs Saks?") But perhaps his most inspired song was "The Ballad of Harry Lewis," which is sung to the tune of "The Battle Hymn of the Republic":

Chorus: Glory, glory, Harry Lewis,
Glory, glory, Harry Lewis,
Glory, glory, Harry Lewis,
His cloth goes shining on!

I'll sing to you a story of a great man of the cloth,
His name was Harry Lewis and he worked for Irving Roth,
He died while cutting velvet on a hot July the fourth,
His cloth goes marching on.

Harry Lewis perished in the service of his lord,
He was trampling through the warehouse where the drapes of Roth are stored,

Figure 9. Allan Sherman.

> He had the finest funeral his union could afford,
> His cloth goes shining on!
>
> With the fire raging 'bout him, Harry stood by his machine,
> And when the fireman broke in, they discovered him between,
> A pile of roasted dacron and some french fried gabardine,
> His cloth goes shining on![44]

The song is a satirical anthem to American Jewish culture, which, while in some sense emancipated from religion, had also become a new kind of secular faith for its adherents. (It's interesting that he dies while working on Independence Day, as if his "Jewish" occupation takes precedence over the national holiday.) No matter what happens to Harry Lewis, "his cloth goes shining on"—his fabric has become interchangeable with his spirit. Yet this is all in the service of mocking the inflated sense of power and importance that the traditional hymn possesses. Sherman is taking it down a peg, showing, in a sense, that the emperor has no clothes. There is an emphatic impudence about the song, a David standing up to Goliath, a Jew standing up to Christian America.

As historian Mark Cohen puts it, Sherman presented the "skewed perspective of a Jewish comedy that knocked American culture off its high-horse and made it mingle with those who had arrived in steerage." Until Sherman came along, "it was not obvious that the frightfully earnest and ur-American 'Battle Hymn of the Republic,' with its evocation of a sword-bearing God delivering justice, had overstayed its welcome." Sherman's song "proved that it had."[45]   Sherman's music playfully celebrates the ascension of Jews in popular culture, their visibility, and influence. As he joked on the jacket to *My Son, the Folk Singer,* "These songs are what would happen if Jewish people wrote all the songs—which in fact they do."[46]

Nevertheless, as critic Lawrence Epstein has pointed out, the song springs from Sherman's conflicts over his Jewish identity—his "insecure, even fearful, sense of American society and the place of Jews in such a society." As Epstein quotes Sherman as saying,

> There was a time when I couldn't find roots because I was ashamed
> to look where they were. When you are running around Madison
> Avenue . . . you carefully avoid mentioning your grandfather the
> ladies' coat presser. You cover up the old roots because something in
> your upbringing has convinced you that they are weeds.[47]

This sense of shame in one's Jewish origins diminished somewhat in one of the most popular television series of the 1970s, *Saturday Night Live.* The show was the brainchild of Toronto-born Lorne Michaels (born Lorne Michael Lipow-itz), and it was to break new ground in the depiction of Jews on screen, with skits like Gilda Radner's "Jewess Jeans," a brazen spoof on the Jewish American Princess stereotype that played on the popularity of Jordache blue jeans. As media scholar Bernard M. Timberg has noted, the Jewess Jeans parody broke a "too Jewish" taboo on network television, in which explicit references to Jew-ishness were seen as limiting the size of the audience. But, as Timberg writes, "it was as a Jewish woman performer relishing a Jewish American stereotype, enjoying it, and turning it on its face that Radner broke a new glass ceiling on this issue."[48]

Nevertheless, even in the 1970s, when multiculturalism was in vogue and Americans were expected to celebrate their ethnic backgrounds, Jews still sensed danger if they stuck their necks out too much. Or at least this was an implicit theme of a series of more than a dozen skits written for Saturday Night Live by Alan Zweibel, some of which dealt with clothing. These skits featured the legendary comedian John Belushi as a samurai who interacts with straight man Buck Henry (born Henry Zuckerman), a Jewish comedy writer and actor.

In each samurai skit, Belushi (modeled on Toshiro Mifune, the star of Akira Kurosawa's film *Yojimbo*) spouts gibberish as he attempts to use his sword to perform an ordinary occupation, such as that of hotel manager, deli-catessen owner, television repairman, stockbroker, optometrist, or psychiatrist. His frustration with his oversized tool invariably leads him both to threaten his customer and, when the customer complains, to pretend to be about to commit hara-kiri. In "Samurai Tailor," Henry comes in for a fitting of a wed-ding tuxedo; he finds Belushi in the process of stabbing a dummy with pins and then beheading it. After trying on the suit, the chatty customer complains about various aspects of the suit, including the fact that there are too many buttons, the suit lacks a vent in the back, and there is no fly. Belushi is able to fix the first two problems with his sword; the routine ends as he prepares to fix the third, which may well castrate his customer.[49]

Just as psychoanalysts tell us that we "play" all the roles in our own dreams, the samurai could also be read as symbolizing a Jewish character. Bewildered by his occupational role, struggling with his sword (an unavoidably phallic symbol), and almost completely unable to communicate, the samurai is somewhat in the position of the Jewish immigrant whose masculinity is far from assured. Yet his mind is always racing; Belushi raises one eyebrow to show that he has an idea that may just save whatever absurd situation has developed with his customer. In the end, the samurai almost always has the last laugh.

Even after *Saturday Night Live* demonstrated that openly Jewish humor could appeal to the mass television audience, it still took another decade until an entire sitcom could center around a Jewish character. That show, of course, was *Seinfeld*, a show about a Jewish comedian and three of his friends—four unrelated New Yorkers who get ceaselessly caught up in trivial details of modern urban life. While it has been famously dubbed "the show about nothing," scholars have had a field day with the show. As the Australian sociologist Jon Stratton has pointed out, the underlying preoccupation of the characters on Seinfeld is with the negotiation of social norms and rules—as Stratton puts it, "what certain forms of behavior are, what they involve, and how to decipher what other people mean when they act in particular ways or say particular things."[50] Indeed, the characters' constant struggle with the forms of etiquette reminded critic Frank McConnell of the novels of Jane Austen, many of which were being turned into Hollywood films at the same time as *Seinfeld* was on the air.[51]

Not surprisingly, given the show's concern with the intricacies of social display, an inordinate number of *Seinfeld* episodes revolve around the theme of clothing. For example, in "The Jacket," Jerry buys an extraordinarily expensive and elegant suede jacket that has one important flaw; it has a pink and white candy-striped lining that makes him look gay. When Jerry and his neurotic sidekick, George Costanza (played by Jason Alexander), go out to dinner with the hyper-masculine father of their friend, Elaine (played by Julia Louis-Dreyfus), Jerry wants to turn the jacket inside out to protect it from the snow, but the father, Alton Benes (played by Lawrence Tierney), refuses to go outside with him unless he turns it back around. In "The Puffy Shirt," Jerry ends up wearing a ridiculous pirate-type shirt on *The Today Show* as a favor to Kramer's girlfriend, who talked so quietly that he did not understand what she had asked him to do.[52] And in "The Reverse Peephole," Jerry wears a fur coat and carries a handbag in order to keep his landlord from discovering that his neighbor Newman (played by Wayne Knight) is having an affair with the landlord's wife.[53]

Seinfeld's clothing matters a lot to him; he is still making his reputation, and he uses clothing to project an image of confidence, an aura of being suave and unruffled. Yet, as David Marc has written, Seinfeld

> lives out a dilemma that is simultaneously his deepest source of anxiety and his richest resource of strength. . . . His sense of humor, the very asset that has allowed him entree to an advantaged hedonistic secular life among the goyim, remains rooted in a marginal point of view that grows out of exclusion. Jerry needs exclusion, and, without his Jewishness, he is unexcludable.[54]

These episodes about clothing are somewhat reminiscent of the ending of "Second Hand Rose"; even though the clothing is new, it still contains the seeds of the wearer's humiliation. Seinfeld is always undone by his own garments. His clothing, rather than building up his self-image, invariably unravels it, making him feel like an outsider. Obsessed with the need for self-display, he tries to turn the older stereotypes inside out and make his garments into a badge of pride rather than a source of shame.

This dynamic continues, to some extent, in *Curb Your Enthusiasm*, the show by *Seinfeld*'s lead producer, Larry David. David himself stars in the HBO series; he plays an exceedingly narcissistic and wealthy Jewish character who is, like the Seinfeld characters, constantly flummoxed by the rules of social behavior. David gets himself into one mortifying situation after another. Clothing remains a major theme, beginning with the very first episode of the show, "The Pants Tent," in which Larry is embarrassed by corduroy pants that bunch up in such a way that it looks like he has an erection. Later episodes include "Chet's Shirt," in which Larry inappropriately asks a woman where her late husband bought a blue and white button-down shirt so that he can buy one for himself; "Krazee-Eyes Killah," in which Larry borrows a jacket from a gangsta rapper so that he can appear in a Martin Scorsese film; and "The Bare Midriff," in which Larry is disturbed by his assistant's short shirt, which exposes her obese stomach.[55]

But perhaps the most striking is "The Smoking Jacket," in which Larry is invited to Hugh Hefner's Playboy Mansion, where Hefner dismisses Larry's father's burgundy velvet smoking jacket, which looks identical to Hefner's, as a "cheap Korean knock-off," leading Larry to switch the jackets when Hefner's back is turned. The idea that Larry's clothing is fake suggests that in some sense, Larry himself is inauthentic, that despite his financial success, he (like Seinfeld) remains marginalized and inferior. According to David Gillota, the show "attempts to reassert the seemingly assimilated, successful American Jew as a cultural other. In doing so, the series critiques reductive attitudes toward race, religion, and other forms of difference and reflects an uneasiness that many contemporary American Jews feel about their own ethnic identity"[56] [Fig. 10].

Nor is insecurity about one's appearance limited to secular Jewish comedians. Leah Foster, an Orthodox stand-up comic, has a routine in which she shows off a dress to her female audience; the dress is a little girl's dress that Foster pretends was the one that she wore at her wedding. In addition to spoofing the weight gain that many women experience after marriage and

Figure 10. Larry David in "The Smoking Jacket." Courtesy of John P. Johnson/HBO.

child-bearing, Foster dances around with the dress and pokes fun at the inane conversations that people have at huge Orthodox weddings, in which women who have not seen each other for years pretend to be close friends; the guests all ask the bride the same questions about where she got her gown and who did her makeup. In this routine, the clothing again serves as an emblem for discomfort with one's appearance, even though the comedian remains entirely within a Jewish context.[57]

This then is the ironic, double-sided nature of clothing in Jewish comedy: it simultaneously symbolizes both success and the persistent fear of inadequacy. Even as Jews have become extremely successful in American society, Jewish comedians still use clothing as a way of grappling with issues of belonging, of self-acceptance, and of comfort in their own Jewish and American skin.

NOTES

[1] Thomas Kessner, *The Golden Door: Italian and Jewish Immigrant Mobility in New York City, 1880–1915* (New York: Oxford University Press, 1977), 38 and 63.

[2] Burton J. Hendrick, "The Great Jewish Invasion," *McClure's Magazine* (January, 1907): 314.

[3] As Marlis Schweitzer has pointed out, one reason that the theater district ended up around Times Square was that it was pushed uptown by an expanding garment industry.

Marlis Schweitzer, *When Broadway Was the Runway: Theater, Fashion and American Culture* (Philadelphia: University of Pennsylvania Press, 2011), 59.

[4] See Neal Gabler, *An Empire of Their Own: How the Jews Invented Hollywood* (New York: Anchor Books, 1989), 5.

[5] See Jonas Barish, *The Anti-Theatrical Prejudice* (Berkeley: University of California Press, 1995).

[6] Harley Erdman, *Staging the Jew* (New Brunswick: Rutgers University Press, 1995).

[7] Quoted in Jenna Weissman Joselit, *A Perfect Fit: Clothes, Character, and the Promise of America* (New York: Henry Holt and Company, 2001), 1.

[8] Ted Merwin, *In Their Own Image: New York Jews in Jazz Age Popular Culture* (New Brunswick: Rutgers University Press, 2006), 19.

[9] Harry Lee Newton and A. S. Hoffman, *The Troubles of Rozinski* (Chicago: T. S. Denison, 1904).

[10] Jews were also often stereotyped as flagrantly dishonest, demonstrated by the fact that they purportedly burned down their own stores to collect fire insurance money. In one joke, a Jewish clothing store owner in Arizona is nonplused when the local police open their headquarters in his basement and the town puts a swimming pool on the floor above him, both of which make it impossible for him to commit arson. *On a Slow Train, and Many Other Humorous Railroad Stories, Best Jokes and Popular Sayings* (Baltimore: I. and M. Oppenheimer, 1905), 54.

[11] Quoted in Esther Romeyn, *Street Scenes: Staging the Self in Immigrant New York, 1880–1924* (Minneapolis: University of Minnesota Press, 2008), 180.

[12] Quoted in ibid., 181.

[13] Quoted in Burns Mantle, "'Abe' and 'Mawruss' At Last Become the Heroes of a Play," *New York Times* (24 August 1913). Mantle, who was not Jewish, noted that he saw the play with a "special audience of cloak and suit salesmen, Abes to the left of me, Mawrusses the right. And they volleyed and thundered with laughter."

[14] "Potash and Perlmutter—A Dramatization of the Cloak and Suit Trade," *Current Opinion* 57:3 (September, 1914): 172.

[15] Walter Hurt, *Truth About the Jews, Told By a Gentile* (Chicago: Horton and Company, 1922), 108.

[16] Quoted in Michael Denning, *The Cultural Front: The Laboring of American Culture in the Twentieth Century* (New York: Verso, 1997), 232

[17] Willa Cather, "New Types of Acting: The Character Displaces the Star," *McClure's Magazine* (February, 1914): 47.

[18] Lisa Marcus, "Willa Cather and the Geography of Jewishness," in *The Cambridge Companion to Willa Cather* (Cambridge: Cambridge University Press, 2005), 70.

[19] Madison Grant, *The Passing of the Great Race* (New York: Charles Scribner's Sons, 1922), 91.

[20] James Martin Miller and Henry Ford, *The Amazing Story of Henry Ford* (Chicago: Midland Press, 1922), 221–23.

[21] See Jesse Eliphalet Pope, *The Clothing Industry in New York* (University of Missouri Social Science Series 1; Columbia: University of Missouri Press, 1905), 48.

[22] Donnie Radcliff, "Heeere's Nancy: First Lady Steals Show at Annual Gridiron Dinner," *Washington Post* (29 March 1982): D1.

[23] Grant Clarke and James F. Hanley, "Second Hand Rose," 1921. First recorded by Ted Lewis and His Band (July 13, 1921). Hanley also wrote "Zing Went the Strings of My Heart," first recorded in 1934 and later sung by Judy Garland, Frank Sinatra, Rufus Wainwright, and many others.

[24] In Shakespeare's *Hamlet*, the title character calls his evil uncle, "a ragtag king, a king of shreds and patches" (*Hamlet* III, iv, 104), comparing him, invidiously, to the ill-dressed mock kings who appeared before the court in tragic dramas. This is quoted most famously in Gilbert and Sullivan's *The Mikado*, in which the "wandering minstrel," Nanki-Poo, calls himself "a thing of shreds and patches" (Act I, Part II).

[25] Michael Wex, *Born to Kvetch* (New York: St. Martin's Press, 2005), 2.

[26] *Glorifying the American Girl*, dir. Millard Webb, Paramount Pictures, 1929. Cantor and Hearn both claimed authorship of the skit; Cantor ultimately sued Hearn over the rights to it. See *Variety* (11 May 1949).

[27] The routine is reminiscent of the old Jewish joke about the man who complains to his tailor that his new suit does not fit. But the tailor blames the problem on the customer, telling him that he does not know how to wear such an elegant suit. In order to make the left sleeve not seem too long, he tells the customer to hitch up his left shoulder; furthermore, to adjust for the right pants leg being too short, he tells the customer to lock his knee. When the customer hobbles out of the store with his uneven shoulders and straight leg, he is spotted by a passerby who stops him and asks him where he got the suit. The customer is flabbergasted—why would anyone want to patronize such a lousy tailor? But as the passerby explains, any tailor who could fit a hunchback like him must be amazingly skillful! This joke is retold in Chris Crawford, *Chris Crawford on Game Design* (London: New Riders Games, 2003), 102.

[28] A similar routine was performed in the third episode of the first season of Sid Caesar's *Your Show of Shows*, an episode in which the plummy English actor Rex Harrison costarred. In the first half of the skit, Harrison pretends to be a secondhand clothing salesman trying desperately to sell Caesar a suit; in the second half, Caesar pretends to be a salesman in a high-end British clothing store who has no interest in selling Harrison anything! Sid Caesar, *Your Show of Shows* (11 March 1950). For a description of the routine, see Sid Caesar and Eddie Friedfeld, *Caesar's Hours: My Life in Comedy, With Love and Laughter* (New York: Public Affairs, 2003), 102–3.

[29] B. Kuppenheimer & Co. was founded in 1863 in Chicago by Bernard Kuppenheimer, who was a Jewish immigrant from Baden, Germany. By 1910, it had become one of the largest clothing companies in the world; it employed 2,000 manual workers and was known for its top coats, "automobile overcoats," "watershed raincoats," and other men's garments. See *Literary Digest* (29 October 1921), vol 71, no. 5, for an advertisement of a Kuppenheimer suit with a "belt in the back" (back of front).

[30] This violent treatment by Jews of their customers might seem uncharacteristic of Jewish businessmen (other than bona fide gangsters), but it did, according to the *New York Times*, actually take place in the clothing establishments of the Lower East Side. As the *Times* reported in 1893, aggressive clothing, hat, and shoe salesmen known as "pullers-in" were known to drag customers into stores on Baxter Street and Park Row. One customer,

Thomas Cowles, was even killed by a "puller-in" when he resisted. ("Outrages by 'Pullers-In,'" *New York Times*, 22 June 1893).

[31] Quoted in Lee Papa, ed., *Staged Action: Six Plays from the American Workers' Theatre* (Ithaca: Cornell University Press, 2009), 235.

[32] Denning, *The Cultural Front*, 300–1.

[33] Rumshinsky's song was popularized by the Yiddish theater and film star Molly Picon, who was the most beloved of all the female Yiddish performers in America.

[34] Mark Schwartz, "Players Club: Memories from the Days of the Mamboniks," *Guilt and Pleasure* 6 (Fall 2007).

[35] There are three other versions of the routine, each one of which prescribes a remedy for a particular ailment: an open window for smelly feet, antacid for indigestion, and castor oil for a cough. Covering up the body with a suit of clothes is connected, in each case, with curing the body of unpleasant or embarrassing conditions. Irv Saposnik links this focus on disease to the fading of Yiddish humor, writing that "Yinglish"—the mix of Yiddish and English—humor was on its way out. "For a culture in decline," he posits, the routine "offers a comic primer on the here-and-now, a how-to manual on how to stay alive." Irv Saposnik, "'Joe and Paul' and Other Yiddish-American Varieties," *Judaism* 49:4 (October 1, 2000).

[36] Quoted and translated in Mark Shechner, "Studies in Hysteria, or Jewish Comedy from Shtetlach to Shticklach," in *What Makes America Different? American Jewry on its 350th Anniversary* (ed. Steven T. Katz; Lanham: University Press of America, 2010), 323–24.

[37] Robert A. Freedman recalls that his father "mostly talked to the salesman, told him 'The boy's getting bar mitzvahed. Let's make him look like a big *macher*.' Then he and the salesman laughed like that was the funniest joke of all time. . . . Dad told me that the blue suit that I picked out looked 'very sharp.' He even bent down and adjusted my collar. I was as happy then as I'd ever been with my father." Robert A. Freedman, *Fancypants: An Autobiographical Novel*. Published on lulu.com (March 24, 2008).

[38] Jenna Weissman Joselit, *The Wonders of America: Reinventing Jewish Culture, 1880–1950* (New York: Hill and Wang, 1994), 93–94.

[39] Saposnik, "Joe and Paul," 438.

[40] Myron Cohen, *Laughing Out Loud: The Funniest Jokes, Anecdotes and Humor by America's Master Story-Teller* (New York: Gramercy Publishing, 1958).

[41] *The Goldbergs*, CBS, Episode 4 (aired on 26 September 1949). See George Lipsitz, "The Meaning of Memory: Family, Class and Ethnicity in Early Network Television," *Cultural Anthropology* 1:4 (November 1986): 355–87.

[42] The show was not particularly successful with critics; *Time* magazine called most of the musical "as quiet as Seventh Avenue [the heart of garment district] on Yom Kippur." *Time* (30 March 1962). It marked Streisand's Broadway debut; her next—and only other—Broadway show was *Funny Girl*, in which she played Fanny Brice.

[43] Phil Rose, *One Dozen Roses: Hilarious Ballads of the Garment Belt* (Phil Rose, 1964). Rose, whose real name was Philip Rosenthal, died just two years later while on a business trip to the Far East. He was killed along with his lyricist and publicity manager, Barbara Logan, as well as 122 others, when their plane crashed into Mount Fuji. It was

the second plane crash in Tokyo in less than twenty-four hours, and the third in a month. See Robert Trumbull, "All 124 on Plane are Dead in Crash Into Japan's Fuji" *New York Times* (6 March 1966): 1. See also "Phil Rose, Ladies Wear Head, Killed," Long Beach *Press-Telegram* (5 March 1966): 1. Allan Sherman also composed an amusing parody of "The Streets of Laredo" that he called "The Streets of Miami." It describes a deadly feud between two business partners. Allan Sherman, *My Son, the Folk Singer* (Warner Brothers, 1962).

[44] Sherman, *My Son the Folk Singer.*

[45] Mark Cohen, "My Fair Sadie: Allan Sherman and a Paradox of American Culture," *American Jewish History* 93: 1 (March 2007): 55.

[46] Sherman, *My Son the Folk Singer.*

[47] Lawrence J. Epstein, *The Haunted Smile: The Story of Jewish Comedians in America* (New York: PublicAffairs, 2002), 177.

[48] Bernard M. Timberg, "Gilda Radner and 'Jewess Jeans': Breaking the Jewish Ethnicity Taboo on Network Television," *FlowTV.org* 9.09, Special Issue: *Saturday Night Live* (20 March 2009).

[49] *Saturday Night Live*, "Samurai Tailor," (originally aired on 22 May 1976).

[50] Jon Stratton, *Coming Out Jewish* (New York: Routledge, 2000), 307–8.

[51] Frank McConnell, "How 'Seinfeld' Was Born: Jane Austen Meets Woody Allen," *Commonweal* 123:3 (9 February 1996): 123.

[52] In 2004, Seinfeld donated the puffy shirt to the National Museum of American History. See Joel Achenbach, "Seinfeld Leaves His Mark on History," *Washington Post* (19 November 2004): C01. Nor is Seinfeld the only character for whom clothing is highly symbolic. Elaine has a job writing catalogue copy for the J. Peterman Company (which was a real company), a clothing store that uses narrative descriptions of its wares rather than pictures. Elaine is hired for the job when the company's owner spots her on the street, wearing a jacket that he describes as "very soft, huge button flaps, deep bi-swing vents in the back-perfect for jumping into a gondola." When they go out for a drink, Elaine replies in an equally absurd manner, this time describing her shirt: "This innocent-looking shirt has something that is not innocent—touchability, heavy, silky Italian cotton; a fine, almost terry-cloth like feeling; five-button placket, relaxed fit; innocence and mayhem at once." Seinfeld, "The Understudy," Season 6, Episode 24 (originally aired on 18 May 1995).

[53] *Seinfeld*, "The Jacket," Season 2, Episode 3 (originally aired on 6 February 1991); "The Puffy Shirt" Season 5, Episode 2 (originally aired on 23 September 1993); "The Reverse Peephole," Season 9, Episode 12 (originally aired on 15 January 1998).

[54] David Marc, "Seinfeld: A Show (Almost) About Nothing," in *Seinfeld: Master of Its Domain* (New York: Continuum, 2006), 23–27. As the comedian later wrote, "To me, everything you have is really a layer of clothing. Your body is your innermost and truest outfit. Your house is another layer of wardrobe. Then your neighborhood, your city, your state. It's all one giant outfit. We're wearing everything." Jerry Seinfeld, *Seinlanguage* (New York: Bantam Books, 2008), 103.

[55] *Curb Your Enthusiasm*, "The Pants Tent," Season 1, Episode 1 (originally aired on 15 October 2000); "Chet's Shirt," Season 3, Episode 1 (originally aired on 15 September

2002); "Krazee-Eyes Killah," Season 3, Episode 8 (originally aired on 3 November 2002); "The Bare Midriff," Season 7, Episode 6 (originally aired on 25 October 2009).

[56] David Gillota, "Negotiating Jewishness: *Curb Your Enthusiasm* and the Schlemiel Tradition," *Journal of Popular Film and Television* 38:4 (2010): 153.

[57] "Leah Foster—Orthedox Jewish Women Comedian." Retrieved from www.youtube.com/watch?v=0pYbKdnU1e4. Downloaded on 12 July 2012.

lack-and-white variety. Women wearing tallitot also has affected men's prac-
nd more variation has been introduced here, in the past thirty years, as well.
ally, Jewish feminists' concerns about the appearance of their tallitot mesh
those of the twentieth-century Orthodox scholar Moshe Feinstein, whose
ngs are followed by most within modern Orthodoxy. In the mid-1970s,
ein stated that a woman who desires to wear a tallit may do so (even though
time-specific commandment, from which women are traditionally exempt,
t forbidden), provided that the tallit is distinctively feminine in appearance.
n my interview-based, oral history of contemporary Jewish women who
allitot, in which I interviewed over fifty women from across the country
fteen to mid-seventies, I was struck by how many women echoed Feinstein,
er or not they were aware of his teaching. These women voiced the need to
nd wear a tallit suited to their personal taste, which generally meant that
not like the traditional, white-and-blue-striped male tallit, but, instead,
signs or colors or material that rendered them female. Gender norms are
lt to cross, even for those dedicated to the task of creating gender equality.
woman in her 30s said to me, "I'm not a woman wearing a man's tallit.
aring a tallit that's meant for me."[4] Fiber artist Rachel Kanter, whose tal-
ve been exhibited at the Jewish Museum in New York City, describes her
or a custom-made, feminine tallit in these terms:

> When I wore a tallit for the first time, it felt uncomfortable, as if
> I were wearing my father's overcoat. If I wanted to wear a tallit, it
> should be made for me. But what would my tallit look like? Using
> history as a guide, I created a tallit inspired by the four-cornered
> robes worn by priests in biblical times and designed using vintage
> apron patterns from the twentieth century. In using traditional sew-
> ing techniques I have become part of a long line of women who have
> created ritual objects using their hands.[5]

was inspired by tradition but also attuned to her embodied experience
ism. Aware that she was reworking the tradition of wearing a tallit by the
her gender, Kanter and her tallit-wearing female peers evince a willing-
create new versions of the old. This flexibility stems, in part, from their
ninist movement awareness that gender is an arena in which power is
.[6] If ideas about gender structure our perceptions of the world, they also
e how we think about Jewish ritual. Members of this first and second
on of tallit-wearing women are generally aware of this potential of their
ractice to shift power relations within their religious communities. (A
point to this desire to signify new relations of power is that women who
not to wear a tallit, in egalitarian communities, may express a discomfort

"What a Strange Power There Is in (Women's Tallitot

Rachel Gordan

In the early 1970s, a milestone in the history of wome
occurred. At the time, the Jewish Theological Seminary co
women as rabbis and the issue sparked national controver
of debate, the Jewish women's study group, Ezrat Nashim,
erful feminist voice, and although not invited, they decide
annual meeting of the Rabbinical Assembly (made up of C
in 1972, "in order to promote their feminist philosophy."[1]

In preparation for the event, Ezrat Nashim members
litot. Their demands to the Assembly included that wome
required quorum for synagogues and prayer groups; that
to participate fully in religious observances; that they be p
rabbis and cantors; and that women be "considered as bou
vot equally with men." The tallitot that the women wore
prayer sessions were a way to visibly proclaim a demand f

One member of the group, Martha Ackelsberg, desc
as a plain piece of sage-green wool material with tzitzit
ners. Like many women who started wearing tallitot in th
crafted hers as a way to personalize the custom. Religiou
Jewish feminist Judith Plaskow described this kind of re
by women in her now-classic book, *Standing Again at Sin*
recognize ourselves as heirs to and shapers of Judaism, as
experiences and integrate them into the tradition, we nec
tradition and shape it into something new."[2]

Arlene Agus, another member of Ezrat Nashim,
of the tallit, cutting armholes into a scarf-like piece of fa
her shoulders and reached down to her knees. Agus sai
different in part because of her Orthodox background; i
men wore tallitot. She wanted to be able to fulfill the coi
without compromising herself in terms of gender by pu
of clothing, which is prohibited by Jewish law.[3]

From the beginning, then, Jewish women who wore
about the look and style of their prayer shawls in a way tha
distinguished their practice from men, who generally wore

silk k
tice,
Ironi
with
teach
Feins
it is a
but n

wear
ages
whet
have
it wa
had a
diffic
As on
I'm w
litot k
desire

Kante
of Jud
fact of
ness to
post-fe
define
structu
genera
ritual
counte
choose

with making a power/political/feminist statement.) The relative newness and elective nature of female tallitot allows Kanter and others to think in terms of creating a right fit, instead of forcing the old to fit the woman. Kanter wanted to situate herself in a line of tradition, but she did so creatively, choosing her own terms and thinking about how to customize the ritual to her tastes.

In this paper—which is more of a report of interview findings—I use what Vanessa Ochs calls a narrative approach to understanding ritual. "With new rituals come stories" that explain the practice's origin or significance.[6] As Ochs writes, narratives are constructed in a variety of ways, expressing how the new ritual builds upon or rejects past ritual, or rehearsing major themes in Jewish history, or exposing the practitioner's fears or excitement about the new ritual. I also found this variety in the interviews I conducted with Jewish women. I asked women to describe their tallit, when they began to wear it, and its significance in their lives. These questions spun off into conversations about family, community, and personal taste. Almost two generations of Jewish women now wear tallitot, and their stories tell us something about how ritual is working in contemporary American Jewish life.

Normally, in my academic life, I am a historian who relies on archival research with the occasional interview. In beginning of this project, I turned to oral history because there is not that much written about women who wear tallitot and because I'm interested in a historiography of Jewish practice that accounts for personal circumstances, cultural anomalies, and religious fears and desires that change over the course of a lifetime, as well as the intellectual, moral, and religious struggles that Jews undertake in coming to their practice. Coming from a religious studies department, I find that scholars attentive to ritual are often overly focused on belief. As a scholar of American Judaism, I feel the need to apply Arnold Eisen's imperative to "look beyond belief and take stock of the social, political, familial, and other imperatives that play a part in influencing Jewish practice."[7]

I want to say something about my conversations with women. My intention was to have a series of wide-ranging, unstructured dialogues about tallitot. I did not hide my reactions to what women told me or respond in completely neutral terms. As a result, I felt that I was able to have more sincere conversations. For example, if I asked a woman if she thought of her tallit as a piece of fashion and she said, emphatically, "Absolutely not," I followed up with my actual question, which was, "Is that because you think of fashion as frivolous and incompatible with the category 'religion'?" She then had the opportunity to disagree with me or explain to me what she really meant, and I had a better opportunity to understand her. I think my style was not combative, but conducive to refining ideas.

In my own historical work, this is the kind of information I try to uncover about a time period. What are the factors shaping women's religious practice? How does feminism, specifically, relate to the ritual at this stage of its history? Where does this ritual fit into women's religious worlds? What kind of refashioning of the self is achieved by wearing a certain tallit?

One of the problems with studying Jewish religious practice, as a historian, is that we do not have a lot of information about how and why Jews in the West behaved religiously—how and why they observed kashrut or *niddah* [separation from her husband during a wife's menstrual period], for instance—so we're often comparing the present to what we think was "traditional Jewish practice." This study is an effort to build that trove of information for the present era.

In this paper, I focus on three features that stood out to me in women's narratives. I will then apply a Mordecai Kaplan framework for understanding how this ritual is working in American Jewish life, today.

First feature: women spoke about their tallit as a means of being part of a community. This was expressed both by women who described feeling part of the Jewish community as a result of wearing a tallit and by women who chose not to wear one in order to feel connected to a more traditional congregation.

Judith K., one of the older women with whom I spoke, at seventy-two, is a married grandmother. She grew up in Philadelphia and graduated from Radcliffe before receiving her PhD in comparative literature from Harvard. She then became a faculty member in English Department at Harvard. She now teaches in the Boston Jewish community. Judith remembers being sixteen when her brother became a bar mitzvah at the Spanish Portuguese shul synagogue in Philadelphia and feeling envious. She wanted some recognition for herself in her community. Judith thinks of herself now as fortunate to have had a mother who listened to her feelings, and consequently spoke with the rabbi, who responded by creating a consecration ceremony for a few sixteen-year-old girls. (It's hard not to wonder about the effect this must have had on Judith's confidence and comfort in the Jewish community—to have her feelings so immediately taken into account). The rabbi taught Judith and the other young women biblical grammar, and their confirmation took place on a Sunday afternoon. As a result, Judith reflects that the confirmation ceremony did not seem equivalent to the boys' bar mitzvahs. Still, the experience was formative, as it shaped Judith into an adult who was seeking "something more" in Judaism.

It wasn't until the 1960s, at Harvard Hillel, while Judith was a faculty member, that she felt real egalitarianism in the service, she says. She saw a few women wearing tallitot in the Hillel minyan, and she started wearing one herself in the 1970s. Judith described this transition to wearing a tallit seam-

"What a Strange Power There Is in Clothing": Women's Tallitot

Rachel Gordan

In the early 1970s, a milestone in the history of women wearing tallitot occurred. At the time, the Jewish Theological Seminary considered ordaining women as rabbis and the issue sparked national controversy. During this era of debate, the Jewish women's study group, Ezrat Nashim, emerged as a powerful feminist voice, and although not invited, they decided to attend the the annual meeting of the Rabbinical Assembly (made up of Conservative rabbis) in 1972, "in order to promote their feminist philosophy."[1]

In preparation for the event, Ezrat Nashim members made their own tallitot. Their demands to the Assembly included that women be counted in the required quorum for synagogues and prayer groups; that women be allowed to participate fully in religious observances; that they be permitted to become rabbis and cantors; and that women be "considered as bound to fulfill all mitzvot equally with men." The tallitot that the women wore during the morning prayer sessions were a way to visibly proclaim a demand for equality.

One member of the group, Martha Ackelsberg, described her 1972 tallit as a plain piece of sage-green wool material with tzitzit attached to the corners. Like many women who started wearing tallitot in the 1970s, Ackelsberg crafted hers as a way to personalize the custom. Religious studies scholar and Jewish feminist Judith Plaskow described this kind of reworking of tradition by women in her now-classic book, *Standing Again at Sinai*: "As Jewish women recognize ourselves as heirs to and shapers of Judaism, as we explore our own experiences and integrate them into the tradition, we necessarily transform the tradition and shape it into something new."[2]

Arlene Agus, another member of Ezrat Nashim, redesigned the shape of the tallit, cutting armholes into a scarf-like piece of fabric that gathered at her shoulders and reached down to her knees. Agus said she made her tallit different in part because of her Orthodox background; in her home, only the men wore tallitot. She wanted to be able to fulfill the commandment of tzitzit without compromising herself in terms of gender by putting on a male item of clothing, which is prohibited by Jewish law.[3]

From the beginning, then, Jewish women who wore tallitot were concerned about the look and style of their prayer shawls in a way that, in the women's view, distinguished their practice from men, who generally wore the traditional wool or

silk black-and-white variety. Women wearing tallitot also has affected men's practice, and more variation has been introduced here, in the past thirty years, as well.
Ironically, Jewish feminists' concerns about the appearance of their tallitot mesh
with those of the twentieth-century Orthodox scholar Moshe Feinstein, whose
teachings are followed by most within modern Orthodoxy. In the mid-1970s,
Feinstein stated that a woman who desires to wear a tallit may do so (even though
it is a time-specific commandment, from which women are traditionally exempt,
but not forbidden), provided that the tallit is distinctively feminine in appearance.

In my interview-based, oral history of contemporary Jewish women who
wear tallitot, in which I interviewed over fifty women from across the country
ages fifteen to mid-seventies, I was struck by how many women echoed Feinstein,
whether or not they were aware of his teaching. These women voiced the need to
have and wear a tallit suited to their personal taste, which generally meant that
it was not like the traditional, white-and-blue-striped male tallit, but, instead,
had designs or colors or material that rendered them female. Gender norms are
difficult to cross, even for those dedicated to the task of creating gender equality.
As one woman in her 30s said to me, "I'm not a woman wearing a man's tallit.
I'm wearing a tallit that's meant for me."[4] Fiber artist Rachel Kanter, whose tallitot have been exhibited at the Jewish Museum in New York City, describes her
desire for a custom-made, feminine tallit in these terms:

> When I wore a tallit for the first time, it felt uncomfortable, as if
> I were wearing my father's overcoat. If I wanted to wear a tallit, it
> should be made for me. But what would my tallit look like? Using
> history as a guide, I created a tallit inspired by the four-cornered
> robes worn by priests in biblical times and designed using vintage
> apron patterns from the twentieth century. In using traditional sew-
> ing techniques I have become part of a long line of women who have
> created ritual objects using their hands.[5]

Kanter was inspired by tradition but also attuned to her embodied experience
of Judaism. Aware that she was reworking the tradition of wearing a tallit by the
fact of her gender, Kanter and her tallit-wearing female peers evince a willingness to create new versions of the old. This flexibility stems, in part, from their
post-feminist movement awareness that gender is an arena in which power is
defined.[6] If ideas about gender structure our perceptions of the world, they also
structure how we think about Jewish ritual. Members of this first and second
generation of tallit-wearing women are generally aware of this potential of their
ritual practice to shift power relations within their religious communities. (A
counterpoint to this desire to signify new relations of power is that women who
choose not to wear a tallit, in egalitarian communities, may express a discomfort

lessly; it felt natural. Although Judith had always felt very Jewishly connected, it was not until she discovered this participatory, egalitarian minyan with an emphasis on Torah study that she found that, "I really always wanted it. When I found it, I embraced it fully."

As Judith remembers it, this was the heyday of the havurah, the *Jewish Catalog*, and studying on your own about traditional Judaism. The tallit was not the first expression of Jewish feminism, Judith remarked, but the tallit became a visible marker of her feminism. "People used to stop me on the street in Cambridge," Judith said, telling her "how important it was for women to wear a tallit." It represented a possibility that women had not known existed, Judith remarked.

Regarding the look of her tallit, Judith remarked that she feels it is important to have something that looks feminine. "I like having something that seems to belong to being a woman," Judith said. Hers is a woven tallit with blue-green stripes.

Judith did not discuss God in relation to her tallit, but she did speak of feeling embraced by the tallit. Moreover, her narrative of the story of beginning to wear a tallit—starting with a description of her family background and feeling excluded from her traditional Jewish community, leading toward her finding a Jewish community that felt like what she always wanted—gave the impression of her tallit being a part of her process of finding her "right fit," Jewishly.

Emily, a twenty-three-year-old graduate student in Boston, began wearing a tallit in ninth grade at the same time that she started wearing tefillin. As she describes it, tallitot were part of the "uniform" of people who were serious about Judaism in her school. At the time of her bat mitzvah—this was in the year 2000—Emily had purposely chosen not to wear a tallit because it seemed like something girls did for their bat mitzvah and then never wore again. This denoted a lack of commitment to her.

Similarly, Rachel S., who just finished her junior year at Brandeis University when we spoke, chose not to wear a tallit at her bat mitzvah because she associated it with something Reform girls did without much thought: "I thought it looked silly. I thought people wouldn't take me very seriously if I wore one." Not wanting to be connected with a Jewish community lacking in seriousness, Rachel did not start wearing a tallit until she became an observant Jew in an observant community in college.

Sarah M., in her mid-twenties, living in Manhattan, and soon to be married, is the daughter of a non-Jewish father and a Jewish mother who divorced when she was a toddler. Sarah grew up in Salt Lake City, where Mormonism was the norm, and she was often identified as "the Jew" in her class. Sarah now lives an observant life with her fiancé in New York, but she remembers receiving a tallit at her bat mitzvah as part of her synagogue's ceremony, where parents presented the child with a tallit on the bimah. To Sarah, these tallitot seemed like accessories. They seemed unconnected to a serious commitment to mitzvoth. Sarah's decision, as an adult, to purchase a larger tallit that she describes as less "girly" than her bat mitvah tallit also was a decision to identify with a more serious and observant Jewish community. As is the case for many of the young women who received tallitot at the time of their bat mitzvah, that practice now seems de rigueur—devoid of religious significance. Selecting a new tallit as an adult thus becomes a way to invest the practice with new meaning.

Arnold Eisen defines this factor in Jewish decision making about ritual as "politics," to denote the impact, in the past, of direct governmental edicts and/or concerted societal pressures designed to shape, elicit, or forbid distinctive Jewish ritual observance.[8] Today, too, considerations about the "desired degree of Jewish distinctiveness" and the likely reactions to it by both gentiles and other Jews are important considerations in ritual practice.[9]

Related to this desire to feel part of the community—and self-consciousness about which community one was being identified with—was the second feature that I found prominent in my research: sending a message about egalitarian values by wearing the tallit. Forty-year-old Rebecca, a Persian retired attorney who lives in Great Neck, New York, with her family, described being the first Persian women in her Conservative synagogue to wear a tallit and said that she hopes to be a "tipping point where other women will follow." Rebecca is aware that these changes in a community take time. After all, her own Persian community, with time, has inched closer to mainstream American Judaism. For Rebecca, wearing a tallit is "part and parcel of a true desire for men and women to have parity in religion."

Rebecca's memories of being marginalized in her Jewish community— because of her gender—spur her resolve to wear the tallit. Growing up in Queens, Rebecca remembered being trained to chant a haftorah for her bat mitzvah in the early 1980s. The man who taught her was an older man with a European accent, she recalled, who walked out of the room when it was time for her to read the haftorah at her bat mitzvah. Rebecca noted this, but she said that she was not aware of it really bothering her until recently.

In her narrative of coming to wear a tallit regularly, Rebecca also recounted the experience of sitting shiva, as an adult, for her maternal grandfather. During the mourning period, neither Rebecca nor her sisters or mother were counted for a minyan by her mother's family. "We had to sit there," she said. "My uncle refused to count us. Chabad sent over some guy [for the minyan]—he had an earring, smoked cigarettes—my uncles would have had no regard for him in any other arena." It was infuriating, Rebecca said, but she also remarked that she decided these offenses were not inherent in Judaism. "It was them," she decided. Rebecca considers herself a Jew who has taken steps to counteract that kind of exclusionary practice.

Similarly, Linda, who is sixty and lives in West Hartford, Connecticut, charts her path to wearing a tallit as beginning with the experience of exclusion. In Hebrew school, she remembered the rabbi at her synagogue coming into her classroom with a shofar to explain what it was. "I'd rather the girls not touch this," he said, and Linda recalled that he "chased me away" from Judaism. As an adult, she was pretty much ready to give up on Judaism entirely, until one year when she went to work on Yom Kippur. Linda had five coworkers she didn't even know that well, and they exclaimed, "What are you doing here?" Linda said she realized that the world saw her as a Jew and that she didn't even know what that meant. She embarked on an adult education path that included meeting other women who wore tallitot, and she was intrigued enough to try it herself.

It may be a surprise that even women in their twenties and younger who felt themselves to be the inheritors of feminism—many of whom had received a tallit at their bat mitzvah as a matter of course—still recognized feminism as part of their ritual practice. Even in congregations where the gains of feminism were largely taken for granted—where there was no "fight"—these women seemed nurtured by the connection that they made with that no-so-long ago fight by an earlier generation of Jewish women. Tamar, who is in her mid-twenties and a graduate of Brandeis University, now living in the Boston area, said she started wearing a tallit regularly in college, once she discovered how much more comfortable she felt in the egalitarian minyan than in the Orthodox service. Tamar said that she has tried to avoid the feminist aspect of wearing a tallit because she doesn't want to seem pushy. She prefers the adjective "egalitarian" to describe her inclusive values. Still, Tamar noted, she feels "empowered" by wearing a tallit because she feels like she is fulfilling a mitzvah and that wearing the prayer shawl is comforting and calming, helping her feel part of a religious community.

The third main feature that I noted in my conversations is that wearing a tallit becomes a means for self-fashioning a personalized connection with Judaism. There has been much derisive talk of American Jews' cafeteria-style approach to Judaism—Jews selecting what they like and not opting for flavors that displease us. Yet in my conversations, women were open and unapologetic about the importance of owning and wearing a tallit that suited their personal tastes. Many described the process of finding the right tallit or outgrowing an old tallit and the search for a new tallit.

Beautifying a mitzvah or *chidur mitzvah* has long been a part of Jewish ritual practice, but these women discussed owning a tallit that was aesthetically pleasing as an essential part of their ritual. God or belief was rarely mentioned in my conversations, although the tallit is traditionally a vehicle for wearing tzitzit, which are meant to remind the wearer of religious obligations. At a time in American Jewish life when nonobservance is a popular option and religious obligation does not carry a strong resonance with most American Jews, Jewish women, I argue, have been in the vanguard of reworking this ritual so that it expresses a contemporary desire for a personalized connection with Judaism.

Annie G., who is thirty-one, lives in and grew up in Toronto. She is studying to become a rabbi and came from a strong Reform background. She received her first tallit when she became a bat mitzvah in the early 1990s. It was a patchwork tallit with squares, given to her by friends and family. She said she received a lot of mogen davids [Stars of David], doves, skylines of Jerusalem, and embroidered squares for her tallit. Her grandmother made a mini Torah scroll that was glued on, pieces of which are constantly falling off, Annie explained. "It's probably beautiful," Annie said, making it clear that she can't quite see it this way. She is happy to have a newer, simpler tallit made of recycled materials that expresses her current style. This was given to her by a friend. Annie also has another design in mind: a tree of life tallit that she spotted on her last trip to Israel and "fell in love with," but she wasn't so keen on the colors they had there. So she has an idea for her next "dream tallit." A better tallit is always around the corner, it seems.

Bethany—in her early thirties and a convert to Judaism—was in the process of moving from Los Angeles to New York when we spoke. She described having a tallit made for her in Bethlehem by a Palestinian woman, made from fabric used to make the garments of Christian clergy and embroidered in a traditional Palestinian style. Bethany said that she feels that it shows her vision of what it would look like to value all cultures living in Israel. It very much represents her vision for a Jewish world.

As a convert from an evangelical background, Bethany tells me that she is disturbed by how little instruction is given to young Jewish women and men about the religious and spiritual meaning of a tallit. To Bethany, tallitot seem to be handed over to thirteen-year-olds who don't understand the garment as a spiritual technology that will enhance their lives. Hearing her describe it this way, I have to say that I agree and that I find her perspective—informed by her Christian background—insightful.

Bethany is my interviewee who speaks most about her tallit in relationship to faith and what she calls "being religious in a heart sense." These terms are not usually part of the Jewish lexicon. Not having had the experience of being gifted a tallit as a teenager, and have chosen Judaism as an adult, Bethany sees the tallit as a tool that connects her to Judaism. It does illuminate for me how many other aspects of life enter into wearing a tallit for women, who are usually not doing it simply as an inherited ritual, if they do wear it beyond the bat mitzvah. As I've discussed, they also value being part of a certain kind of Jewish community and want to embody its egalitarianism, and they want to self-fashion a ritual into something of their own so that it is a personal connector to Judaism.

This desire for connection to Judaism that the tallit represents to women who could—more easily than adult men—elect not to wear it, but for their strong desire, is also a sign, I want to suggest, of being in the posture of seeking, and of not yet having arrived. Bethany, the convert from evangelical Christianity, expressed a much greater at-homeness in religion and spirituality than most other women with whom I spoke. It was clear that the tallit was helpful for putting women in the proper mind-set, like a baseball player's uniform. This was how so many of them phrased the experience, but there was still a searching mentality that most women described. The not having—whether as a result of some experience of gender exclusion or knowledge that exclusion still exists in certain Jewish communities that prevents individuals from having the desired kind of Judaism and the world that we want—creates a need for ritual, like wearing a tallit, to help some women refashion a world (through fashion, we might say) that more closely suits their vision.

Unlike having an aliyah or leading a service—other results of Jewish feminism—wearing a tallit also evokes the possibility of crossing gender lines and the need, among contemporary women, to define a distinctive, feminine identity at this boundary.

There was a tension between the first feature of these narratives—of wearing a tallit (or deciding not to wear a tallit) in order to fit into a community—and the third—wanting a distinctive tallit that represented one's personal style. To me, this represented contemporary Jewish women's desires to participate in a traditionally male ritual without nullifying their female identity.

Three features became most salient: 1) wearing a tallit as a means of belonging to a community, 2) wearing the tallit as an embodiment of egalitarian values in Judaism, and 3) wearing a tallit as a means for Jewish woman to fashion a personalized connection to Judaism—by selecting the style and color and material. These are all ways of using this ritual in order to craft new kinds of Jewish selfhood and new world visions.

These contemporary Jewish women also seemed to be wearing tallitot as a way to employ a Mordecai Kaplan approach to Jewish ritual, as he explained it in his 1934 *Judaism as a Civilization*. What I mean here is that they supply meanings for their practice that are at least partly self-conscious inventions, without worrying too much about what the practices in question meant to previous generations of Jews. For Kaplan, as suggested by the title of his magnum opus, Judaism was not to be conceptualized as merely a religion; it is also a civilization, and as such, it concerns the whole of life. Just as a Jewish communal center ought to replace the synagogue for Kaplan, so too the notion that Judaism is a civilization must replace the idea that Judaism is a religion. As Kaplan wrote in 1934, "Paradoxical as it may sound, the spiritual regeneration of the Jewish people demands that religion cease to be its sole preoccupation."[10] Kaplan's proposal, that Judaism be reconstructed as a civilization, called for understanding Judaism in terms of the collective life of the Jewish people. Ritual can be conceptualized in these same functionalist terms as to how it coheres in the everyday life of Jews.

My research suggests that the female tallitot are transforming people, just as the best ritual often does, whether it makes two individuals a married couple or helps the grieving get through the process of mourning. But Judaism is changed, too, by female tallitot, which, depending on where you stand, may be to the cost or the benefit of this new ritual practice.

NOTES

[1] Rebecca Shulman Herz, "The Transformation of Tallitot: How Jewish Prayer Shawls Have Changed Since Women Began Wearing Them," in *Women in Judaism Contemporary Writings* (University of Toronto, 2003), 2.

[2] Judith Plaskow, *Standing Again at Sinai: Judaism from a Feminist Perspective* (New York: Harper Collins, 1991), vii.

[3] Herz, "The Transformation of Tallitot." In some Ashkenazic communities, unmarried men do not wear the tallit. The reason given is that the biblical verse about the wearing of a garment with fringes is followed by the verse (Deut. 22:13): "If a man marries a women," indicating that a tallit is not to be worn until one is married.

[4] Interview with Becky Deitsch, May 8, 2011.

[5] Danya Ruttenberg, "Heaven and Earth: Some Notes on New Jewish Ritual," in *Reinventing Ritual: Contemporary Art and Design for Jewish Life* (New Haven: Yale University Press, 2009), 77.

[6] Joan Wallach Scott. *Gender and the Politics of History* (New York: Columbia University Press, 1999), 45.

[6] Vanessa Ochs, *Inventing Jewish Ritual* (Philadelphia: Jewish Publication Society, 2007), 57.

[7] Arnold Eisen, *Rethinking Modern Judaism: Ritual, Commandment, Community* (Chicago: University of Chicago Press, 1997), 17.

[8] Eisen, *Rethinking Modern Judaism*, 12–13.

[9] Ibid., 13.

[10] Mordecai Kaplan, *Judaism as a Civilization: Toward a Reconception of American Jewish Life* (New York: Macmillan, 1934), 345.

Aboriginal Yarmulkes, Ambivalent Attire, and Ironies of Contemporary Jewish Identity

Eric K. Silverman

How should a Jew dress? The question is far from trivial.[1]

Traditionally, Jews—mainly men—prayed in certain distinctive garments. Wearing a skullcap or yarmulke, draped in a prayer shawl [*tallit*], and, in the morning, enwrapped in *tefillin* or phylacteries, a devotional Jew looked unmistakably Jewish. He dressed for Judaism.

But what about on the streets? How should a Jew dress in public? In distinctively Jewish attire? Like everybody else? Should a Jew intentionally dress to stand apart—or to blend with the rest of society? Are there certain non-Jewish garments that must be avoided? How, in other words, should clothing reflect Jewish identity?

The classic rabbis spoke with an almost singular voice on the matter: Jews must dress distinctively. At the very least, Jews should never seek to emulate Gentiles. Any such garb was tantamount to apostasy. The classic rabbis of old thundered, century after century, against the donning of non-Jewish garb. The rabbis often enlarged on biblical edicts, thus creating a religious "fence" [*seyag*] that would protect Jews from inadvertently transgressing divine law. Clothing served as one such hedge. Dress, too, functioned as a crucial sign of Jewish difference that would thwart acculturation and the mirroring of Gentiles. Or so the rabbis hoped.

"Learn not," declared the prophet Jeremiah (10:2), "the ways of the other nations." The rabbis interpreted this and similar biblical passages to specify that Jews should dress in distinct attire. Indeed, Jews should suffer martyrdom, declared the Talmud (*b. Sanh.* 74a–74b), rather than renounce the slightest commandment or custom, even "changing the strap of one's shoe." One father was quite clear on this point in his fourteenth-century ethical will penned to his children: "you must not adopt non-Jewish fashions of dress. . . . Never change the fashions of your fathers."[2]

Other rabbinic legal decisors, known as *poskim*, were more liberal. They objected only to non-Jewish clothing specifically tied to taboo behaviors, such as idolatry and immodesty.[3] Some rabbis allowed Gentile garb so long as the intent was not to pass as a non-Jew,[4] or, as the Talmud discussed (*b. B. Bat.* 83a), if a Jew wished simply to avoid embarrassment when interacting with non-Jewish officials. In the main, though, all rabbinic authorities until the nineteenth century rise of Reform Judaism and the Haskalah or Jewish Enlightenment subscribed to the dictum that Jews should not "walk in the ways of the Gentiles," a principle known as *chukkat ha-goy*.[5] Jews should dress like Jews, that is, in clothing that upholds the key social boundaries that separate men from women, the learned rabbinic elite from the common folk, and especially Jew from Gentile. How should a Jew dress? For his or her place in the divine order of society and the cosmos.

Figure 1. Australian yarmulke with kangaroos.

KOSHER KANGAROOS?

As a self-professed Australiaphile and an anthropologist with long-standing field-work experience in Papua New Guinea, a former Australian colony, my interests in Jews and Antipodean indigenes rarely correspond. So it is not difficult to imagine my delight upon espying a few years ago yarmulkes ornamented with Aboriginal designs [Figs. 1–3]. They are manufactured by Design Kippah in the eastern suburbs of Sydney. (Yarmulke is Yiddish; *kippah* is Hebrew.) The patterns are colorful, vibrant, and, most significantly, unmistakably Aboriginal. What do these non-Jewish motifs mean on these quintessentially Jewish garments?

Figure 2. Yarmulke made from Julie Nabangardi Shedden's Aboriginal Australian "Bush Tucker" design.

In 2011, I conducted an impromptu e-mail query facilitated through the Australian Association of Jewish Studies.[6] My interlocutors reported a range of sentiments in regard to these designs: a generic sense of Australian citizenship, national pride, a fashion statement, a bit of fun in the pews, solidarity with another oppressed

Figure 3. Australian yarmulke with boomerang pattern.

people, and a moral commitment to social justice phrased as the Jewish value of *tikkun olam* [repairing the world]. These yarmulkes allow Jews to announce their affinity with another long-persecuted people whose very identity is threatened by the forces of assimilation. Ever since the British established a penal settlement in Botany Bay in the late eighteenth century, the clash between Euro-Australians and indigenous Australians has been one of unrelenting tragedy. Why should Jews not "root," as one person said, for the oldest, original Australians? Indeed, one could read these yarmulkes as a stylish comment on the often complex relationship between Jews and Aborigines.[7]

From a religious perspective, however, Aboriginal-themed yarmulkes potentially pose certain complications and impious innuendo. As one devout Jew said to me in an e-mail exchange, the depiction of animals on these yarmulkes might violate Jewish religious law, or *halacha*. For one, some of these yarmulkes depict decidedly non-kosher animals, such as kangaroos [Fig. 1] and honey ants [Fig. 2; the yarmulke was cut from a larger cloth that also depicted stylized lizards, snakes, and witchetty grubs]. For another, many of the patterns derive from the Aboriginal cosmological concept known in English as The Dreamtime. The Dreamtime or The Dreaming, called the "everywhen" by the noted anthropologist W. H. Stanner,[8] "denies creative significance to history and human action" and "denies the erosions of time," since The Dreaming "represents all that exists as deriving from a single, unchanging, timeless source."[9] We humans, like everything else in the cosmos, were created by anthropomorphic and theriomorphic ancestral spirit-beings. Facets of The Dreaming might evoke certain dimensions of the biblical deity. But there is no place for The Dreamtime in the Torah, Israelite religion, or the rabbinic worldview. Consequently, Aboriginal yarmulkes could be seen in a broad sense as violating the first commandment of the Decalogue and thus repudiating the most basic premise of monotheism. Last, religious Jews, as I noted earlier, normally should shun distinctively non-Jewish clothing. Not only are the Aboriginal patterns obviously Gentile, but they seemingly celebrate that very non-Jewishness.

The rabbis of old, however, did offer one possible resolution to the conundrum of the Aboriginal yarmulke. The rabbis, always fearful of idolatry, largely banned jewelry ornamented with heathenish images such as suns, moons, and dragons.[10] Other rabbis barred only costly ornaments, assuming that worthless baubles were made simply for fashion, not ritual and worship. Still another opinion tolerated pagan gems but only after a non-Jew nullified the idolatrous intent or aura of the item, for example, by marring or spitting upon the image. In fact, a recent set of Jewish girls' dolls dressed in modest clothing befitting a "Torah-observant lifestyle," called Mini Mishpacha,[11] addressed this very issue. If a local community sees these dolls as a form of *avodah zara* or idol worship, advised the website for Mini Mishpacha, "an adult can snip off a piece of the nose or a finger of each doll."[12] This mutilation signifies a Jew's commitment to never view or use the dolls impiously. One could conceivably perform a similar marring on an Aboriginal yarmulke or perhaps awkwardly ask an Aboriginal person to expectorate on the item.

Ancient rabbinic authorities forbid Jews from dressing in garments directly connected to pagan worship.[13] Thus a cloak presented to an idol as a ritual offering is categorically taboo. It can never be worn by a Jew. But if an idolater wore the cloak for warmth and afterward slung it on the effigy for storage, then a Jew could rightly wear the garment. The rabbis were particularly concerned with censoring behavior that might appear, however unintentional, to signal Jewish respect for a heathen deity. Might one apply similar logic to Aboriginal yarmulkes? Perhaps. But surely no reasonable person would view these caps as ritual objects used in non-Jewish rites. Still, the patterns might nonetheless convey a degree of respect for a non-Jewish religious outlook. Worse, the motifs could imply the intent to introduce a non-Jewish ritual element, or deity, into Jewish worship. The Aboriginal yarmulke, I suggest, evokes a quality of taboo precisely because it blurs normative boundaries between sacred and profane, Jew and non-Jew.

There is more we need to consider in determining the religious status of Aboriginal yarmulkes. The pattern in Figure 2 is sewn from a copyrighted fabric titled "Bush Tucker," designed by the Northern Queensland Aboriginal artist Julie Nabangardi Shedden. On the Internet, one can readily find the very same pattern and variations on tablecloths, scarves, bandannas, tote bags, and coffee mugs. I applaud Design Kippah for using an authorized Aboriginal pattern, which ensures that the artist receives rightful remuneration. The unauthorized reproduction of Aboriginal designs, and the parroting of faux patterns, is a long-standing, degrading, and shameful form of cultural colonization.[14] By donning an authorized Aboriginal-themed yarmulke, a Jew stands with other progressive citizens seeking to redress the continued exploitation and muting of Aborigines in the Australian nation-state.

Despite these non-Jewish meanings and political stances, what could possibly be more distinctively, obviously, and publicly Jewish than a yarmulke? What other garment so quintessentially proclaims a Jewish identity? How could one possibly walk in the footsteps of Gentiles while attired in this cap?

Figure 4. Yarmulke designed after the Aboriginal flag.

The Aboriginal yarmulke, then, blurs the very rabbinic "fence" it aims to uphold. In other words, this garment evidences the very acculturation the rabbis so strenuously opposed even as it announces an unmistakable Jewish identity. Indeed, Aboriginal yarmulkes vibrantly illustrate the long-standing tension in Jewish clothing between what I call ethnic or religious particularism and generic citizenship—between dressing like a Jew and dressing like others.

Another, similar-themed yarmulke displays the Aboriginal flag [Fig. 4]. This banner was designed in 1971 by Harold Thomas, a descendent of the Luritja people of the Western Desert. The black represents Aboriginal people, the red signifies the earth, ochre, and the Aborigines' spiritual affiliation with the land, and the yellow symbolizes the life-giving sun. These are hardly classic rabbinic or Jewish significations. This yarmulke, then, raises the same complexities as the previous caps I discussed. But this yarmulke also displays the friction between garbing Jewish identity in a Jewishness that resists colonization by European Christian cultural hegemony and affiliating Jewishness with the Aboriginal struggle against the very same colonization of which Jews are a part. After all, Jews arrived with the first convict fleet in 1788. Moreover, many Aborigines today assert intellectual ownership over the flag and wish non-Aborigines to cease its reproduction for commercial purposes. (In 1997, the Federal Court of Australia recognized Mr. Thomas, the sole designer of the flag, as protected by the Copyright Act of 1968.) It is, in many respects, a yarmulke fraught with tension about how a Jew should, or should not, dress to announce Jewishness. From any angle, Aboriginal yarmulkes represent the irreducible complexities of modern Jewish identity.

ANCIENT HEADBANDS AND FRINGES

But how modern are these complexities of Jewish identity as encoded in clothing? Judaism, of course, postdates the biblical era of hereditary priests, animal sacrifice, and the Jerusalem Temple. Indeed, the main practices of the religion, such as rabbis leading congregants in collective prayer inside local synagogues, did not emerge until after the destruction of the Second Jerusalem Temple in the first century CE. Nonetheless, Jewish religious authorities anchor Judaism to the biblical era and the code of law enshrined in the Torah, or Five Books of Moses. In fact, the vestimentary tensions I identified in regard to Aboriginal yarmulkes go back as far as Ancient Israel. Let me offer several examples.

Exodus 13:9 alludes to an item of ancient ritual apparel: "And it shall serve as a sign on your hand and as a reminder between your eyes, that the teaching of the Lord shall be in your mouth; that with a strong hand the Lord freed you from Egypt." Seven verses later, we learn "It shall be for a sign upon your hand and *totafot* between your eyes, for with a mighty hand the Lord freed us from Egypt." Deuteronomy 6:8 and 11:18 repeat the edict with slight variation. The ancient authors of these decrees, as was their wont, failed to describe with any precision either the hand "sign" or the *totafot*.

Jews today associate these objects with *tefillin*, or phylacteries in Greek. But *tefillin*—biblical passages[15] encased in black leather boxes and strapped to the forehead and arm for morning prayer—assuredly differ from the ancient amulets and the headband or pendant.[16] The Hebrew Bible records many charms, ornaments, and bodily markings such as circumcision (Genesis 17) and Cain's "mark" (Genesis 4:15). At the same time, the Israelite deity forbid many bodily insignia, including funerary gashing (Leviticus 19:28), idolatrous lacerations (1 Kings 18:28), and fraudulent prophetic stigmata (Zechariah 13:6). In this regard, Israelite bodies did and did not resemble their neighbors. And this is a crucial point. Although the exact nature of the biblical *totafot* and hand signs remain uncertain, these ritual items fit into a wider biblical and ancient pattern of marking and unmarking the Israelite body to designate exclusive membership in their society. The Israelites partly stood apart on account of their bodily adornment. Aboriginal yarmulkes now appear as a recent rendition of an ancient conundrum: how to dress the covenantal community.

In the book of Numbers (15:37–41), God tells the "sons" of Israel to attach "fringes" or "tassels" [*tzitzit*] to their garments. The deity also prescribes a thread or cord of blue, a color called *tekhelet*. "Look at it," continues God, "and recall all the commandments of the Lord and observe them, so that you do not follow your heart and eyes in your lustful urge" or, more literally, "go whoring." A similar command, albeit lacking mention of the blue cord, occurs in Deuteronomy 22:12.

Both passages require the Israelites to affix fringes to a feature, called the *kanaphayim*, of their garments—generic garments, I note, not particular items. The word *kanaph* variously refers to corners, wings, borders, skirts, extremities, and hems. Rabbinic authorities since the Talmudic era favored "corners" and so required Jewish men to wear a fringed shawl for prayer, called a *tallit*, and a fringed undergarment [*tallit katan*] throughout the day. But these items, which now signify only Jews, are postbiblical. What, in the original context, did the fringes and blue cord mean? And did these fashion accessories tag only Israelites?

The fringes, like the *totafot* and hand sign, likely instance the cross-cultural utilization of knots as mnemonic devices for sealing vows.[17] Indeed, the Numbers passage commands the Israelites specifically to recall the law when looking at the fringes. In Proverbs, the Israelites tied divine commandments to their necks (3:3), hearts (6:21), and fingers (7:3). Metaphoric knots appear throughout the Torah (e.g., Isaiah 8:16, Hosea 13:12, Job 14:17). I see the biblical fringes, the *totafot*, and the hand "sign" as memorial devices affixed, as in so many other cultures, to the body and clothing. To a large degree, these ritual fashion accessories were not exclusively Israelite.

Knots also figure prominently among the Iatmul people of the middle Sepik River in Papua New Guinea, among whom I have conducted anthropological fieldwork since the latter 1980s.[18] To remember the date of a market, women traditionally untied knotted cords, one knot representing each passing day. Maternal uncles, even today, lash ensorcelled bands to the wrists, ankles, and necks of their nieces and nephews to promote health and fortune—to keep sisters' children, we might say, intact. Mourners wear similar knotted twine to contain their souls lest they fatally lose themselves in grief. Throughout Iatmul culture, knots and ties represent memory, permanence, and security. The biblical fringes did likewise: bind the people to the law, their deity, and the community. But was this custom unique in the ancient world? The answer is, yes and no.

Many ancient peoples throughout the Mediterranean used tassels and ornamental cords as regal and ritual insignia.[19] The hem was often the most ornate part of a garment, symbolizing rank and authority. Mesopotamian texts reveal that clay imprints of hems sometimes served as legal signatures and that people cut hems in exorcisms and divorces. The Babylonians seized the fringes of their deities in an act of supplication. They also grasped hems to gain "coercive power" during business negotiations.[20]

Of course, as I repeatedly intimated, the biblical adornment of hems and fringes to communicate messages about identity was hardly unique in the ancient world. Yet why adorn the hems of *every* Israelite? Why not just the wealthy and powerful, as in other Near Eastern societies? Because the Israelites wished to dress the *entire* society as God's elite, not just the privileged few.[21]

This message was unique in the ancient world. Even the poorest Israelite was symbolically attired as divinely chosen royalty.

Now we can explain the blue thread. The ancients paid dearly for their blue—really, deep indigo. A gram of blue, painstakingly extracted in miniscule amounts from a certain sea snail, was so exorbitant that only the wealthy and powerful dressed in blue and purple.[22] It is precisely from the ancient value of this hue, especially during the Roman Empire, that we now speak of certain colors as "royal blue" and "imperial purple." At any rate, the Torah implies that all Israelites could afford a few blue threads, and thus the entire Israelite community again symbolically dressed in regal garb to signify the divine election of Israel above all other peoples. Israelite tassels, then, swayed between ethnic distinctiveness and acculturation or blending—just like Aboriginal yarmulkes.

BLENDS AND BOUNDARIES

The central motif in the book of Leviticus, a long register of ritual laws, is holiness. In Hebrew, the linguistic root of "holy" means "keep apart." Israelite religion enshrined myriad rules concerning the separation of distinct categories. Mixtures were ordinarily polluting. Leviticus 19, for example, forbids the Israelites from crossbreeding domestic animals and sowing different seeds in their fields. The same chapter, further defined by Deuteronomy 22:11, bars wool and linen blends, called *sha'atnez*. Why?

Rules governing everyday life in Ancient Israel, to repeat, stressed boundaries and separations. The sacred Temple, however, represented divine unity, and thus priests encountered mixtures largely forbidden to other Israelites.[23] Since natural dyes adhere poorly to plant cellulose, such as flax, the ancients could dye only wool, not linen.[24] The *sha'atnez* rule thus barred colorful blends from most Israelite wardrobes. But the High Priest's robe, as well as regular priestly sashes and certain Tabernacle curtains, all conspicuously violated this edict. These textiles paralleled cosmic creation by symbolizing the formation of worldly order from primal disorder. These fabrics, too, I suggest, inverted the everyday dress code of commoners to visualize the prominence of the law. Of course, the commandment to wear a blue thread necessarily dressed all Israelites in the taboo blend, thus tying the entire community to the priesthood. But regular folk were permitted no further garments spun from the sacred mixture. This way, the *sha'atnez* prohibition symbolized social order, cosmic creation, and the distinction between sacred and profane. But the law, too, likely attired the Israelites apart from other ancient peoples.

The Torah also commands "There shall not be a man's gear on woman, and a man shall not wear a woman's garment" (Deuteronomy 22:5). Much later, the rabbis understood this rule plainly to prohibit cross-dressing. But the original meaning was rather different and fine-grained.[25] The rule prevents, first, any woman from taking up the emblem or military armor of an elite man called a *geber*. Second, the law prevents a *geber* from dressing like women. Other men could seemingly dress as they pleased—even in women's garb. No passage in the Torah expressly forbids gendered cross-dressing. Many scholars also suggest that this rule censured ritual transvestism, commonly practiced in the ancient world. This rule, then, originally served to protect the privileges and manhood of an elite group of men while separating, yet again, the Israelites from their neighbors.

In the early seventh century, the prophet Zephaniah (1:8) thundered against Israelites who, among other indiscretions, "don a foreign garment." This rebuke was perhaps narrowly directed at vestments worn for the worship of Baal (see also 2 Kings 10:22). But Zephaniah's rant might also suggest the presence of certain vestimentary boundaries between the Israelites and their neighbors. Nowhere does the Torah outright specify a national dress code. But I have argued that many, albeit not all, biblical laws nonetheless hint at an effort to dress the Israelites apart from their neighbors. Israelite dress thus sustained and blurred the communal boundary.

CAPS, BADGES, AND EMANCIPATION

There is no textual evidence in all the writings of late antiquity that Jews dressed distinctively.[26] In the Maccabean literature, for example, we read about the brutal occupation of Palestine by the Seleucid Greeks and the triumphant Jewish revolt celebrated annually on Chanukah. Less well known is that the Maccabees also slaughtered Jews who embraced Hellenistic culture by, among other things, wearing a Greek hat (2 Maccabees 4:12). But the tale never refers to Jewish caps or any other item of national attire. In fact, the evidence suggests that Jews did not, despite several laws and prophetical exhortations recorded in the Hebrew Bible, dress distinctively.

Flavius Josephus, writing in the first century, often remarked on clothing. But he, too, fails to comment on any sort of universal Jewish dress code. In the New Testament, neither the Gospels nor Jesus spoke about Jewish attire. New Testament Jews, like all Roman citizens, dressed in standard Greek garb (e.g., Mark 13:16, Matthew 5:4). Archaeological excavations and ancient mosaics reveal that Jew and non-Jew both favored the same tunics and adornments.[27]

Interestingly, second-century Jews living at the Dead Sea, unlike the Greeks and Romans, dressed in two-piece tunics.[28] But no other author comments on this feature. It was a difference that did not make a difference. In sum, any effort by the Torah or Israelite authorities to institutionalize an ethnic dress code failed. Perhaps the best evidence for this assertion derives from the Letters of Paul, composed in the second half of the first century, which lambasted nearly all public affirmations of Judaism, such as circumcision, the dietary code, and the Sabbath rest. But Paul said nothing about Jewish clothing. Jews were clearly distinctive—but there was no distinctively Jewish style of dress.

Indeed, the central texts of the classic rabbis, such as the Talmud, also offer no concrete evidence for distinctive Jewish attire. Rabbinic garb was plucked entirely from the standard Greco-Roman lexicon and wardrobe.[29] Nonetheless, the classic rabbis consistently demanded that Jews dress apart. They even specified a particular method for tying shoes.[30] But few Jews heeded these calls. The folk largely lived and dressed apart from their rabbinic leaders.

In the early High Middle Ages, Rashi typified a male Jew's outfit as consisting of an undershirt, robe attached to stockings, garters, coat secured at the waist by chords, and a variety of shoes.[31] Women dressed in midriff garments to enforce chastity and various head-coverings such as woolen caps and kerchiefs. None of these articles were uniquely Jewish. Illustrated medieval manuscripts inked by Jews likewise show little evidence for any distinctively Jewish sleeves, necklines, patterns, colors, headgear, buttons, and so forth.[32] These manuscripts do portray Jewish ritual practices. Jews thus remained distinct. But everyday Jewishness was not reflected in clothing. Jews, with the exception of the rabbinic elite, dressed as much as possible in local, non-Jewish styles.

Additionally, we need to consider the role of the Church. Beginning with the Fourth Lateran Council, summoned by Pope Innocent III in the early twelfth century, church and state in Europe imposed a seemingly endless series of derisive dress codes on Jews. These decrees essentially aimed to prevent any intercourse, sexual and otherwise, between God-fearing Christians and the despised race, forever besmirched by the betrayal of Christ.[33] These regulations included the infamous patch, in various shapes and hues, and an assortment of distinctive hats as well as, in parts of Italy, earrings. For centuries, in fact, Europe remained committed to marking Jews as disdainfully Otherly.[34] Only when Jews submitted to the purifying waters of baptism could they dress, at least legally, like everybody else.

What is quite remarkable about these anti-Jewish dress codes, which endured for almost seven centuries across Europe, is the regularity with which they were renewed. By implication, I suggest, many Jews ignored these laws, at least whenever possible. Most Jews dressed, as I stated earlier, in local rather than legislated fashions. Wealthy Jews, too, could in some regions of Europe endeavor to purchase dispensations. Enforcement also varied in accordance with local economic conditions and the political concerns of ruling elites. The idea of branding Jews with peculiar clothing remained an important part of European culture until the eve of modernity. But the translation of this idea into practice was hardly uniform.

Jews, too, like all other European communities, regulated consumption and display in order to protect the privileges of their own communal elites and to regulate social life more generally. Such sumptuary legislation, too, aimed to stem non-Jewish envy.[35] For most of European history, then, Jewish clothing was stitched from several competing forces: biblical law, rabbinic rulings, local political and economic exigencies, the church and widespread anti-Judaism, and sumptuary legislation. Jewish clothing, then, symbolized a wide-ranging conversation about the role of the Jew in society—a role that pivoted between distinctiveness and acculturation.

The vestimentary apartheid imposed on Jews by their own religious leaders as well as church and state lasted well into the eighteenth century in some European countries. One outcome of these edicts was that Jews generally dressed in attire that seemed anachronistic. They appeared old-fashioned. Jews represented the past, as befitting a people beholden to the old covenant. For centuries, this "look" of the Jew was not only tolerated but actively encouraged as a way to recognize the execrable race. But on the eve of modernity, Europe switched ideological suit: Jews were now encouraged, and outright ordered in Russia and the Polish territories, to dress like ordinary citizens. That is, Jews were finally admitted into European society—but only on condition that they cease to appear Jewish.[36] Many Jews profoundly bemoaned these changes, seeing the new dress code as an outright assault on Judaism. Yet Jews swept up in the democratic promises of the era, especially adherents of the Haskalah or Jewish Enlightenment and the emergent Reform movement, enthusiastically donned modern garb in the second half of the nineteenth century. Most Jews now dressed for the ideals of citizenship, social mobility, individual morality, and modernity.

In America, most Jewish immigrants during the classic period of immigration from the 1880s to 1924 were thrilled to shed their Old World garb and dress in mass-produced, off-the-rack clothing that materialized the promises of wealth, equality, consumerism, and free choice.[37] Jews thrillingly dressed like all other citizens. In her 1912 novel *The Promised Land*, Mary Antin recalls journeying:

> to a wonderful country called "uptown," where, in a dazzlingly beautiful palace called a "department store", we exchanged our hateful homemade European costumes, which pointed us out as "greenhorns" to the children on the street, for real American machine-made garments, and issued forth glorified in each other's eyes. (p. 187)

Abraham Cahan penned similar sentiments in his autobiographical novel, *The Rise of David Levinsky* (1917). "The well-dressed crowds of lower Broadway," tells the narrator, "impressed me as a multitude of counts, barons, and princes" (p. 91). Despite the wrenching poverty of the Lower East Side in New York City, "these people were better dressed than the inhabitants of my town" in Lithuania (p. 93). In 1833, congregants in the Crosby Street Synagogue, New York City, draped their prayer shawls "over modern broadcloth coats, and fashionable pantaloons with straps."[38] They prayed not simply as Jews but as stylish Americans. And therein these Jews, seeking to dress both for Judaism and acculturation into the wider society, enacted a time-honored ideal and dress code throughout Jewish history. My task in the rest of this essay is to trace this tension in two recent genres of Jewish garb: yarmulkes and T-shirts.

POP CULTURE RELIGIOUS CHIC

I want now to illustrate the continuing tension between Jewish distinctiveness and acculturation by exploring a particular genre of contemporary yarmulkes.[39] These caps, which I dub pop culture yarmulkes, vividly illustrate the predicament of most Jews who aspire to fuse their Jewish identity with a commitment to full participation in the modern nation-state. Despite the unmistakable Jewishness of this small cap, contemporary yarmulkes often display images and phrases far removed from traditional identity and theology. Yarmulkes now express personal preferences for sports teams, cartoon characters, rock-and-roll bands, hobbies, consumer goods, and wry humor. The yarmulke, in other words, wonderfully illustrates the ongoing tension between Judaism as a distinct religion, set apart from the wider society, and Judaism as just another ethnic group, defined by the very same individualism embraced by everybody else, and so hardly distinct at all.

In the 1940s, a unique yarmulke style emerged in the United States that would eventually dominate synagogue celebrations as a quasi-religious souvenir. These yarmulkes are purchased by the hosts of major ritual occasions, such as weddings and the bar or bat mitzvah coming-of-age rite. The caps are made from glossy satin or plush velvet, often lined with cotton, and frequently bordered by faux silver or gold filigree. Guests wear these yarmulkes during the religious service, then bring them home as keepsakes. The distinguishing feature of these yarmulkes, which has changed little over the past sixty years, is the machine-stamped autograph on the lining that generally records the names of the honorees, the date and type of event, and the location.

These souvenirs first appeared through caterers as part of the overall wedding and bar mitzvah package.[40] This novelty represented the tensions as well as the successes of American Jewry at mid-century. Both the yarmulke and the ritual occasion it commemorated symbolized the retention of Jewish tradition—even if that tradition was only recently invented, as in the case of the bat mitzvah. Even the yarmulke itself emerged as a universal signifier of Jewishness only in the 1930s and 1940s. Before then, Jews donned all manner of caps, including bowlers, top hats, fedoras, berets, turbans, pillbox hats, and peaked caps. There was no particular headcovering that unmistakably communicated Jewish identity. Moreover, the public norm was for all men to wear hats in public. A Jew covered his head like everybody else. Only when secular fashion doffed hats, and religious Jews retained their caps as a "fence" against further acculturation or assimilation, did the yarmulke become a vestimentary token of Jewishness. Indeed, the smallish yarmulke appeared as an acceptable compromise between the Orthodox mandate of headcovering and the secular custom of bareheadedness. Although the yarmulke today seems unequivocally Jewish, it is, I have suggested, as much a creation of secular fashion as it is of Jewish theology.

Still, both the yarmulke and the occasion it represented signified that American Jews remained Jewish. Nonetheless, the stamping on the now-classic American yarmulke exemplified the transformation of tradition and community into a special celebration of unique lives and fortunes, that is to say, the classic American values of social mobility and individualism. Personalized yarmulkes, too, celebrated the material and consumerist successes of American Jews as they ascended into the middle class *en masse* during the post-World War II era. Actually, the commercialization of American bar mitzvah and wedding celebrations began as early as the 1920s with the rise of lavish menus, ornate ice sculptures, calligraphic place settings, and other expressions of bourgeois opulence.[41] By the mid-1970s, personalized yarmulkes had become so much a part of mainstream or non-Orthodox American Judaism that they became almost obligatory for any large celebration. The personalized yarmulke weaves together consumer capitalism, conspicuous consumption, the individualization of ritual, and Jewish identity. These yarmulkes communicate the inescapable conclusion that most American Jews are as thoroughly acculturated into the premises of modernity as they are Jewish.

Today, Jews can select from a wide range of yarmulke fabrics, including silk, denim, terylene, chino, and seersucker. To accessorize, one can order various trims, buttons, metallic embossing, photographs, and all manner of colors, patterns, images, logos, and phrases. Until fairly recently, four manufacturers, all based in Brooklyn, all managed by Orthodox Jews, dominated the yarmulke market in the United States: A1 Skullkap (www.skullcap.com), Weinfeld Skullcap Manufacturing (http://yarmulkes.com), Mazel Skullcap (www.kippah.com), and Brucha Yarmulke (now, Yofah Religious Articles, www.yarmulka.com). The website for A1 Yarmulke lists the typical array of styles available today: satin, deluxe satin, moiré, brocade, velvet, velour, knit, design suede, suede, leather, custom, and sport. A click on satin brings up twenty-six colors: aqua, black, brown, burgundy, dark grey, dusty rose, forest green, gold, hot pink, ivory, kelly green, lavender, light blue, light grey, light pink, lime green, navy blue, orange, peach, purple, red, royal blue, teal, turquoise, white, and yellow. Each yarmulke can also receive one of eleven different trims: ivory, black, navy, royal blue, white, gold, silver, silver/white, gold/white, silver/black, and gold/black. In total, A1 Yarmulke offers an astounding 241 possible combinations, not including variations for trimming and personalized stamping. One wears such a yarmulke to convey one's Jewishness. But one shops for a yarmulke amid a bewildering variety of choices that bespeaks the American values of consumerist free choice and variety. American Jews now shop for yarmulkes much as they do for any other commodity.

For Conservative and Reform Jews, yarmulkes no longer merely convey a commitment to religious tradition. Rather, yarmulkes now express the thoroughly modern values of individualism, taste, and sometimes mere amusement—the precise qualities associated with secular fashion. As A1 Yarmulke advises on its website, "choose a color to suit your taste, or your décor." For my own wedding in 1996, my fiancée and I asked a non-Jewish seamstress to make yarmulkes from fabric we purchased from an Asian store in Hawaii that displayed a Polynesian *tapa* cloth pattern [Fig. 5]. To see our yarmulkes as merely Jewish is to ignore the thoroughly multicultural dimensions of these garments, never mind a certain level of affluence that allowed for a trip to Hawaii—a state that many native Hawaiians view, not unlike Australian Aborigines, as part of an ongoing and illicit colonization. In fact, it was my own experiences as an anthropologist in the Pacific Islands that gave rise to

Figure 5. Yarmulkes made from fabric displaying Polynesian tapa cloth pattern—from the author's wedding.

my desire to have our wedding yarmulkes loosely evoke both the exotic and romantic allure of Hawaii and a diffuse sense of non-Jewish indigeneity.

The smorgasbord of yarmulke styles now available suggests the transformation of Jewishness into an ethnic identity that matches, like one's wallpaper or iPod, wider societal tastes, trends, and lifestyle options. No longer does the yarmulke appear solely to push against assimilation. Rather, contemporary yarmulkes represent the contrary relationship between Judaism and modern society, a suggestion nowhere more in evidence than on the pop culture yarmulke.

Yarmulkes today appear cute, playful, witty, and sometimes transgressive. They display almost every icon, insignia, slogan, and pop culture character imaginable. No longer is the market dominated by a few unassuming retailers in Brooklyn. Jews today can point their web browsers to Kippah King, Kool Kipah, Design Kippot, Best Kippah, Kippa Connection, Kippah Corner, Kippot World, Mazel Tops, Ego Kippot, and Lids for Yids, among others. A quick perusal of online yarmulke retailers reveals an almost limitless variety of painted, printed, embossed, and crocheted patterns. Today, yarmulkes express Jewishness through the quintessential traits of modernity: self-expression, consumerism, and popular culture. Contemporary designs include:

- Sports team logos and mascots [Fig. 6] from mainly American baseball, basketball, football, and ice hockey, but also the occasional British soccer team such Manchester United. There is probably no professional team, in any sport, that lacks representation in the pews.

- Comic book and television superheroes: Batman, Superman, Spiderman, Green Lantern, and so forth.
- Movie characters: Yoda and Obi-Wan Kenobi (*Star Wars*), Buzz Lightyear and Woody (*Toy Story*), *Little Mermaid, Beauty and the Beast, Cinderella,* James Bond's 007, and so forth.
- Beloved figures from Disney and various children's television programs: Mickey Mouse, Big Bird, Cookie Monster, Bart Simpson, Blue's Clues, Pikachu, the Wiggles, Snoopy, Charlie Brown, SpongeBob SquarePants [Fig. 7], Avatar, Tinkerbell, Bob the Builder, Telletubbies, and others.
- Rock and roll iconography: The Beatles crossing Abbey Road, Phish's logo, the symbols from Led Zeppelin IV, the Rolling Stones tongue, the iconic image from Pink Floyd's album *Dark Side of the Moon,* AC/DC, The Who, Metallica, Black Sabbath, and the dancing bears from the Grateful Dead.

Yarmulkes display the national emblems of military branches, consumer preferences for Hershey kisses and Apple computers, Harry Potter on his broomstick, the Cat in the Hat, Winnie the Pooh, Hello Kitty, Teenage Mutant Ninja Turtles, Shrek, Clifford the Big Red Dog, Curious George, Garfield, Thomas the Tank Engine, Bart Simpson, poker hands, Scooby Doo, Super Mario, bagpipes, drum sets, electric guitars, bowling pins, golf clubs, paw prints, national flags, dolphins, Godzilla, NASCAR, chess pieces, smiley faces, Yin and Yang, hearts, sailboats, fishing rods, construction machines, Harley Davidson motorcycles, tie-dyed patterns, karate kicks, shamrocks, flowers, fish, and even the occasional

Figure 6. Sports yarmulkes.

Figure 7. *SpongeBob SquarePants* yarmulke.

Jewish motif such as stars of David, menorahs, and matzah patterns. Seemingly no aspect of secular culture is barred at the sanctuary doors. Contemporary yarmulkes all but dissolve the boundary between sacred and profane.

The L.E.D. Kippah (http://ledkippah.com) flashes a personalized message on a programmable display. A search for "yarmulke" on eBay today yields 1,242 results. Krazy Keepas (www.krazykeepas.com) makes yarmulkes from corduroy, men's suit fabrics, fleece, argyle, flannel, and sports mesh. They also offer plastic "krok *kippas*" to match popular Croc footwear. Kids Kippot (www.kidskippot.com) sells patterns of dreidels and Hebrew letters as well as camouflage, airplanes, butterflies, soccer balls, flames, safari animals, dogs, hippos, sea life, and dragonflies. At UncommonYarmulke.com, you can download the book *Yarmulke-gami: E-Z Paper Fold Jewish Art Hats.*

You can even buy "kosher *kippot*" certified sweatshop-free by the Progressive Jewish Alliance (www.pjalliance.com). Three sources supply kosher *kippot*: Justice Clothing (www.justiceclothing.com), a unionized apparel cooperative in the United States and Canada; Maya Works, dedicated "to the economic development of women and girls" in Guatemala (www. mayaworks.com); and Global Goods Partners, a nonprofit "alleviating poverty and promoting social justice by strengthening women-led development initiatives for marginalized communities in Asia, Africa, and the Americas" (www.globalgoodspartners.org). In the United Kingdom, the Jewish Social Action Forum offers "fair trade *kippot*" woven from "cotton yarn which has been ethically sourced and made by cooperatives in India," specifically, the Godavari Delta Women Lace Artisans Co-operative in Tamil Nadu (www. faritradekippot.org). You can also find colorful, fair trade yarmulkes, woven by Mayan women, at A.M Stein Art Imports in Utah (www.amsteinart.com) and Mayan Hands (www.mayanhands.org).

African Home (www.africanhome.co.za), based in Cape Town, offers under the category of "township art" tin yarmulkes made from discarded soft drink cans. A similar sense of liberal environmentalism recently fueled the rise of yarmulkes made from recycled cardboard, also called "eco-suede," which Zara Mart (www.a-zara.com) calls "The eco-friendly vegan alternative to suede-leather *kippot*." And kosher *kippot* are not the only form of political Jewish headgear. American Jews often cast symbolic votes for presidential elections on their yarmulkes. In the 2008 season, Jewish voters could pray in the "Obama-kah" or the "McCippah."

One day in 2003, a high school student named Dan Torres in upstate New York asked his friends to wear yarmulkes in school as a humorous response to the Santa hats allowed by the teachers who for Christmas waived the normal ban on caps. A few years later, this "joke" expanded into an annual Yarmulke Day that celebrates difference and tolerance.[42] In this context, the yarmulke shifted from a local symbol of youthful quasi-rebellion to a global emblem of pluralism. Yarmulke Day even has its own line of T-shirts and messenger bags, which celebrate Judaism through one of the most ubiquitous contemporary American slogans, "I ♥ Yarmulke Day" (http://yarmulkeday.spreadshirt.com/). It is hard for me to imagine the classic rabbis of old ♥'ing anything! This, as much as any other dimension of contemporary American Jewry, attests to the full incorporation of Jews and yarmulkes into modern society.

Figure 8. *Dora the Explorer* yarmulke.

Figure 9. *Dragon Ball Z* yarmulke.

Several years ago, I purchased for my daughter a yarmulke displaying Dora the Explorer [Fig. 8], the popular Latina girl, and her decidedly non-kosher pet monkey, Boots. For my son, I selected a picture of Goku from the anime series Dragon Ball Z [Fig. 9]. These yarmulkes comment wonderfully on the prominence of globalization, ethnic fluidity, and multiculturalism in contemporary Jewish culture. They also, at least in regard to my daughter, evidence the impact of feminism on religious practices for many, if not most, American Jews. Above all else, these two yarmulkes show that the vestimentary boundary between the Jewish and non-Jewish worlds, a boundary so important to the classic rabbis and even certain edicts in the Torah, remains porous for many acculturated Jews. We don yarmulkes to signal our affiliations with Judaism—but also our affiliation with the rest of society.

OUTFITTING THE NEW JEW COOL

About a decade ago, groups of young American Jews—known variously as Hipster Jews, Generation-J, Heebsters, Cool Jewz, and New Jews—embarked on a far-reaching program to reinvent Jewish identity and to challenge the hegemony of mainstream Jewish institutions. New Jews yearn to push Jewishness to the cutting-edge of contemporary culture by making Jewishness relevant to the wider society. In this effort, New Jews wear their Jewishness on their sleeves.[43]

The New Jew Cool, to borrow one journalist's moniker,[44] is drawn to "entertaining, playful, ironic [and] generationally distinctive" expressions of Jewishness.[45] New Jews aspire to un-assimilate.[46] But they anchor their Jewishness not to religious practices, but to an ethnic identity that stresses what the theorist James Clifford calls "cultural hybridity" and "inventive impurity."[47] Specifically, we will see, New Jews ironically dress their Jewishness in T-shirts that display the same racy, swaggering tones that characterize contemporary pop culture—much as I argued in the previous section with regard to recent yarmulkes.

For example, one can purchase a T-shirt that shows a gun-toting chasid who taunts, after a famous wisecrack uttered by Clint Eastwood's character Dirty Harry in the 1983 film *Sudden Impact*, "Go Ahead, Make My Shabbos." You can readily find shirts, thongs, panties, and other undergarments that declare Jewcy, Jewlicious, Jewtastic, and "Jews Kick Ass." The latter shirt, voicing a classic expression of American bravado, features six heterodox Jewish figures: Henry Winkler, better known as "The Fonz" on the television sit-com *Happy Days*; Albert Einstein; Sammy Davis, Jr.; William Shatner, famous as Captain Kirk on *Star Trek*; Bob Dylan; and Jesus Christ. This shirt vividly illustrates the irreverent, sardonic fashion of the New Jew Cool.

A central venue of the New Jew Cool is *Heeb* magazine, "brewed in Brooklyn in 2001 as a take-no-prisoners zine for the plugged-in and preached-out." The title, which *Heeb* also prints on T-shirts, attempts to refashion an ethnic slur into an emblem of pride. The term thus resembles the provocative and pervasive use of "nigga" by younger African Americans today and the wider hip-hop community. *Heeb* and many other T-shirt vendors also offer shirts stating "Jesus Saves, Moses Invests." This phrase transforms the old canard of Jewish wealth, dating to the New Testament and Judas Iscariot's betrayal of Jesus for thirty pieces of silver (Matthew 26), into a comical expression of ethnic bluster. Indeed, many garments in the New Jew Cool play with the very stereotypes that earlier generations of Jews found degrading and unsettling. Instead of hiding stereotypical traits of Jewishness to "pass," the New Jew Cool emblazons those clichés on their garments in order *not* to pass.

The "Jesus Saves, Moses Invests" shirt also defines Judaism not from within, as Jews traditionally defined their identity, but in terms of Christianity. We are, the shirt says, what they are not. That said, many contemporary Jew-

ish T-shirts respond brusquely to Christianity in ways that surely would have
made earlier generations shudder. YidGear printed "I didn't kill your God;
get off my back" (http://yidgear.com). In the 1990s, American evangelicals
often displayed WWJD on their garments and jewelry, an acronym for "What
Would Jesus Do?" To this, Rotem Gear responds with "What Would Maimonides Do?" (www.rotemgear.com). *Heeb* printed a shirt with the likeness of
Barbara Streisand and "WWBD" or "What Would Barbara Do?"

Many shirts merge Jewishness with a generic American identity. PopJu-
daica.com, also called ChosenCouture.com, sells a "Yo Semite" shirt that
symbolically maps Jewishness onto the classic American landscape. This shirt
thus adds a new voice, in a sense, to the long-standing dialogue between
Jewish distinctiveness and generic citizenship. Another PopJudaica garment
proclaims "No Limit Texas Dreidel." LuckyJew.com offers a similar comedic
repertoire, such as "I Prefer Kosher," "Jews for bacon," and "Jews for cheeses"
(a play on messianic "Jews for Jesus"). The "chosen shirts" at Everything's
Jewish include "You had me at shalom" (www.cafepress.com/oygevalt). This
garment is a variant of "You had me at hello," a famous line uttered by Renée
Zellweger to Tom Cruise in the 1996 film *Jerry Maguire*. Everything's Jewish
also promotes a "Schmutz Happens" shirt that puns with the crude witti-
cism "shit happens." Judaism thus appears as a variant of the wider cultural
cadence, not a language all of its own.

Cool Jewish T Shirts sell a "Just
Jew It" slogan [Fig. 10] with a ram's horn
[shofar] that resembles the Nike swoosh
logo (www.cooljewishtshirts.com). This
amusing shirt dresses Jews in the very
same footwear worn by the rest of society
while allowing Jews to stand apart. The
shirt simultaneously assimilates and un-
assimilates. It offers a humorous comment
on the same historical tension that has
shaped Jewish dress over centuries.

JUST JEW IT.

Figure 10. "Just Jew It" T-shirt
design. Courtesy of Oron Berkow-
itz, Israeli-T, www.israeli-t.com.

Designs by the oxymoronic clothing
company KosherHam (www.kosherham.
com) include "Winnie the Jooh" (with a
yarmulke atop the famous bear) and, beside
a jar of gefilte fish, a Dr. Seuss-like rhyme, "One fish, two fish, red fish, Jew fish"
[Figs. 11–12]. Jtshirt.com offers a "Shofar Hero" motif that visually recalls the

Figure 11. "Winnie the Jooh" T-shirt design. Courtesy of Jeremy Bloom, www.kosherham.com.

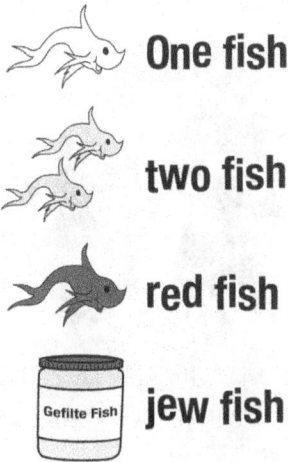

Figure 12. "One Fish, Two Fish, Red Fish, Jew Fish" T-shirt design. Courtesy of Jeremy Bloom, www. kosherham.com.

Nintendo Wii game Guitar Hero. Shalom Shirts (www.shalomshirts.com) sells "Do the Jew," which resembles the logo for the soft drink Mountain Dew, and a dancing Hasid listening to an MP3 player accompanied by the phrase "חי Pod." The latter, pronounced *chai* pod, refers to the talismanic Hebrew word for "life." Shalom Shirts also parodies rock-and-roll bands. Instead of Guns N' Roses, they offer "Guns N' Moses," complete with a skull sporting a beard, long earlocks or *payess*, and a black hat.

Many vestimentary proclamations of new Jewish identity playfully blur ethnic boundaries. These garments celebrate Judaism both as ethnically distinct as well as multicultural. Judaism thus again appears as a variant of American culture, not as a distinctive tradition defined on its own terms. Several T-shirt designs, for example, allude to hip-hop and African Americans. Of course, Jews and blacks in America have long shaped their respective identities in contrast to each other. Indeed, in the racial hierarchy of America, Jews partly achieved their status as legitimate "white" people, rather than besmirched ungodly Jews, by darkening their faces with burnt cork in the popular amusement of blackface. This "racial cross-dressing" allowed Jews to mock the only group that dwelled beneath themselves in the urban social hierarchy.[48] By turning black in theater and film, Jews "passed" in everyday life. Ironically, this racist burlesque also gave rise to Jewish empathy with the plight of blacks during the civil rights era unmatched by other ethnic groups. Thus Jews marched in solidarity with African Americans in the 1960s; the Irish and Italians, for example, did not. I see contemporary Jewish T-shirts that draw on hip-hop as the latest voice in the ongoing dialogue between Jews and blacks over their kinship, differences, and roles in American society.

For example, YidGear offers a shirt with the catchphrase "Strictly Ghetto." This design depicts not the rapper King Sun, who released a Strictly Ghetto album in 1994, but the silhouette of Chasidic Jews with long fringes. The slippery semiotics of this T-shirt allows Jews, as in blackface, to borrow the cultural capital normally associated with African Americans. Yet the design also reclaims the ghetto for Judaism—a word first used in reference to the Jewish quarter of sixteenth-century Venice. This shirt, then, portrays Jewishness in a fluid relationship with another ethnic identity.

Similarly, the "Too Cool For Shul" design by Jtshirt.com depicts a young man dressed in hip-hop garb, including Star of David "bling." (*Shul* is Yiddish for synagogue.) They also offer a shirt with the phrase "True Jew!" tattooed, prison-style, on a man's knuckles. Cool Jewish Shirts sells "Jewboyz" and "Jewgirlz" (www. cooljewishtshirts.com). At KosherHam, one can purchase "Jew-Tang," which plays with the rap group Wu-Tang Clan, "Jew

Figure 13. "Jew Jitsu" T-shirt design. Courtesy of Jeremy Bloom, www. kosherham.com.

Figure 14. "Gin and Jews" T-shirt design. Courtesy of Jeremy Bloom, www.kosherham.com.

Jitsu" [Fig 13], and "Gin and Jews" [Fig. 14]. The latter, which includes the silhouette of two Chasids holding a bottle, mimics Snoop Doggy Dogg's 1995 hit, "Gin and Juice." Shalom Shirts offers "Ninjew" and "Fu Man Jew" (www. shalomshirts.com). YidGear puns with ethnic distinctions through its "The Notorious Y.I.D." shirt. This design features a photo of the late Lubavitcher rebbe, Rabbi Menachem Schneerson, to spoof The Notorious B.I.G., the stage name of Christopher George Latore Wallace, a rapper murdered in a drive-by shooting in Los Angeles in 1997. And Rotem Gear, with a witty nod to the famous African American coiffure that also characterized many young Jewish men, offers "Gotta love that Jewfro hairdo" [Fig. 15].

Many shirts express Jewishness through ribald messages. Most Jews will undoubtedly recognize the OU as the imprimatur of the Orthodox Union

Figure 15. "Gotta Love that Jewfro hairdo" T-shirt design. Courtesy of Jean Roth, www.rotemgear.com.

that certifies foods as strictly kosher (www. oukosher.org). This emblem stands for the scrupulous adherence to religious tradition. However, the icon briefly appeared on a YidGear T-shirt accompanied by the ribald phrase "Eat me—I'm kosher." YidGear promotes itself as "the shirts your rabbi warned you about." Alas, those very same rabbis strenuously objected to the provocation and especially the unauthorized reproduction of their copyrighted logo. YidGear pulled the design. YidGear also offers a drawing of *tefillin* with the naughty phrase "Get Laid." This design presumes knowledge of the very Orthodoxy it offends, for only someone familiar with traditional Judaism would know that one "lays," or wraps, *tefillin.*

Tough Jew Clothes (www.cafepress.com/toughjew) and LuckyJew.com offer a similar sexualized repertoire on men's boxers, including "Temple Mount," "Spin My Dreidel," "Blow Me" (accompanied by a drawing of a ram's horn or *shofar*), and "Let's Get חי [*chai*]." ShalomShirts sells an image of a man in a yarmulke holding a large pistol, taunting "Jew Talkin' to Me?" KosherShirts.com proclaimed "I have a Kosher Salami," "I hit a home run at Rachel's Bat Mitzvah," "Once you go Jew, nothing else will do," "I put the syn in synagogue," and, next to the face of Ron Jeremy, the Jewish porn star, "Ultimate Role Model."

Many expressions of the New Jew Cool offer rejoinders to the passive stereotype of Jewish women, specifically, the Jewish American mother and Jewish American princess clichés. For example, Rotem Gear sells a "Jewtilicious" shirt that encourages women to express their "Jewish bootiliciousness!" Likewise, a brand of clothing called Jew.Lo, which took its cue from J.Lo, or Jennefer Lopez, the fabulously successful Latina entertainer, promoted:

> . . . the new Jewish female, bold, strong, invincible, and available.
> Jew.lo sees that Jew and cool are not incompatible . . . that the Jewish female has been underrepresented in the world of pop culture, or worse, hidden, and seeks to change that.

These garments mobilized humor to critique the absence or neglect of Jewish women in hip-hop, multiculturalism, and normative Judaism. Similarly, Rabbi's Daughters, another line of clothing and accessories, offers slogans such as "Goy Toy" [non-Jewish plaything], "Shiksa" [non-Jewish woman], and, on their panties, "Tush" and "Kish Mir In Tuchas," the Yiddish equivalent of "Kiss My Ass." Jewish Fashion Conspiracy ("putting the racy back into conspiracy") sold "Sexxxy men's briefs and hot ladies' low rise panties . . . sweatshop free and positively smokin'!" One panty punned with the dreidel game played at Chanukah and printed "a great miracle happened here!" atop the crotch. These garments acknowledge Jewish tradition while communicating the classic American values of unrestrained individualism and hypersexuality. They dress Jews apart, as a distinct people, even as they allow Jews to "pass" as just another ethnic group posing in the latest fashions on the great American, multicultural catwalk.

CONCLUSION

I argued in this chapter that Jewish clothing throughout history often served as a commentary on the great warp and waft of Jewish identity, namely, the desire for ethnic particularism and the yearning for acculturation. This was true for clothing endorsed by the rabbis, imposed by an anti-Jewish church and state, and simply donned by the Jewish folk as a matter of local preference and availability. I also showed that the most recent voices in this ongoing dialogue include pop-culture yarmulkes and T-shirts promoted by the New Jew Cool.

Surely the most ribald use of the yarmulke today is the yarmulkebra—a brassiere fabricated from a pair of actual yarmulkes. This garment, such as it is, derives from a lyric by MC Paul Barman, a witty Jewish hip-hop rapper, "I couldn't stay calm because/she revealed a bra made of two yarmulkes" (www. yarmulkebra.com). The yarmulkebra comes in several sizes, including *Batmitzvah* and *Boobooshka*. A parallel item was the bramulke, a yarmulke fashioned from a bra.[49] More tame is the Mazel Tov Curly Teddy, complete with yarmulke and prayer shawl, available from the popular Build-A-Bear chain of shops (www.buildabear.com).

I sometimes wonder what the rabbis of the talmudic era would have said about the yarmulkebra, Dora the Explorer, Yarmulke Day, the iKippa app for your iPhone (for when you need a yarmulke and don't have one; alas, no longer available), and the unorthodox canine ceremony practiced by some American Jews, complete with a pet-yarmulke, the "bark mitzvah." Surely the rabbis would be appalled. Or maybe not. For however much yarmulkes and T-shirts today display the quintessential signs of modern identity, they also allow Jews to resist, even as they embrace, acculturation, a process, I have shown, that is as traditional to Jewish life as any ritual precept. Indeed, pop culture yarmulkes and New Jew Cool T-shirts are recent renditions of a time-honored predicament: how to dress for Judaism as much as for integration into the wider society. The phrasing of this predicament might appear new on these recent garments. Ironically, the message is not, namely, that Jews continue to dress their Jewishness as an ongoing, irresolvable conversation between particularism and generic citizenship.

ACKNOWLEDGMENTS

This essay derives from a much larger project recently published as a book, *A Cultural History of Jewish Dress* (London: Bloomsbury, 2013). There, I offer extensive acknowledgments. Here, I want to extend my sincerest appreciation to Leonard Greenspoon, Professor and Klutznick Chair in Jewish Civilization at Creighton University, for so kindly inviting me to present my work at the Twenty-Fourth Annual Klutznick-Harris Symposium, "Fashioning Jews: Clothing, Culture, and Commerce," at Creighton in 2011. The conviviality, conversation, and scholarship was exemplary, and I learned much from Leonard and the other participants, especially Kerry Wallach. I also wish to acknowledge Wheelock College and the Women's Studies Research Center at Brandeis University. I am also indebted to the many shop proprietors, online yarmulke and T-shirt vendors, and congregants who tolerated my questions, and allowed me to reference their garments in this essay. Lest I forget, I also wish to acknowledge Sam and Zoe. After all, it was my quest to find them appropriate yarmulkes that in many respects started this whole project.

NOTES

[1] For a more comprehensive exploration of this topic, from which this essay derives, see Eric Silverman, *A Cultural History of Jewish Dress* (London: Bloomsbury, 2013).

[2] Israel Abrahams, "Jewish Ethical Wills," *The Jewish Quarterly Review* 3:3 (1891): 463.

[3] Sacha Stern, *Jewish Identity in Early Rabbinic Writings* (Leiden: E. J. Brill, 1994), 191–92.

[4] See, for example, Jeffrey R. Woolf, "Between Law and Society: Mahariq's Responsum on the 'Ways of the Gentiles' (Huqqot Ha-'Akkum)," *AJS Review* 25:1 (2000–2001):45–69.

[5] Biblical sources for this principle include Leviticus 18:3, 20:23, and Deuteronomy 21:30.

[6] I owe a debt in this regard to Marianne Dacy of the University of Sydney and Secretary of the Australian Association of Jewish Studies.

[7] On Jews and Aborigines see, for example, Tatz Colin, "An Essay in Disappointment: The Aboriginal-Jewish Relationship," *Aboriginal History* 28 (2004): 100–21. See also Suzanne D. Rutland, *The Jews in Australia* (Port Melbourne: Cambridge Univ. Press, 2005).

[8] W. E. H. Stanner, "The Dreaming," in Australian *Signpost: An Anthropology Edited for the Canberra Fellowship of Australia Writers* (ed. T. Hunderford; Melbourne, 1956), 51–65.

[9] Fred R. Myers, *Pintupi Country, Pintupi Self: Sentiment, Place, and Politics among Western Desert Aborigines* (Berkeley: University of California Press, 1986), 52.

[10] Tziona Grossmark, "Laws Regarding Idolatry in Jewelry as a Mirror Image of Jewish-Gentile Relations in the Land of Israel during Mishnaic and Talmudic Times," *Jewish Studies Quarterly* 12:3 (2005): 213–26.

[11] In Hebrew, *mishpacha* means "family."

[12] The website, www.minimishpacha.com, is now off-line, but it was up and running for several years prior to July 2012.

[13] Grossmark, "Laws Regarding Idolatry."

[14] See Vivien Johnson, *Copyrites: Aboriginal Art in the Age of Reproductive Technologies* (Sydney: National Indigenous Arts Academy Association and Macquarie University, 1996).

[15] Exodus 13:1–10, 11–16, and Deuteronomy 6:4–9, 11:13–21.

[16] For a recent, rather comprehensive review of the voluminous literature on ancient *tefillin*, see Yehuda Cohn, *Tangled Up In Text: Tefillin and the Ancient World* (Providence: Brown University Press, 2008).

[17] See Solomon Gandz, "The Knot in Hebrew Literature, or from the Knot to the Alphabet, *Isis* 14:1 (1930): 189–214.

[18] See, for example, Eric Kline Silverman, *Masculinity, Motherhood, and Mockery: Psychoanalyzing Culture and the Iatmul Naven Rite in New Guinea* (Ann Arbor: The University of Michigan Press, 2001).

[19] See Jacob Milgrom, "Of Hems and Tassels," *Biblical Archaeology Review* 9:3 (1983): 61–65; Paul A. Kruger, "The Hem of the Garment in Marriage: The Meaning of the Symbolic Gesture in Ruth 3:9 and Ezek 16:8," *Journal of Northwest Semitic Languages* 12 (1984): 79–86.

[20] Ferris Stephens, "The Ancient Significance of *sisith*," *Journal of Biblical Literature* 50:2 (1931): 59–70. King Saul botched a similar gesture after unsuccessfully begging forgiveness from Samuel for violating a divine decree (1 Sam 15). As the prophet turned to leave, Saul grabbed Samuel's hem, tearing the garment. The significance of this insult was not lost on Samuel. "The Lord has this day," he responded to Saul, "torn the kingship over Israel away from you." Much later, David also offered a retort by stealthily snipping Saul's hem while the king defecated in a cave (1 Sam 24).

[21] Milgrom, "Of Hems and Tassels."

[22] Most researchers on this topic attribute the ancient blue dye to the colorless mucus secreted from the hypobranchial gland of the banded-dye murex snail, or *Murex trunculus*. For the process of obtaining the dye, see Milgrom, "Of Hems and Tassels," and Irving Ziderman, "The Biblical Dye Tekhelet and its Use in Jewish Textiles," *Dyes in History and Archaeology* 21 (2008): 36–44.

[23] Gildas Hamel, "Sacred and Profane Clothing in Ancient Israel: *Sha'atnez*," in *The World of Religions: Essays on Historical and Contemporary Issues in Honour of Professor Noel Quinton King for His Eightieth Birthday* (ed. G. W. Trompf and G. Hamel; Delhi: ISPCK, 2001), 29–42.

[24] Milgrom, "Of Hems and Tassels."

[25] Harold Torger Vedeler, "Reconstructing Meaning in Deuteronomy 22:5: Gender, Society, and Transvestitism in Israel and the Ancient Near East," *Journal of Biblical Literature* 127:3 (2008): 459–76.

[26] See Shaye Cohen, "'Those Who Say They Are Jews And Are Not': How Do You Know A Jew In Antiquity When You See One?," in *Diasporas in Antiquity* (ed. S. J. D. Cohen and E. S. Frerichs; Atlanta, Scholars Press), 1–45.

[27] For example, John W. Welch and Claire Foley, "Gammadia on Early Jewish and Christian Garments," *BYU Studies* 36:3 (1996): 252–58; Michael P. Knowles, "What Was the Victim Wearing? Literary, Economic, and Social Contexts for the Parable of the Good Samaritan," *Biblical Interpretation* 12:2 (2004): 158–59.

[28] Lucille A. Roussin, "Costume in Roman Palestine: Archaeological Remains and the Evidence of the Mishnah," in *The World of Roman Costume* (ed. J. L. Sebesta and L. Bonfante; Madison: University of Wisconsin Press), 183–84.

[29] See *b. Shabbath* 120a; Alfred Rubens, *A History of Jewish Costume* (New York: Crown, 1967), 21–22; Roussin, "Costume in Roman Palestine," 183.

[30] *b. Shabbat* 61a; Howard Jacobson, "Shoes and Jews," *Revue des Etudes juives* 161:1–2 (2002): 233.

[31] Esra Shereshevsky, "Some Aspects of Life in Rashi's Times," *Jewish Quarterly Review* 65:2 (1974): 98–114.

[32] Thérèse Metzger and Mendel Metzger, *Jewish Life in the Middle Ages: Illuminated Hebrew Manuscripts of the Thirteenth to the Sixteenth Centuries* (New York: Alpine Fine Arts, 1982).

[33] Sources include Nicholas Vincent, "Two Papal Letters on the Wearing of the Jewish Badge, 1221 and 1229," *Jewish Historical Studies: Transactions of the Jewish Historical Society of England* 34 (1994/96): 209–24; and Rubens, *History of Jewish Costume*, 82–88. For earlier derisive garb imposed on Jews and other non-Muslims in the Islamic world, see Mark R. Cohen, *Under Crescent and Cross: The Jews in the Middle Ages* (Princeton: Princeton University Press, 1994): and Bat Ye'or, *The Dhimmi: Jews and Christians under Islam* (trans. D. Maisel, P. Fenton, and D. Littman; Rutherford: Fairleigh Dickinson University Press, 1985).

[34] The literature of Jewish patches and hats is vast. Select sources include Guido Kisch, "The Yellow Badge in History," *Historia Judaica* 4:2 (1942): 95–127; Raphael Straus, "The 'Jewish Hat' as an Aspect of Social History," *Jewish Social Studies* 4:1 (1942): 59–72; Diane Owen Hughes, "Distinguishing Signs: Ear-Rings, Jews and Franciscan Rhetoric in the Italian Renaissance City," *Past and Present* 111 (1986): 3–59; Benjamin Ravid, "From Yellow to Red: On the Distinguishing Head-covering of the Jews of Venice," *Journal Jewish History* 6:1–2 (1992): 179–210; Ruth Mellinkoff, *Outcasts: Signs of Otherness in Northern European Art of the Late Middle Ages*, Volumes 1, 2 (Berkeley: University of California Press, 1993); Barbara Wisch, "Vested Interest: Redressing Jews on Michelangelo's Sistine Ceiling," *Artibus et Historiae* 24:48 (2003): 143–72; and Flora Cassen's article in this volume.

[35] For examples of Jewish sumptuary legislation, see Cecil Roth, "Sumptuary Laws of the Community of Carpentras," *Jewish Quarterly Review* 28:4 (1928): 357–83, and Rubens, *History of Jewish Costume*, 184–99.

[36] See Simon M. Dubnow, *History of the Jews in Poland and Russia* (trans. I. Friedlaender; Philadelphia: Jewish Publication Society, 1918); David W. Edwards, "Nicholas I and Jewish Education," *History of Education Quarterly* 22:1 (1982): 45–53; Michael Stanislawski, *Tsar Nicholas I and the Jews: The Transformation of Jewish Society in Russia, 1825–1855* (Philadelphia: Jewish Publication Society, 1983); and Eugene M. Avrutin, "The Politics of Jewish Legibility: Documentation Practices and Reform During the Reign of Nicholas I," *Jewish Social Studies* 11:2 (2005): 136–69.

[37] See Jenna Weissman Joselit, *The Wonders of America: Reinventing Jewish Culture, 1880–1950* (New York: Henry Holt, 1994), and Andrew R Heinze, *Adapting to Abundance: Jewish Immigrants, Mass Consumption, and the Search for American Identity* (New York: Columbia University Press, 1990).

[38] Lee M. Friedman, "Mrs. Child's Visit to a New York Synagogue in 1841," *Publications of the American Jewish Historical Society* 38:1–4 (1948–49): 178.

[39] For the history of yarmulkes, see Gunther Plaut, "The Origin of the Word 'Yarmulke,'" *Hebrew Union College Annual* 26 (1955): 567–70; Samuel Krauss, "The Jewish Rite of Covering the Head," *Hebrew Union College Annual* 19 (1945–46): 121–68; David L. Gold, "The Etymology of the English Noun *yarmlke* 'Jewish skullcap' and the Obsolescent Hebrew Noun *yarmulka* 'idem' (With An Addendum on Judezmo Words for 'Jewish Skullcap')," *Jewish Language Review* 7 (1987): 180–99; Suzanne Baizerman, "The Jewish *Kippa Sruga* and the Social Construction of Gender in Israel," in *Dress and Gender: Making and Meaning in Cultural Contexts* (ed. R. Barnes and J. B. Eicher, Oxford: Berg, 1992), 93–105; Eric Zimmer, "Men's Headcovering: The Metamorphosis of This Practice," in *Reverence, Righteousness, and Rahamanut: Essays in Memory of Rabbi Dr. Leo Jung* (ed. J. J. Schacter; Northvale: Jason Aronson, 1992), 325–52; and Dan Rabinowitz, "Yarmulke: A Historical Cover-up?," *Hakira: The Flatbush Journal of Jewish Law and Thought* 4 (2007): 221–38.

[40] Abraham G. Duker, "Emerging Culture Patterns in American Jewish Life," *Publications of the American Jewish Historical Society* 39:104 (1949–50): 379.

[41] Joselit, *Wonders of America*, 98.

[42] See http://www.myspace.com/yarmulkeday; and Alice Hunt, "Yarmulke Day Stresses Tolerance; Student Started Tradition As a 'Joke,'" *Poughkeepsie Journal*, (19 December 2006).

[43] For contemporary Jewish ethnicity, Walter Zenner, "Jewishness in America: Ascription and Choice," *Ethnic and Racial Studies* 8:1 (1985): 117–33; Caryn Aviv and David Shneer, *New Jews: The End of the Jewish Diaspora* (New York: NYU Press, 2005); Barbara Kirshenblatt-Gimblett, "The 'New Jews': Reflections on Emerging Cultural Practices," Paper delivered at Re-thinking Jewish Communities and Networks in an Age of Looser Connections, Wurzweiler School of Social Work, Yeshiva University, and Institute for Advanced Studies, Hebrew University (New York: 6–7 December 2005, online at http://www.nyu.edu/classes/bkg/web/yeshiva.pdf); and Vivian Klaff, "Defining American Jewry From Religious and Ethnic Perspectives: The Transitions to Greater Heterogeneity," *Sociology of Religion* 67:4 (2006): 415–38.

[44] Sue Fishkoff, "New Jew Cool," *Reform Judaism* 33: Fall (2004): 20–27, 32.

[45] Steven M. Cohen and Ari. Y. Kelman, "Cultural Events and Jewish Identities: Young Adult Jews in New York," 2005. New York: The National Foundation for Jewish Culture,

UJA-Federation of New York, Commission on Jewish Identity and Renewal. On-line at http://bjpa.org/Publications/details.cfm?PublicationID=2911.

[46] Joanna Smith Rakoff, "The New Super Jew," *Time Out New York*, 427 (4–11 December): 13–14, 16, 18.

[47] James Clifford, *Routes: Travel and Translation in the Late Twentieth Century* (Cambridge: Harvard University Press, 1997), 176.

[48] Here, I draw on Michael Rogin, *Blackface, White Noise: Jewish Immigrants in the Hollywood Melting Pot* (Berkeley: University of California Press, 1998).

[49] The website for the *bramulke* is no longer active (www.bramulke.com). But information about the item is available at http://www.dailyjews.com/articles/69_wear_a_bra_on_your_h.htm.